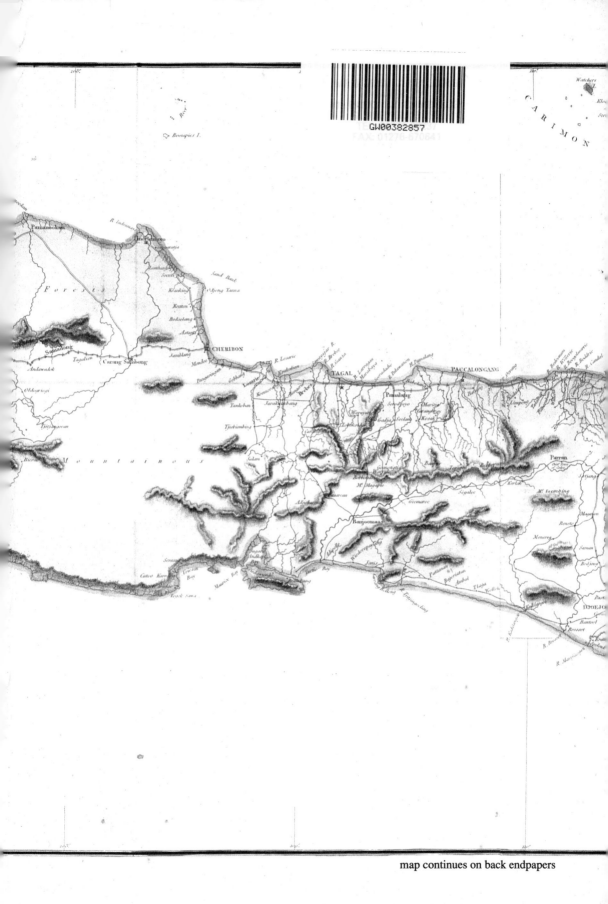

map continues on back endpapers

THE CONQUEST OF JAVA

BY

Major William Thorn

PERIPLUS
EDITIONS
LIMITED

Originally published in 1815 by T. Egerton,
Military Library, Whitehall, London

Reprinted in 1993 by Periplus Editions (HK) Ltd.
with the cooperation of Antiques of the Orient Pte. Ltd., Singapore

Publisher:
Eric M. Oey

Cover Design:
Peter Ivey

Distributors:
Singapore and Malaysia: Berkeley Books Pte. Ltd.
Farrer Road P.O. Box 115, Singapore 9128

Indonesia: C.V. Java Books
Box 55 JKCP, Jakarta 10510

Hong Kong: Pacific Century Distribution Ltd.
G/F No. 14, Lower Kai Yuen Lane, North Point

Australia: CIS Publishers
245 Cardigan Street, Carlton, Victoria 3053

North America: Weatherhill Distribution, Inc.
420 Madison Avenue, 15th Floor,
New York, NY 10017-1107

ISBN 0-945971-86-9

PRINTED IN THE REPUBLIC OF SINGAPORE

MEMOIR

OF THE

CONQUEST OF JAVA;

WITH THE SUBSEQUENT OPERATIONS

OF

THE BRITISH FORCES,

IN

The Oriental Archipelago.

TO WHICH IS SUBJOINED,

A STATISTICAL AND HISTORICAL SKETCH OF

JAVA;

BEING THE RESULT OF OBSERVATIONS MADE IN A TOUR THROUGH THE COUNTRY;

WITH AN ACCOUNT OF ITS DEPENDENCIES.

BY MAJOR WILLIAM THORN,

Late Deputy Quarter-Master-General to the Forces serving in Java.

ILLUSTRATED BY PLANS, CHARTS, VIEWS, &c.

LONDON:

PRINTED FOR T. EGERTON, MILITARY LIBRARY, WHITEHALL.

1815.

SIR,

THE permission to inscribe this Memoir to your ROYAL HIGHNESS, flattering as it must be to the feelings of a Soldier, is only an evidence of that benign attention, under the influence of which the Military Character has risen in this country to an unrivalled degree of excellence, diffusing the glory of our arms over every part of the globe. While the most powerful exertions were making to rescue the people of Europe from the chain of a despot, whose object was to yoke all Sovereigns to his chariot-wheels; it must have been peculiarly gratifying to the friends of humanity to find, that correspondent efforts were carried on with equal vigour, in remote regions, for the accomplishment of the work of universal deliverance. Though the operations which took place in the farthest parts of Asia, to curb the aspiring domination of France over the commerce and liberties of the world, were in a great measure eclipsed by the rapid succession of brilliant achievements in the Peninsula, under the command of the first Captain of modern ages; the value and splendour of those which attended the Conquest of Java, were not without the praise of Government, or the gratitude of the nation.

Thus, amidst the revolutions which it has been the lot of your ROYAL HIGHNESS to witness, the perseverance and energy of Britain have commanded the admiration of mankind; and afforded a solid ground of confidence, that whatever changes other States may be destined to endure these Islands, under the paternal rule of the House of Brunswick, will ever continue to be a check to ambition, and an example of loyalty, presenting a barrier against the encroachments of licentious power, and a refuge to the persecuted and afflicted of every land.

That your ROYAL HIGHNESS may be long instrumental in maintaining these blessings, by promoting the interests of that important Service over which you preside, is the prayer of,

Your Royal Highness's

Most dutiful and obedient Servant,

WILLIAM THORN.

PREFACE.

THE ISLAND of JAVA and its immediate dependencies, present so many interesting objects for the consideration of intelligent observers, that no relative change with respect to the possession and government of these remarkable portions of the globe, can affect their importance, or lessen the desire of being more intimately acquainted with countries which have been too much secluded from examination by local difficulties and commercial jealousy.

It may well excite surprize, that while the Dutch fixed here the seat of their Eastern Empire, and for above two centuries drew from hence immense supplies of wealth, so little should have been comparatively done under their direction, either for the improvement of such valuable possessions, or in satisfying the natural desire of men to acquire a knowledge of regions, the productions of which have been sought with avidity. This frigid insensibility to the concerns of science, and to the progress of the human mind, certainly did not arise from any apathy in respect to the value of their Oriental settlements,

or for the want of energy in turning them to the most lucrative advantage. On the contrary, the entire history of the Dutch dominion
in the eastern world, exhibits a perpetual spirit of encroachment, and
of incessant activity to prevent the intrusion of others on a trade which
they considered as their exclusive property. With this view of uphold-
ing their power, and of making a deep impression on the nations
among whom their settlements were formed, these people, who have
been proverbially plain and frugal in Europe, were as much distinguished by the splendour of their foreign establishments.

The City of BATAVIA might well obtain the appellation of being the
Queen of the East, on account of the wealth of its inhabitants, the
grandeur of its buildings, and the vast extent of its commerce. This
was indeed the heart of the Dutch empire in India, as the Island of
Java itself constituted the principal source of all its opulence and
strength. The kingdom of Bantam formed the western division of this
large territory, while in the opposite direction the Dutch enjoyed the
sole command of the rich and beautiful line of coast on the north side
of the island, abounding with populous towns and numerous harbours.
Possessed of so much power, it could not be a matter of wonder that
the influence of these enterprizing people should be felt and obeyed
through the neighbouring seas; and that with such multiplied means
of increasing riches in their hands, the most valuable productions of
this prolific part of the earth should be emptied as it were with exube-

rance into that celebrated mart, which united in itself the pomp of Asiatic luxury, with the activity of European industry.

But this ready accumulation of wealth, connected as it was with a very defective system of internal administration, proved the source of corruption to the members employed by the state, and of idleness and debauchery to the mass of the people. Large fortunes, it is true, were made by individuals, but the revenue became deteriorated, so that for some time before the French revolution, the affairs of the Dutch in the East were in a declining condition; and the subjugation of Holland to the gigantic power which arose out of that event, accelerated their absolute ruin. Deprived of the protection afforded by an alliance with Great Britain, the Dutch soon had to lament the loss of Ceylon, Malacca, and the Spice Islands; besides their settlements on the Continent of India. JAVA indeed remained, but the trade was in a great measure annihilated; and the resources of this great possession, however considerable they might be intrinsically, could hardly be of much benefit to the parent state. The local government had, in fact, long exercised an arbitrary rule over every branch of commerce and cultivation for present interests, rather than for the general good; looking only to the proceeds of the sales, and the immediate returns of colonial produce. But the annexation of Holland to France, after the temporary mockery of erecting the United Provinces into a Monarchy, opened enlarged views with respect to the destination of Java, and it was rightly considered, that this important island would yield many advantages to the new empire, independent of the prospect which it held out of creating a rival power in the East. Accordingly, some of the most sagacious statesmen of that nation, turned their thoughts closely to this subject, and endeavoured to kindle in their countrymen a spirit of emulation and enterprize, by setting before them a brilliant picture of the benefits to be gained in a migration to the distant regions which were now added to the French dominion. This artful policy was admirably calculated to free the country of a dangerous and redundant population, at a period when the revolutionary tempest had scarcely subsided, and when there yet remained many disaffected and turbulent spirits who wanted employment, and were guided by no principles of morality. On the other hand, the successive changes which had taken place throughout France and her dependent states, had thrown multitudes of unfortunate persons into poverty, from which they were now flattered with the assurance of being delivered, by pursuing the certain course to affluence in the oriental settlements.

The ardent and aspiring, the inquisitive and industrious, were alike stimulated to turn their minds towards the colonial establishments, for the acquisition of riches and the retrieval of their misfortunes. The avaricious were lured by the promise of gain, and the ambitious were fired by the prospect of glory. Thus did the intriguing Government of France endeavour to profit by the possession of this remote appendage to the Empire, in holding out such allurements as were most powerfully adapted to render it beneficial in itself, and instrumental to the general object of natural aggrandizement. Nor can it be denied, that the exertions of France to improve the Island as a military position, to strengthen its relative connexions, and to make it answerable to the professions which had been artfully thrown out in the way of temptation, were such as denoted equal energy and ability.

But it could not escape the observation of those who felt the importance of this settlement, that the change which had taken place must necessarily call the particular attention of the British nation to the possession of Java by France. This was indeed a matter of such pressing and unavoidable moment, that the most vigorous measures were immediately taken to secure the island from the attempts which it was natural to expect would be made, to wrest the settlement from the hands of those who were known to entertain other views in the possession of it, than such as were merely commercial and pacific.

General Daendels, one of the most active and intelligent officers in the French service, was therefore appointed to this government; and immediately on his arrival, he began to prepare for any attack which might be made upon the island by the British naval and military forces in India. The plans of this officer were for the most part exceedingly judicious, and his means were commensurate with the important trust of which he had the care, and the opposition which he had reason to expect. His powers were unlimited, and he had twenty thousand well-disciplined soldiers at his disposal; while over the actual resources of the colony he had an absolute controul, and he made no scruple of applying them at his pleasure to the accomplishment of the designs which he conceived to be the best for the defence of the island against an invading force. At an immense charge, therefore, and with a prodigious waste of human life, roads were constructed throughout the island; while Fort Ludowyck was erected to command the straits between Java and Madura In pursuance of the same plan, the seat of Government was removed to the suburbs of Batavia, and a more salubrious military station was also chosen in the interior, where the new fortifications, aiding the natural advantages of the position, seemed to render the settlement impregnable. But this enterprizing Commander did not confine his views to mere measures of defence only, for in the true spirit of the new master whom he served, his mind was inspired with the desire of conquest, and the Moluccas were already threatened, and our spice trade would soon have fallen, had the preparations been suffered to go on for naval purposes, and the French continued much longer in the absolute command of the island of Java, from whence they could sweep the seas and annoy our settlements.

The subversion of this rising power, therefore, became an imperious duty on the part of the British Government in India, and it was happily accomplished under the judicious and personal direction of Lieutenant-General Sir SAMUEL AUCHMUTY, and by the overbearing valour of our troops. Of this great achievement, and of the arduous services with which it was attended, a detailed Memoir appeared necessary, as the authentic record of an interesting event, and to enable the public in Europe to appreciate the value of the acquisition, and the nature of the operations by which it was attained.

Any apology for such a performance would be justly treated as superfluous, where, from the nature of the subject, criticism must be ill employed in censuring what could not obtain the advantages of literary composition, without the chance of doing injury to the simplicity of the narrative. The sketches and details of operation reported in the following sheets, were, for the greatest part, noted down on the spot, after the close of each action; consequently, no merit can be claimed for any thing beyond a diligent attention to passing occurrences, and a scrupulous regard to fidelity in the representation of them. The inclination of the author to mark the esteem which he entertains for his companions in arms, would have led him to notice their particular exploits, in language suited to the high sense which he entertains of them; but in so doing he is aware, that he should thereby have justly incurred the charge of presumption. But while he is silent on the distinct merits of the living and the dead, he must be permitted to say, generally, that no terms could be found adequately to express his sentiments of those with whom he was happily associated in the labours here narrated; and he can, with great propriety, adopt the glowing lines of the poet, which are perfectly responsive of the emotions that animate the breast of the patriotic soldier.

> Oh War! thou hast thy fierce delight
> Thy gleams of joy intensely bright!
> Such gleams, as from thy polish'd shield
> Fly dazzling o'er thy battle field!
> Such transports wake, severe and high,
> Amid the pealing conquest-cry;
> Scarce less, when after battle lost
> Muster the remnants of a host,
> And as each comrade's name they tell,
> Who in the well-fought conflict fell,
> Knitting stern brow o'er flashing eye,
> Vow to avenge them or to die!
>
> SCOTT'S "LORD OF THE ISLES."

On the passage to England, the leisure afforded by being detained six months at St. Helena for the want of convoy, suggested the idea of adding to the Memoir a brief statistical view of the Islands of Java and Madura, substantially compressed from personal observations made in a tour through those parts; which, with some interesting sketches of the Oriental Archipelago, constituting the dependencies on the government at Batavia, may be relied on in respect to accuracy of description, and the authenticity of the details with which the writer was favored, concerning the operations that added the Moluccas to the British possessions.

When it is considered that the jealous policy of the Dutch had succeeded but too effectually for two centuries, in preventing any correct
information relative to their eastern territories from being made known
in Europe, this addition to the stock of geographical knowledge,
though simple in its particulars, and unadorned in the language, may
probably have some claims for an indulgent attention on the ground
of practical utility. Similar pretensions may be urged in behalf of the
Plans and Views, which, though the nature of the volume rendered
them indispensible, yet are they to be esteemed in no other light than as
mere graphical illustrations of the objects they represent, and correct
surveys of the countries and districts which they delineate.

On the candour of the Public, the work must now rely for that favour
which rarely fails to reward those who seek rather to deserve credit for
what they relate, than for their skill and address in cloathing and
embellishing the History.

London, April 5, 1815.

CONTENTS.

PART I.

Page

Tract of the several Divisions of the Fleet   1

Rendezvous at Penang—Malacca—High Islands—Sambar, on the south-west coast of Borneo—Difficulties of the Navigation—Arrival in the Bay of Batavia.

PART II.

ACCOUNT OF THE CAMPAIGN.

SECTION I.

From the Landing of the Army to the gaining Possession of Batavia   17

Disembarcation—Position of the Army—Its Movements—Passage of the Anjole—The Suburbs—Surrender of Batavia—A Night Attack—The Enemy foiled—Providential Discovery.

SECTION II.

The Action of the 10th of August, near Weltervreeden   .   .   30

SECTION III.

Bombardment and Battle of Cornelis .   .   .   41

French Orders—Measures of Defence—Batteries erected before Cornelis—Sortie of the Enemy—Bombardment—Strength of the Enemy—Preparations for the Assault

c

Page

—Columns of Attack—Perplexing March—Advanced Picquet surprized—The
Lines forced—Dreadful Explosion—Reserve defeated—Pursuit—Charge of the
Cavalry—Rout of the Enemy—Flight of Generals Janssens and Jumel—Possession
of Buitenzorg—Official Report—General Orders.

Review of the Battle of the 26th of August, 1811 75
Sir Samuel Auchmuty's Dispatch to Lord Minto 80
Lord Minto to the Earl of Liverpool 88

SECTION IV.

Conclusion of Lieutenant-General Sir Samuel Auchmuty's
Campaign in Java 90

Escape of the French Frigates from Sourabaya—General Janssens' Report—Possession
of Cheribon, and General Junot taken Prisoner—Taggal Fort surrendered—Capture of Samanap, and Surrender of the Island of Madura—Expedition to Samarang
—Proposals to General Janssens—His Answer—Gun-boats taken—Landing effected
at Samarang—Action of the 16th September—Cessation of Arms—Capitulation
and Surrender of General Janssens, with the whole Island of Java and its Dependencies—Possession of Sourabaya and of Fort Ludowyk—Character of the
Expedition in Official Documents—The Prince Regent's Approbation.

PART III.

SUBSEQUENT OPERATIONS OF THE BRITISH FORCES.

SECTION I.

Disturbed State of Java . . . 121

SECTION II.

Expedition to Palimbang under the Orders of Colonel Gillespie   127

Page

Nanka Island—Palimbang River—Difficulties of the Passage—Order of Sailing—
Malay Duplicity—Batteries at Borang taken, 1812—Flight of the Sultan—Colonel
Gillespie gains possession of Palimbang, by surprize—Appalling Spectacle Con-
flagration—Account of the Massacre of the Dutch—Pangerang Adipaty—Character
of the Court—Unlucky Affray—Tranquillity restored—Coronation—Description
of Palimbang—Articles of Commerce—The Sultan's Family—Settlements in
Sumatra—Banca, named Duke of York Island, formally annexed to the British
Dominions—Fort Nugent—Minto the Capital—Official Document.

SECTION III.

Hostilities with the Sultan of Mataram, and Capture of
Djoejocarta 174

Court of Mataram—Policy of the Dutch—General Confederacy—Dangerous Crisis—
Provoked Hostilities—Bombardment commenced—Cavalry Skirmish—Important
Junction—Conflagrations—Preparations for the Assault—Magnitude of the Object
—Storm and Capture of Djoejocarta—The Sultan taken Prisoner—Dissolution of
the Confederacy—Character of this Exploit—Peace established.

General Order, by Major-General Gillespie 192
—————— by Lieutenant-General Sir George Nugent, Commander-in-Chief in
India 197
—————— by the Earl of Minto, Governor General . . . 200

STATISTICAL AND HISTORICAL SKETCH OF JAVA,

Being the Result of Observations made in a Tour
through the Country 203

State of the Island—Face of the Country—Military Roads—Climate—Produce—
Animals—Manufactures—Exports and Imports.

Internal Administration . . . 219

Revenue Department—Old System abolished—New Landed Tenure—Port Regulations.

  Page

                Judicial Department   226

Courts of Justice—Native Jury—General Police—Its Divisions—Village Adminis-
    tration.

            Population and State of Society . . .   232

Of Malays and Javanese in General—Inhabitants of Batavia—Enfranchised Slaves—
    Arabs—Baliers—Buggese—Amboynese—Madurese—Chinese—Dutch—The City
    and Environs—The Bay—Rivers—Roads and Avenues—Molenvliet—Ryswyck—
    Tanabang—Markets—Weltervreeden.

                        ITINERARY.

            From Batavia to the Westward . . .   260

Tangerang—Kingdom of Bantam—Ceram—City and Court of Bantam—Change of
    Administration—Marack Bay—The Bantamese—Anjier—North-west Coast—In-
    land Districts—Edible Birds'-nests.

            From Batavia to the Eastward . . .   271

Route to Samarang—Tjimangis—Tjiloar—Soucarajah—Buitenzorg—Dutch Farms—
    Blue Mountains—Tjiceroa—Tjipanas—The Hill Regencies—Tanjore—Bandong—
    Samadong—Karang Sambong—Cheribon—Forts on the Coast—Taggal—Pacca-
    longang—Samarang.

            From Samarang to the South Coast . .   285

Oonarang—Salatiga—Boyollalie—Volcano—Selo—Carta Soura—Chain of Forts inland
    —Soulo, or Soura Carta—The Soosoohoonan, or Emperor—Klattan—Sultan of
    Mataram—Djoejocarta—Water-Palace—Guard of Amazons—Tiger Fights—Euro-
    pean Town—The South Coast.

        From Samarang—Eastern Route continued . .   296

Damack—Japara—Joanna—Rembang—Lassem—Toubang—Zedayo—Sourabaya
    River—Fort Ludowyck—Harbour of Gressie—Town of Sourabaya—Environs—
    De Noyo Cantonment—Passarouang—Probolingo—Melancholy Catastrophe—
    Insurrection suppressed—Eastern Extremity of the Island—Banyowangy—Straits
    of Baly.

Page

Island of Madura 311

Samanap—Parmacassan—Bancallan—Gallion and Pondi Isles—Carimon Java.

DEPENDENCIES ON JAVA.

The Eastern Archipelago . . . 314

Timor—Coupang Town and Fort Concordia—Tributary Isles—Roma—Kisser—
Semao—Rotto—Savu—Sumbawa—Beema—Harbour—Horses—Volcanoes—Allas
Strait—Lombock—Baly—Inhabitants.

Borneo, Banjirmassin and Fort Tatar . . 324

Pontiana—Sambas—Account of the Capture, 1813—Trade of Borneo.

Macassar Town and Fort Rotterdam . . 333

Island of Celebes—Assassinations—The Buggese—Native Chieftains—Fort Bulo
Comba—Expedition of General Nightingale—Rajah Boni—Dependencies of
Macassar—Maros—Salayer and Booton Isles—Buggese Bay—Goonong Tella
River—Manado and Fort Amsterdam.

MOLUCCA ISLES. 343

Ternate and Tidore—Account of the Capture of Ternate—Gillolo—Bachian—Xulla
Isles.

Amboyna . . . 349

Account of its Capture—Produce of Amboyna—Population—Clove Islands belonging
to Amboyna—Ceram—Bouro.

Banda Isles . . . 356

Nutmeg Plantations—Inhabitants.

Commercial Intercourse with Japan . 360

Factory at Desima in Nangasacki—Articles of Trade—Institutions—Conclusion.

ERRATA.

LIST OF PLATES.

		Page
1. Map of Java	facing the Title page	
2. Tract of the Fleet		1
3. View of High Islands		13
4. Plan of the Brigades of the Army		17
5. Plan of the Landing		19
6. Route of the British Army		23
7. View of the Town-House at Batavia		26
8. View of the Wharf at Batavia		29
9. Plan of the Action near Weltervreeden		31
10. Plan of the Battle of Cornelis		57
11. Plan of the Town and Environs of Samarang		97
12. Sketch of the Action near Samarang		99
13. Harbour of Gressie and Sourabaya		105
14. Tract of the British Force against Palimbang		127
15. Sketch of the River of Palimbang		129
16. Sketch of the Batteries at Borang		137
17. The Fort, Batteries, and Palaces, at Palimbang		143
18. View of Palimbang		157
19. Plan of the Assault on Djoejocarta		185
20. View of a Chinese Funeral		246
21. Fort of Cheribon		279

Page

22. Ditto of Taggal - - - - - - 282

23. View of Samarang - - - - - - 284

24. Fort of Salatiga - - - - - - 286

25. The Water-Palace at Djoejocarta - - - - 292

26. View of Damack - - - - - - 296

27. View of Japara - - - - - - 297

28. View of Joana - - - - - - ib.

29. View of Rambang - - - - - - 298

30. View of Gressie - - - - - - 302

31. View of Sourabaya River - - - - - 303

32. View of Passarouang - - - - - 305

33. Chart of the Eastern Archipelago - - - - 314

34. Amboyna - - - - - - - 349

35. Banda Isles - - - - - - - 356

MEMOIR

OF THE

CONQUEST OF JAVA.

PART I.

TRACT OF THE SEVERAL DIVISIONS OF THE FLEET.

Rendezvous at Penang—Malacca—High Islands—Sambar, on the South-West Coast of Borneo—Difficulties of the Navigation—Arrival in the Bay of Batavia.

———

AT no period in the history of the British dominion in India, have the power and prosperity of that empire shone with a lustre so brilliant, as at the present moment. Among other great results which distinguished the splendid government of the Marquess Wellesley, whose brother here commenced his illustrious career, the historian will have to record two remarkable facts, that of the British standard waving on the banks of the antient Hyphasis, and the terms of a general peace being dictated by Lord Lake, at the head of his gallant army, on that very border which was already celebrated by the altars of Alexander. Such were the events which closed the administration of that great statesman in the eastern world ; while, to his successor, the late Earl of Minto, was reserved the glory of carrying into effect, the important object of strengthening our political and commercial interests by the conquests of the isles of France and Bourbon, of Java and its dependencies.

Without weakening the parent state by draining its resources, the government of India equipped and dispatched in rapid succession, two expeditions, proportioned to the magnitude of their respective objects, and to insure the absolute subjugation of those establishments yet remaining in the hands of the enemy ; and which for position, strength, and connexion, were always considered as their most formidable possessions in the oriental seas.

The expedition destined against Java, having completed its preparations, the first division under the command of Colonel Robert Rollo Gillespie, sailed the eighteenth of April, in the year 1811, from Madras Roads, under the convoy of His Majesty's ship Caroline, Captain Cole. The remainder of the troops followed in about a week after, under Major General Wetherall.

A tremendous hurricane, which came on the very day after their departure, threatened to involve the whole in a general and direful wreck. His Majesty's ship the Dover, and all the other vessels that had remained in the Roads, were driven on shore by the violence of the tempest, and were lost ; but happily, all the transports, having left the place in time, escaped ; thus, the first setting out of the Expedition was surprizingly marked with that wonderful good fortune, which by the mercy of Providence continued to attend it, during a long and dangerous passage, and through unknown seas.

A slight part only of this violent storm overtook the last convoy, and occasioned in one of the ships the loss of forty cavalry horses, which died of suffocation. This was the principal, and, indeed, almost the only loss sustained by the troops during the passage.

The salutary regulations laid down by Colonel Agnew, Adjutant General, by order of the Commander in Chief, for the treatment of both men and horses, on board the transports; and the provident care of Sir Samuel Auchmuty, who, like an affectionate parent, was attentive to every suggestion that could contribute to the preservation of the health of the troops, were productive of the most beneficial effects, during a voyage of nearly four months. The few casualties which happened either among the men or horses during so long a passage, and that too in an Indian climate, ought to be recorded as a circumstance which, considered in every point of view, is without a parallel.

In the first division, scarcely any losses were sustained; for the long experience acquired by Colonel Gillespie in the West Indian expeditions, and his particular acquaintance with the means necessary to be adopted in all hot climates, caused him frequently to inspect the several transports, during the passage, and to enforce a strict observance of the prescribed orders. In this he was ably assisted by all the officers embarked in that convoy. By this attention and care, both men and horses, notwithstanding the almost insufferable heat and long confinement on board the ships, preserved perfect health and spirits, and were all able to enter into immediate action.

On the eighteenth of May, we anchored in Penang harbour; the first rendezvous of the expedition. The Akbar frigate, with his Ex-

B 2

cellency the Commander in Chief, arrived on the thirteenth, and departed again on the twentieth for Malacca. The Modeste frigate, with Lord Minto, had touched at this place, and continued her passage to Malacca before our arrival. Mr. Seton, governor of Prince of Wales' Island, had also proceeded on to Malacca with his lordship.

On the twenty-first of May, the second division under Major General Wetherall, arrived under convoy of His Majesty's ship Phaeton, Captain Pellew.

PENANG, or Prince of Wales' island, is a flourishing settlement, and the troops, during their stay, received a plentiful supply of fresh (buffaloes) beef, which was procured from the opposite coast, in consequence of the permission granted by the King of Queda, who had himself come over to Penang on a visit to the governor.

This island extends from latitude 5 degrees 16 minutes, to 5 degrees 30 minutes N. being nearly fifteen miles in length, and seven or eight miles in breadth. The entrance into the harbour is very picturesque. Mount Olivia and several villas agreeably interspersed among the shady groves near the shore, pleasingly attract the eye; whilst the lofty signal mountain, covered with immense trees up to the very summit, adds greatly to the beauty of the scene. The perpendicular height of this mountain is 2170 feet above the level of the sea, and the signals for ships approaching the island are here displayed; but at a small distance from hence is another mountain, higher than the former by about seventy feet. Both within the town and in the environs are many houses, which in their construction unite elegance with accommodation. That of the governor, three or four miles in the country, is particularly handsome, and well adapted to the climate. At the foot of the signal mountain, there is an establishment for grinding corn and baking bread and biscuit, belonging to a Chinese named Amie. This building is erected on a water course which turns the machinery; and here, ships that touch at this place are abundantly supplied with the necessary articles of life. Pulo Penang was erected into a colony, in the year 1786, when Captain Light, to whom the King of Queda presented the island, as a marriage portion with his daughter, took possession of it, for the use of the East-India Company. Considering the comparatively infant state of the settlement, we may be justly astonished at the rapid rise and progress of George Town in so short a time; and the population is proportionably great, consisting of Europeans, Chinese, Malays, and others from Hindostan and other parts of India. Cultivation however has not yet extended far; except towards the Southern part, and on the Eastern side of the island where the town is situated, and where the land, being low and contiguous to the sea, admits of improvement. The body of the island is high, uneven, and covered with trees.

Fort Cornwallis is built on the N. E. point of the island, close to the town. It is in latitude 5 degrees 24½ minutes North; longitude 100 degrees 21½ minutes East. Ships are constructed here of all sizes and dimensions. The trade of Junk Seylon, Queda Selanger, and other Malay ports, has, since the establishment of this colony, concentrated here; and for the loss of which the king of Queda has a grant of ten thousand piastres from the Penang government, as a compensation. The commerce here consists in commodities of exchange, pepper, beetle nut, rattans, and some gold, brought hither from the main land, as well as from Sumatra and other islands to the

Eastward, by the Malay prows, and for which they receive opium, piece goods, arrack, dollars, and other articles.

The harbour, which appears like a river, is about two miles across, from the Fort point to the main, where a considerable tract, fronting the island, has been added to the Company's possessions, and whence bullocks and poultry are brought over in great abundance. We went out by the North channel, the same way that we came in; as the South channel is too dangerous for large ships, unless a good pilot can be procured. This last passage is bounded by the long sand which begins about three quarters of a mile to the Southward of the fort, and stretches nearly to the North point of Pulo Jarajah, having a small channel of three, four and five fathoms betwixt it and the western shore.

On the twenty-fourth of May we sailed for Malacca, which we reached on the first of June. The weather during this time was generally clear, with moderate breezes, but now and then it was very rainy and squally, and we were often obliged to come to an anchor. The Bengal troops, under convoy of his Majesty's ship the Cornelia, Captain Edgell, had arrived here five or six weeks before us, and were encamped along the shore; Lord Minto, Sir Samuel Auchmuty, and Commodore Broughton, had also arrived.

A dreadful accident happened while we lay at this place. One of the store ships from Bengal, laden with gunpowder, &c. accidentally caught fire, and when it was found that she could not be saved, the people were taken out, and the vessel was set adrift; fortunately she blew up soon after, otherwise, as she drifted towards the fleet, many of the squadron might have been destroyed by the explosion.

On our landing we observed a cloud of smoke ascending from a funeral pile, which was formed of various instruments of torture, as the rack, the wheel, &c. which had been in use among the Dutch, but which Lord Minto had now ordered to be burned; the more equitable laws of England having superseded the former system of terror in the administration of justice. It was highly gratifying to the liberal mind to see these dreadful machines, the invention of ingenious cruelty, consigned to the flames; and as this sacrifice on the altar of humanity, was the spontaneous act of honourable feeling, it was no doubt propitious to the great cause in which we were now engaged; for what could be a more striking contrast than a gloomy despotism, which, by refining on the penal laws, prolongs the sufferings of the victim doomed to death, and the spirit of a mighty power, marking its progress in arms by acts of mercy, and a solicitude for the rights of human nature?

The fourth of June, being the anniversary of His Majesty's birth-day, was celebrated as splendidly as circumstances in this remote part of the world would permit. Royal salutes from the men of war of the expedition, and from the batteries on shore, announced the happy day, and at noon the discharge of cannon proclaimed the number of years our venerable and beloved sovereign had attained. Lord Minto held a levee in the morning, and at four o'clock he gave a dinner to a great part of the naval and military officers, when many loyal toasts were drank with enthusiasm, and afterwards the noble lord himself was drank to, as a volunteer on the present service, with three times three. In the evening a ball closed the fête.

MALACCA has suffered a considerable declension from its former state of prosperity. The few Dutch families who inhabit the town, carry on very little commerce. Idle habits, even among this people, so proverbially industrious in Europe, have gained such an ascendency as to weaken the spirit for mercantile pursuits ; while the desolate, wild, and impenetrable woods, which run up close to the town, debar the inhabitants from any intercourse or communication with the inland parts of the Peninsula.

This city, originally founded by the Mussulmans in the thirteenth century, became early a powerful and flourishing settlement of the Portuguese. The Dutch laid siege to it in 1640, and on the fourteenth of January, 1641, they carried it by storm after an obstinate resistance. The Portuguese had four churches in the town and one in the fort, which last is the only one now in use. It stands on a hill in the center of the fort, and is seen at a great distance off at sea; on the spire a flag is hoisted when a ship is seen coming in. Its latitude is 2 degrees 12 minutes N. Longitude 102 degrees 15 minutes E. The fort is now little better than a heap of rubbish ; and some batteries on the tops of commanding hillocks, constitute the only defence of the place. These batteries are on the south side of the river, and as the town lines the sea shore on the north side, the communication is maintained by a drawbridge. The town, which is inhabited by Dutch, Chinese, Malays, and various Indians, contains a number of very good houses. Of this mixt assemblage of people, professing different religious tenets, the followers of Mohammed are the most numerous. It is remarkable, that though the land adjoining the town is low, with offensive mud banks, which dry every tide, close to the houses, and the country around is almost an impenetrable forest, this is notwithstanding the most healthy place known in India, so near to the Equator. Several very commodious villas and pleasant garden-houses are interspersed along the sea shore, among cocoa nut topes, and other fruit trees; with the much esteemed mangosteen, whose growth is confined to very few places.

About seven leagues and a half inland is a high mountain called Goonong Ledang, also Queen's Mount, or Mount Ophir, whose height is 13,842 feet above the sea, which is only about two thousand feet less than Mont Blanc.

Malacca, at the time when the Portuguese were masters of it, carried on a considerable trade with Japan; but the Dutch, when they gained possession of the place, made a total alteration in its commercial character, by transferring that as well as every other source of wealth, which lay in their power, to Batavia. But though the trade of Malacca has been ever since gradually decreasing, still the importance of this place is evident, from its advantageous position in commanding the straits, which are only sixteen miles broad, and through which every vessel must pass, that is bound to Java, Sumatra, Borneo, and the Moluccas. Possessed of Malacca, therefore, a very small cruizing squadron suffices to command the entire intercourse, and the whole coasting trade of the eastern seas. It was this consideration of its importance which first induced the Portuguese to establish themselves here, and the same reason urged the Dutch to drive them from it; who in their turn were expelled by the English. This acquisition has of course afforded a safe passage for our China fleet through the straits of Malacca, during a time that the Sunda straits were rendered impracticable, or at least when they were considered as unsafe, so long as Java continued in the hands of our enemies.

C

Owing to the shallowness of the water, ships are obliged to lie off at a considerable distance from the shore. Boats proceeding into the river must steer for the church on the hill, keeping it rather on the starboard bow, and when the bar is approached, the channel may be discovered by the stakes at the entrance of the river. Fish is very plentiful, and a variety of excellent fruit, yams, sago, poultry, and Buffaloes may here be obtained, besides grain which is imported from Java, Sumatra, or Bengal. Dammer for caulking is an article of trade, and spars for masts brought over from Siak river, on the opposite coast of Sumatra, are bartered at Malacca.

Intelligence was received here that General Daendels had been recalled from the government of Java, in which he was succeeded by General Jansens, who, it was also reported, had already arrived at Batavia with a numerous body of troops from France.

Before leaving Malacca, it became expedient to decide on the best course to be pursued for reaching the place of our destination. It was universally allowed, that a passage through the straits of Banca was, at that advanced season of the year, totally impracticable. It was at the same time extremely doubtful whether one could be effected by coasting along the south side of Borneo, within the Caramatta passage, so as to gain the benefit of the land and sea breezes, and to be able to stretch across the Java sea from Sambar point. It was, however, considered, in favour of this last navigation, that if it should prove successful, the fleet would be thereby enabled to fetch any station to the westward of Cheribon.

A third, and, as it should seem, the only certain passage, was that round Borneo, and by *Celebes*. This course, it was considered, would enable the fleet to attack any of the posts in Java, as they would approach from the eastward; and consequently the eastern monsoon would thus give them the command of the whole line of coast. Such were the advantages which recommended the choice of this passage in preference to the others; but on the other hand, the extreme length of it made it doubtful whether the fleet could reach Java in sufficient time to accomplish the object of the expedition, before the rainy season, which there commences in October, should have set in; added to which weighty objection, very serious apprehensions were entertained with respect to the health of the troops, during a passage and subsequent operations, conducted in tracts subject to violent rain. These were the considerations that induced Sir Samuel Auchmuty to decline this route, if it could well be avoided; and that more particularly, as he had already resolved to attack the capital; and therefore it was not an essential object to be able to reach the eastern part of the island. Fortunately, at this time, a small vessel, which had been sent to explore the southern coast of Borneo, returned with a favourable account of that navigation; upon which information it was immediately determined to proceed in squadrons to *Sambar,* and from thence to stretch across the Java sea towards Cheribon.

Accordingly, the army having been brigaded, and the ships supplied with water, the different convoys again got under weigh, on the eleventh of June.

The Bengal division sailed first, followed by the first division from Madras, and so on in succession; and in a few days the fleet entered the straits of Sincapore. Here we experienced occasional squalls, with sharp lightning, thunder, and rain; and the tide drifting forcibly over

c 2

to the Malay coast, obliged us frequently to come to an anchor. The depth of water through these straits, is generally from sixteen to seventeen fathoms; and the scenery along the shores is highly beautiful.

After passing through the straits, the fleet stood direct for Borneo, for the purpose of profiting by the land breezes, which blow over that vast line of coast. Having passed *Timbalan*, and a number of other islands, we arrived, on the third of July, at the High Islands, which constituted the third rendezvous of the fleet.

The High Islands, which form an extensive Archipelago, from their number and unknown positions, render navigation in those seas extremely difficult and dangerous.

The Island, where the greater part of the fleet anchored, has two watering places, which supplied all the ships with that necessary article, of an excellent quality, as fast as they arrived ; and this essential service was completed in the course of a week. Hogs, mousedeer, and monkies are found here, but no inhabitants of the human species have hitherto been discovered ; and only a few Malay fishermen and pirates pay occasional visits to these places.

On the morning of the tenth of July, while preparing to get under weigh, a stiff squall with rain came on, which lasted a considerable time, and brought a great portion of the fleet into imminent danger. Several horse-transports drifted from their anchorage close in shore, and a violent pitching, which was rendered more perilous on account of the shallowness of the water, threatened destruction to the ships. A more frightful sight can scarcely be conceived ;---large vessels with a hundred horses, and double that number of men on board, were tossed up into the air at one instant, and precipitated the next to the bottom of the ocean, with such violence that their keels actually struck the ground, and the earth which was thereby torn up with great force, gave the sea all around a thick muddy appearance.

At last, the wind abated a little ; and after many efforts, the distressed ships having succeeded in getting off at a late hour in the evening, they came to an anchor in thirteen fathoms.

We continued sailing through a cluster of islands, leaving Carramata to our right, the coast of Borneo on our left, generally close in land ; and on the twentieth of July, reached Point Sambar, which was the fourth rendezvous of the expedition, at the extremity of the south-west coast of Borneo.

The information which had been received by Sir Samuel Auchmuty, before his departure from Madras, and which was confirmed both at Penang and Malacca, had finally determined him to attack Batavia. From the intelligence which was imparted to him, he was induced to believe, that though the enemy would, in all probability, endeavour to present obstacles to any operations that might be attempted in other quarters, yet, that the great stand would be made near Batavia ; that, in fact, their greatest force was collecting there ; strong positions were taken up at Cornelis and Buitenzorg ; and finally, that all the principal magazines were removing to that spot.

The only point upon which any indecision as yet remained, was the choice of the place of landing. The coast was favourable within few miles of Batavia, after which it became altogether impracticable from thence to Cheribon. In the one case, a vigorous opposition was to be expected at landing ; and some risk, and much loss must of course attend a disembarkation in the face of an army of twenty thousand men; for such, according to computation, was the disciplined force with which we should have to contend. On the other hand, in the event of landing at Cheribon, a long march of nearly two hundred miles was to be encountered through a mountainous and intricate country, in the entire possession of a hostile foe, having every advantage of annoyance, while the invading army would be without the means of moving their guns, and of transporting the provisions and other stores. That the general might be the better enabled to come to a positive conclusion, immediately on his reaching Java, without being there perplexed by delay or uncertainty, he detached Lieutenant-Colonel Mackenzie, of the engineers, and another able officer, Lieutenant Blakiston, with suitable instructions, the purport of which pointed out that Sir Samuel Auchmuty would prefer landing at Batavia, if the Sourabaya division had not been called thither; but that should the whole army be there collected, it would be, in his opinion, most prudent to land near Cheribon.

The armament having thus, after a very tedious, but in other respects most fortunate navigation, assembled on the twenty-sixth of July, at this last point of rendezvous; on the day following the whole made sail for Java. On the thirtieth, the fleet reached Bumpkin Island, on that coast, near Indramay river, and the same night they had a very narrow escape, being close to a reef off that island. Here we continued from this time till the second of August, in expectation of the frigates which were to have joined with intelligence, but as it was determined to wait no longer, the fleet proceeded towards Batavia. This unavoidable delay afforded an opportunity to the enemy of discovering the fleet, and General Jansens was accordingly apprised of our being off the island. In the course of the day, the expected ships, with Colonel Mackenzie, joined ; and from him it appeared that he had reconnoitered the whole coast, and that a landing was most advisable at the village of Chillingching, a situation well known to the navy, and lying about ten miles from Batavia. The Colonel having been induced to land with a few men, was surprized by a corps of the enemy stationed there for the purpose of capturing those, who, according to the customary practice of the ships, might be sent on shore for cattle. The Colonel and his suit escaped, but an officer and a few men of the sixty-ninth regiment were taken, though the enemy obtained no discovery from them, as they all pretended to be marines belonging to the squadron.

From the information now received, and which agreed perfectly with his previous inquiries and intentions, the Commander in Chief resolved upon landing at Chillingching. The fleet, therefore, which had brought to in the afternoon, again got under weigh, and every preparation was completed for effecting the disembarkation without delay.

On the evening of the third, the squadron made Cape Carawang, and early the next morning ran in for the mouth of Marandi river. The ships anchored during the interval between the land and sea breezes, but when the latter came in they again stood in, and before four, being off Chillingching, the signal was made for the troops to land.

BAY OF BATAVIA.

The Fleet employed in this Expedition consisted of the following Ships:

LINE OF BATTLE SHIPS.

Scipion, Rear Admiral Stopford, joined at Batavia.
Illustrious, Commodore Broughton—Captain Festing.
Minden, Captain Hoare.
Lion, Captain Heathcote.

FRIGATES.

Akbar	- -	Captain Drury		Hussar	- - Captain	Crawfurd
Doris	- -	Lye		Drake	- -	Harris
Nisus	-	Beaver		Phœton	- -	Pellew
President	- -	Warren		Leda	- -	Sayer
Bucephalus	-	Pelly		Caroline	- -	Cole
Phœbe	- -	Hillyar		Cornelia	- -	Edgell
Modeste	- -	Elliot		Psyche	- -	Edgecumbe

SLOOPS.

Barracouta	-	Captain Owen		Samarang	-	Captain Drury
Hesper	- -	Reynolds		Harpy	- -	Bain
Hecate	- -	Peachey		Procris	- -	Mansell
Dasher	- -	Kelly				

HON. COMPANY'S CRUIZERS.

Malabar	- -	{ Com. Hayes { Capt. Maxfield	Vestal	- Captain	Hall
Aurora	- -	Watkins	Ariel	- -	Macdonald
Mornington	-	Pearce	Thetis	- - -	Lieut. Phillips
Nautilus	- -	Walker	Psyche	- - -	

Fifty-seven transports and several gun-boats, amounting in all to one hundred sail.

PART II.

ACCOUNT OF THE CAMPAIGN.

SECTION I.

From the landing of the Army, to the gaining possession of Batavia.

When the conquest of Java is attentively considered with a due regard to the magnitude of the object, the means employed, and the formidable obstacles which were opposed to the enterprize, it will not shrink in the comparison with the most splendid achievements of modern history. The votes of thanks which passed both houses of parliament, to those who were engaged in this addition to the glory of the British empire, affords indeed a sufficient proof of the high importance of the acquisition and the value of their services by whom it was obtained.

The fleet, about one hundred sail, including gun-boats, anchored, as before stated, in the Bay of Batavia about two o'clock P. M. on Sunday the fourth of August, 1811; and the landing was immediately carried into effect at Chillingching, a village about ten miles to the eastward of Batavia.

D

The army was divided, agreeably to the arrangements ordered at Malacca, into four brigades; one forming the advance, two the line, and one the reserve*.

The Leda frigate, Captain Sayer, having been off this coast before, and reconnoitred this part, ran in close to the shore to protect the landing on our left, whilst on the right were stationed several gun-boats which had been captured from the enemy, and also several of the Company's cruizers, or gun-brigs.

The place of our landing is one of those spots which, like that of Cap Malheureux at the Isle of France, are generally left unguarded, being considered as points of such difficulty on account of their natural obstacles, that no invading army, it was reasonable to suppose, would there attempt to make a descent. This idea of security on the part of the enemy enabled us to effect our debarkation without loss, in the same manner as happened at the Isle of France.

The advance under Colonel Gillespie proceeded first on shore, followed by his Excellency the Commander in Chief, and immediately moved forward, taking up a position beyond the village, to gain pos-

* General Abstract of the Army under the command of Sir SAMUEL AUCHMUTY, MALACCA, June 4, 1811.

	Officers.	Native Officers.	Non-commissoned Officers and Privates.	Total.
European Force	200	—	5144	5344
Native Force -	124	123	5530	5777
	324	123	10,674	11,121
Pioneers, Lascars, &c.	-	-	-	839
Grand Total -	-	-	-	11,960

But of this number about twelve hundred were sick at Malacca, and about fifteen hundred on landing at Java.

session of the road to Cornelis, and protect the landing of the remainder. The brigades of the line when landed occupied the road to
Batavia *.

* THE FOLLOWING ARRANGEMENTS WERE ORDERED:—

G. O. By the Commander in Chief.

When the army is ordered to land, the various corps of which it is composed will prepare
to disembark in the following order of succession.

First division—The Infantry and dismounted troop of Native Cavalry of the advance, reinforced by the flank battalions of the Line—the Royal Artillery and Lascars attached, and the
detachment of Bengal Pioneers—the whole under the orders of Colonel Gillespie:

1 The Right Flank battalion of the Line.

2 The Left ditto.

3 The battalion of Royal Marines.

4 Detachment, H. M. 89th regiment.

5 The Royal Artillery with their Lascars and six six-pounders complete, with their
ammunition and persons for conveying it when on shore.

6 The Governor General's Body-guard.

7 The Light Infantry Volunteer battalion.

8 The Bengal Pioneers.

9 Horses for officers on the Staff.

Second division—The Line under Major General Wetherall, with the Bengal Artillery,
guns, Madras Pioneers, and Lascars.

RIGHT BRIGADE, Colonel Gibbs:

1 H. M. 14th regiment.

2 H. M. 59th regiment.

3 Fifth Bengal Volunteer battalion.

4 Bengal Artillery and Lascars, with ten six-pounders and ammunition complete, as
ordered, with persons to convey it when on shore, and a party of Artificers.

LEFT BRIGADE, Lieutenant Colonel Adams.

5 H. M. 69th regiment.

6 H. M. 78th regiment.

7 Sixth Volunteer battalion.

The arrangements ordered for the landing were most judicious; but a considerable delay in the operation occurred, owing to the insurmountable obstacles the boats met with in their attempt to assemble round their respective rendezvous ships: both wind and tide were against them, and prevented their proceeding in the prescribed order. It became therefore necessary at last to direct the boats to land as expeditiously as they could, without attending to order. Fortunately there was no opposition, and though certainly this was the most con-

  8 Madras Pioneers.

  9 Madras Tent Lascars.

10 Ditto Dooly Bearers.

             THIRD DIVISION—The Reserve under Colonel Wood:

1 The Flank battalion of the Reserve.

2 First battalion 20th regiment Native Infantry.

3 Third Volunteer battalion.

4 Fourth Volunteer battalion.

Par. 2. The horse artillery, the cavalry, and the remaining staff, horses, and bullocks for the artillery, to be landed as soon as possible after the infantry of the army, &c. &c. &c.

Par. 4. Colonel Gillespie will immediately on landing occupy such posts in the vicinity of the landing-place as will cover it completely, and he will limit his operations in the first instance to this object, until the Line has landed, when Major General Wetherall will form that part of the army to cover the landing of the remainder, while Colonel Gillespie with the advance moves forward to a moderate distance and occupies such advantageous positions as may present themselves more in front, but not so far separated from the line as to risk a possibility of interruption to their communication, or to deprive his own corps of the advantage of certain and immediate support if necessary. The movements of the Line will be made to co-operate on this subject, &c. &c. &c.

                      (Signed)   P. AGNEW, Adj. Gen.

N. B. The Order goes into great length and embraces every essential subject, in the most satisfactory manner.

venient place near Batavia for the purpose of defence, not a man in arms was found in the village.

The corps of the army had ground allotted to them as they landed, on which they were to form, and as soon as the principal part of each battalion was on shore it was marched off to gain the position where it was intended the whole should halt during the night.

Though the country is low, and intersected with swamps, salt-pits, and canals, yet before night the whole of the infantry, with their guns, were on shore; the advanced posts were pushed on, two miles from the landing-place, and the troops were formed in two lines, one fronting Batavia and the other Cornelis.

Notwithstanding the strength of the position, which was sufficient to secure the army, the Commander in Chief was not without some uneasy apprehensions with respect to the consequences that might attend an alarm during the night, as the troops were of necessity totally unacquainted with their relative situations, and a fire rashly commenced would in all probability have been the cause of much mischief. Every precaution was taken to guard against this inconvenience, and happily with effect; for though a patrole of the enemy's cavalry galloped during the night into the advanced posts, on the Batavia road, where they received the fire of two six-pounders and that of a picquet of infantry, no farther firing or unnecessary alarm ensued. An Aid-de-Camp of General Janssens was with this party, of whom an officer and two or three soldiers were killed.

On the fifth the horse artillery and cavalry were landed, and the position of the army was advanced towards Batavia. The country here is low, but the ground occupied is strong, as from the Marandi river, close on our left, a canal runs parallel to the shore nearly a mile in length to the Anjole river. General Wetherall occupied this point with his right to the sea and his left to the canal. The great road to Batavia intersected this position. The village Chillingching was directly inland from the landing-place, beyond the canal, over which the enemy had very imprudently suffered a bridge to remain standing. Colonel Gillespie occupied the ground some distance beyond the village, and guarded the road leading from thence to Cornelis.

The reserve remained at the landing-place, to support each point. Had the enemy destroyed the bridge at Chillingching, they might securely and at their leisure have cannonaded our position, but they never ventured near the line. Information, however, was obtained that a column had approached within four miles of Chillingching, and accordingly on the fifth the advance was pushed forward for the purpose of attacking them.

This detachment marched a considerable distance, and took post at Suyrannah Chapel, about six miles on the road to Cornelis; but it was soon ascertained that the enemy had immediately retreated upon hearing of this movement. The heat was so excessive that several of the party were attacked with coups-de-soleil, which proved instantaneously fatal to some, while others lingered out till the evening, and died after our return. The labours of this day, which of themselves were exceedingly severe, were rendered still more so by the circumstance of our having but just landed.

As this was the road by which the General intended to advance, preparations were made for the conveyance of the necessary stores and provisions, since a communication with the shore must be uncertain, and no dependence could be placed on resources in a country where the enemy had it in his power to remove or destroy all that might be of any benefit to the invader.

It was arranged therefore that every man who did not bear a musket should carry a load; and that every private follower, except one to each officer, should be taken for the public service. The troops would have been obliged to carry five days provisions; and by these means it was hoped that the army might calculate on enduring an absence of ten days without any material inconvenience. But the consequence of so short a march as that already mentioned, performed by the advance, induced the General to practise the men and horses before the commencement of his operations. It was his determination to feel the enemy on the side of Batavia, and when he had engaged their attention in that quarter, then to fall back rapidly, and advance on the road to Cornelis.

On the morning of the sixth, Colonel Gillespie accompanied by the officers of his staff, and Captain Dickson, Aid-de-Camp to the Commander in Chief, with a small escort of dragoons, reconnoitred the road and country all along the coast towards Batavia, proceeding as far as Anjole Point, about two miles from the capital. The videttes of the enemy were discovered on the other side of the water, but the bridge across the Anjole river was already burnt.

From the report made to the Commander in Chief, his Excellency directed the advance to countermarch that evening, and occupy a new position at Tanjong Priock, some distance in front of General Wetherall, and about six miles from the capital. The reserve took up the ground which had been quitted by the advance beyond Chillingching.

The country to the Anjole river was so intricate, as to occasion no small surprise at its being surrendered to us without any opposition. The inactivity of the enemy, the little appearance of force on the Batavia side of the river, and a very serious conflagration in that city, fixed the resolution of the Commander in Chief to attempt a passage the next night. Accordingly, on the seventh of August, the infantry attached to the advance pushed forward and crossed the Anjole river at ten o'clock at night, over a bridge of boats which had been rowed in after dark for that purpose, under the direction of Captain Sayer of the Leda, and Captains Reynolds and Mansell of the Hesper and Procris.

The troops could only pass over in single file, having to step from one boat to another, which delayed the passage considerably.

A part of the horse artillery and the Bengal light infantry battalion, were drawn up behind the banks of the river, which concealed them, and served as a parapet to protect the passage, and to act as a reserve, according to circumstances. It was, indeed, natural to have expected that the passage of the Anjole river would have been warmly contested by the enemy, as they could not fail to be apprised of our intention, by observing the boats that had been rowed up the river; and certainly few countries exhibit greater difficulties than this, to an attacking army, and such as when proper advantage is taken of them are peculiarly favourable in defensive warfare.

By midnight the whole party had crossed over, and at the dawn of day the advance was posted near the suburbs, about one mile from the town, in positions which the nature of such an intersected country pointed out as most eligible, amongst the numerous canals and rivulets ; the bridges over which had all been broken down and carried away or burnt by the enemy, in the view of impeding our approach by every difficulty they could throw in the way, without hazarding the consequences of actual engagements. While the advanced troops were thus gaining ground, the line was moved forward to the river, ready to support them ; the reserve, reinforced by a battalion of marines and a troop of cavalry remaining at Chillingching.

The following morning, the eighth of August, Captains Tylden and Dickson, Aids-de-Camp to the Commander in Chief, having summoned the town, returned with the head magistrate, Mayor Hillebrink, who was deputed on the part of the burghers to crave our protection. Though no correct information, could hereby be obtained ; yet it was evident that the whole of the enemy's force was in the neighbourhood of Batavia, at Weltervreeden and Cornelis ; and might, for any thing we knew to the contrary, even occupy part of the suburbs, or be concealed in the town.

The houses all along our present position were deserted ; as all the respectable inhabitants had been compelled to retire into the interior by positive orders from General Janssens, to prevent the possibility of their giving to the British any assistance or intelligence. By a general proclamation no more than one jar of water was permitted to be kept in any house or family for their own consumption ; and lastly, as we advanced, the conduits by which the water used for drinking was conveyed from the inland parts of the city, were destroyed, in order to distress the army by cutting off that indispensable article.

Thus situated, surrounded by every thing inimical, it became necessary to proceed with great caution. A small party only was directed to enter the town, to feel their way and make a report.

E

This consisted of the rifle and light company of the fifty-ninth regiment under Captain Watts, accompanied by Captain Thorn, Brigade Major of the advance. Several of the enemy's scouts shewed themselves as the party marched through the suburbs; but they instantly gallopped off in the direction of Weltervreeden. The detachment repaired immediately to the town-house, which they occupied, and by their presence put a stop to the plundering which had been carried on by the Malays since our landing, and thus several large stores of colonial goods were timely saved from plunder or the flames.

Colonel Agnew, Adjutant General, arrived shortly after, and communicated to the assembled magistrates and captains of the different classes of native inhabitants, the pleasure of the Commander in Chief with respect to such local and civil arrangements as the case required; the town having surrendered at discretion.

A royal salute was fired from the shipping in the Roads, on hoisting the British colours at the Crane Wharf. In the evening Colonel Gillespie with the greater part of the advance entered the town, and after drawing up in the grand square in front of the town-house, and taking formal possession of the place, the troops were dismissed to their quarters.

Various reports were circulated in the course of this evening of a meditated attack from the enemy, who were at Weltervreeden, not more than three miles distant. The suspicious and extraordinary manner of several of the French officers in the town, whose conduct could not escape notice, with other concurring circumstances, rendered it but too probable that these rumours would be soon verified ; and this apprehension received additional strength from the consideration of the smallness of our force, which, in the town, did not exceed eight hundred men. And as there were no guns or defences to the place, our vigilance was increased, and every precaution of course was adopted to prevent a surprise. Captain Robison, Aid-de-Camp to Lord Minto, who carried a summons to General Janssens to surrender the island, returned about ten o'clock P. M. with his answer, wherein he stated that he was a French General, and would defend his charge to the last extremity. Captain Robison was conducted blindfolded through their lines ; but as he went along he heard a great bustle of men and horses, with the moving of wheel carriages of the artillery, which served still more to confirm our suspicions.

About eleven o'clock at night, the troops were silently called out, and ordered to lie on their arms in the grand square in front of the town-house. Scarcely had they reached the square, when the head of the enemy's column appeared, and opened a fire of musquetry upon our picquet that was stationed at the bridge leading from Weltervreeden to the town, under the orders of Captain Trench of the eighty-ninth regiment, who had just time to raise the drawbridge.* The firing was now heard in all directions round the town, when Colonel Gillespie sallied out at the head of a party, at a gateway on the west side of the city, with the intention of suddenly falling upon

* On hearing the firing, the Mayor, who had been observed particularly alarmed the whole time of supper, and the officers before mentioned, who were present at the Commanding Officer's quarters, instantly started up and attempted to escape ; but they were stopped, and a guard was placed over them.

the enemy's advance by surprize and charging them in flank. This movement had the desired effect. The firing soon afterwards ceased, and the enemy were no more heard or seen during the remainder of the night.

Several of the assailants were killed by our videttes posted on the outside of the drawbridge, who fired into their column to give the alarm; but not one casualty happened on our side. The darkness of the night, and the positive orders given to our troops not to fire unnecessarily, but to trust to their bayonets, prevented the enemy from discovering our several posts; and consequently this want of direction for his fire, rendered it ineffectual.

The enemy had imagined that the two companies which marched into the city in the morning would fall an easy sacrifice, not having been aware at first of the reinforcement which very fortunately joined them in the evening.

On being informed of it by their emissaries in the city, and finding that the rest of the British army was still at a distance, separated from the town by the river Anjole, they still flattered themselves with the expectation of realizing their project by employing a larger force, and accordingly marched a strong column on this night attack; the rear of which, it was reported, extended to Weltervreeden, when the head of the column reached the suburbs.

They had also relied on the effects which they expected would have been produced on our soldiers from the great quantity of deleterious liquor stored up in every house, and which the Chinese and other inhabitants (in conformity doubtless to instructions from the enemy) pressed on the soldiers in lieu of water, which they wanted; but all these contrivances were timely counteracted, and their ill effects prevented, by the decisive measures adopted by Colonel Gillespie, who commanded in the city.

The troops continued under arms the whole night, and the next day part of the horse artillery and a troop of dragoons joined our little garrison.

In the Castle, and the arsenals at the Wharf, a number of guns were found, mostly of brass, together with a great quantity of naval and military stores.

In the following night the town had nearly been destroyed with every soul in it, by a Malay, who most fortunately was discovered in time, with a fire-brand in his hand, in the act of firing wooden magazines, which contained a great quantity of gun-powder. It was at two o'clock in the morning of the tenth of August, when relieving the guards, preparatory to an attack on the enemy's positions near Weltervreeden, that this circumstance happened, and its providential discovery saved the town and thousands of people. The incendiary was hanged the next day.

SECTION II.

The Action of the Tenth of August.

THE bridge over the Anjole river having been rendered sufficiently strong to bear the passage of guns, the army prepared to cross early on the morning of the tenth of August; while the advance marched from Batavia under the orders of Colonel Gillespie, amounting to about one thousand European troops, and four hundred and fifty natives.

This force moved at four o'clock in the morning from the town, and continued along the road to Weltervreeden, through Molenvleet, in profound silence†.

† The Commanding Officer's quarters, which the magistrates had allotted to Colonel Gillespie, were kept by a Frenchman who had been a menial servant of General Daendels. This man, just before we mounted our horses, poisoned the coffee which had been called for, with some villainous drug; and it had such an immediate effect, that Colonel Gillespie and every officer of his staff, and others who had tasted of it, were all at once seized with most violent pains and vomitings. The fellow had a cup poured down his own throat, though very much against his will; and it produced the same effect on him, only a little more powerful. The occupation of the moment, and other more serious matter which then engaged every person, prevented a farther examination into this abominable act, of which the motives were but too obvious—at a moment when the fellow well knew that we were going into action. He afterwards got off to America.

The houses, mostly very superb buildings, all along this tract, were deserted for the reasons already mentioned.

Various signals, blue lights, &c. were exhibited by the enemy as we approached the Champ de Mars. At the break of day we arrived at the cantonment of Weltervreeden, and found it abandoned; the enemy's troops having all retrograded to their strong position, about a mile further on the road towards Cornelis. We advanced to the attack in two columns. The enemy's right was protected by the Slokan; their left by the Great River, over which there was a bridge, at that time in flames. Pepper plantations covered and concealed their line, and an abbatis had been felled to block up the road leading to Cornelis, which was a continuation of the one on which Colonel Gillespie's left was advancing, and behind this the enemy had placed four horse artillery guns, which opened their fire as soon as our troops composing the left column arrived within range of their grape. The infantry of the enemy occupied two villages which ran along the wood on both sides of this road, and from which they kept up a very brisk fire of musquetry.

The enemy's guns were answered with great effect from one twelve and two six pounders horse artillery attached to the British advance, whilst our sharp-shooters made sure of their aim along the whole front. Dispositions had already been made for turning the enemy's flanks; which object was carried, after surmounting very great obstacles from the nature of the country. The villages occupied by the enemy were set in flames, and the British troops, rushing forward, charged their guns at the point of the bayonet.

About this time our Commander in Chief, having preceded his

army, arrived at the scene of action, where he had the satisfaction of beholding a handful of heroes defeat five times their own number.

The action lasted full two hours, owing to the abbatis and other impediments which had been thrown in our way, and which the troops were obliged to remove before they could close with the enemy, who during all this time maintained a very severe fire. They were however completely defeated, with the loss of their guns, a number of killed, wounded and prisoners, both Europeans and Natives, amongst whom were several officers of distinction. General Alberti, Chef d'Etat Major, who arrived recently from France with General Janssens, after having served three campaigns in Spain, was very severely wounded, and narrowly escaped being taken prisoner. General Jumel commanded the post; Brigadier Lutzow was second; and the whole were under the general directions of General Janssens himself, whose head-quarters were at Struiswyk; but being chased from thence by our victorious advance, he removed to Cornelis.

The army had now come up and supported the troops in the pursuit, and Colonel Gillespie at the head of a squadron of the twenty-second dragoons pressed hard upon the fugitives, who were followed close under the works of Cornelis, when a shower of grape and round shot opened upon them from their batteries, but without any injury, as their guns were too highly elevated, and before they could be depressed our cavalry were sufficiently withdrawn to be covered from their sight. The infantry now occupied the advanced posts within eight hundred yards of the French redoubts, covered by the jungle from the view of the enemy. A very heavy cannonade was kept up all the day. In the arsenal of Weltervreeden were found upwards of three hundred pieces of ordnance and a quantity of military stores, &c. which the French had abandoned on our approach.

This affair was highly creditable to all the troops who were engaged in it, particularly to the eighty-ninth regiment, who charged the guns, and the grenadier company of the seventy-eighth. The consequence of it was that the enemy shut themselves up in their works, and gave up to us the undisturbed possession of Batavia and of the adjacent country. Their loss on this occasion was about five hundred men and four horse artillery guns, remarkably well found in every respect. A few prisoners were also taken from them. But the most material object gained by this brilliant action was the immediate possession of the very salubrious cantonment of Weltervreeden, which was most essential to the preservation of the health and lives of our soldiers. The capture of this place was therefore of the greatest importance to the success of the expedition, as it had always been the policy of General Daendels, in case of invasion, to tempt us with the possession of Batavia, well aware that the unhealthiness of the town and the noxious climate of the sea-shore would in a short time destroy our troops and compel the crippled remains of an exhausted army to return without effecting their purpose. This appears to have been also the idea of General Janssens; but these views were completely frustrated by the success of this day; and the severe blow thus inflicted on the *élite* of the French army gave them a foretaste of what they had to expect hereafter, and augured their defeat as certain in the event of a general action*.

* A strict regard to the sound military maxim, that soldiers ought never to be deprived of the glory which is their due, and which is the most potent stimulant to great actions, will

F

Brigade Orders by Colonel Gillespie.

Weltervreeden, 11th August, 1811.

" Colonel Gillespie, in appreciating the gallantry of the troops whom he had the honor to command in the action of yesterday, cannot find words adequate to express his thanks, and the admiration which their heroic behaviour has excited. He will take the earliest opportunity of particularizing to His Excellency the Commander in Chief, the meritorious conduct of the officers and men during the whole of that brisk affair, and trusts that the victory gained will be considered worthy the glory of adding a sprig to the laurels already worn by the distinguished troops composing the advance.

(Signed)

" WM. THORN, Maj. Brig."

Copy of Colonel Gillespie's Official Report to Colonel Agnew, Adjutant General.

" Weltervreeden, 11th August, 1811.

" SIR,

" I Have the honor to report to you, for the information of His Excellency the Commander in Chief, that in conformity to His Excellency's

be a sufficient reason for the insertion in this place, of the official reports, the brigade and general orders, wherein are detailed the names of those officers whose services were deemed worthy of being particularly noticed. This in fact is no more than an act of simple justice to the memory of those who fell in the field, that their relatives and friends may have the mournful satisfaction of knowing that their loss was properly felt by those who could best judge of their merits; while the survivors will consider the record as an incentive to pursue with unabated ardour that course which has been stamped with public approbation.

permission, I moved with the advance from Batavia yesterday morning, at 4 A. M. with the corps detailed in the margin *.

" After passing through the cantonment of Weltervreeden, in two columns, I found the enemy strongly posted beyond it, in a difficult country, having a battery of guns on the road to Cornelis, behind an abbatis.

" The action commenced soon after day dawned. From the disposition made for the advance, we succeeded in attacking the enemy in front and both flanks, which enabled us to force their position ; and this appears, from what we afterwards saw of the ground, and the very great strength of the post they occupied, to have prevented a greater effusion of blood on our side.

" After an action of full two hours we pursued the enemy under their works of Cornelis ; and when on the point of advancing the cavalry to attack, a very heavy fire opened from the batteries, which obliged me to recall them under shelter of the wood.

" His Excellency had the opportunity of witnessing a part of this business ; it is unnecessary therefore to enter into a further detail.

* CONSISTING OF THE FOLLOWING DETAILS :

Horse artillery, four guns, Captain Noble.

Troop of the 22d dragoons, Captain Chadwick.

Right flank battalion, Major Miller.

Left flank ditto, Major Fraser.

Detachment of the 89th regiment, Major Butler.

Governor General's body-guard, Captain Gall.

Detachment of the 22d dragoons dismounted, Lieutenant Dudley.

Detachment of the Bengal light infantry battalion, Captain Leys.

Madras pioneers, Captain Smithwayte.

The enemy's guns were taken at the point of the bayonet, after a defence of the most determined and obstinate nature.   It is reported that the greater part of the European force of Marshal Janssens were at that spot; and from the number of European officers killed and taken, we have every reason to suppose that it was so.

" In appreciating the heroic conduct of the troops in this sharp service, I can hardly find words to express myself.   The fatigue they have suffered since they came on shore, and the almost impassable country through which they had to penetrate and push the enemy, will I hope be considered by his Excellency the Commander in Chief as it deserves.

" Of the conduct of the Officers commanding different corps and companies, (as in many parts, from the thickness of the jungle, companies and even sections were detached,) I have to express my admiration—particularly Major Fraser and the left column under his command, who bore the severest part of the action.   In the capture of the guns, Major Butler and Captain French eighty-ninth foot, Captain Forbes seventy-eighth, and the officers and men composing these corps, I have particularly to mention: Captain Lindsay commanding the light company of the sixty-ninth regiment, Captain Cameron commanding the rifle company of the seventy-eighth regiment, Captains Oakes, Nunn, Rose, and Ramsay, which last was severely wounded, and Lieutenant Young eighty-ninth, in fact all the officers and men of this column fought like British soldiers; and their gallant commander Major Butler, ably seconded by Captain French, deserve my warmest acknowledgments, as does Captain Forbes of the seventy-eighth regiment for the same gallantry.   I cannot say too much of Captain Noble, and the officers and men under his command, who so gallantly fought the two guns that drew a most terrible fire from the enemy ; indeed the zeal and ability displayed by Captain Noble throughout this service demand my particular commendation.

" I must also express my acknowledgments to Major Miller commanding the right column, to Captain Stanus of the 14th light infantry company, Captain Watts of the 59th regiment, Lieutenant Cochlan commanding the rifle company of the 14th regiment, and Lieutenant M'Pherson commanding the rifle company of the 59th regiment, and the officers and men of their different corps, as that column contributed much to the success of the day, by turning the enemy's left flank. I have also to thank Captain Leys, officers and men of the Bengal light infantry battalion, and Captain Evans and Captain M'Pherson, the officers and grenadiers under their command of the 5th and 6th Bengal volunteer battalions attached to the flank battalions. Captain Leys commanded the detachment of Bengal light infantry in the absence of Captain Fraser and Major Dalton, whom I found it necessary to leave in command of Batavia.

" I have also to thank Captain Gall of the body-guard, Lieutenant Dudley of the dismounted dragoons twenty-second regiment, and Captains Smithwayte and M'Craith of the Madras pioneers, for their support during the affair.

" To Captain Taylor, of His Majesty's twenty-fourth dragoons, military secretary to the Governor General, I have to return thanks for his indefatigable assistance during the whole affair, and his very zealous exertions during the whole time since we landed, as also to Captains Dickson and Blakiston, his Excellency's Aid-de-Camp, from whom

I experienced every assistance, and whose conduct has been most gallant.

" Captain Mears of the seventeenth Madras native infantry, who volunteered with me on this service, Lieutenant Hanson of the Quarter Master General's department, and Lieutenant Taylor twenty-fifth dragoons, who have been attached to me since the commencement of the service, I have to thank for their gallantry, activity, and persevering conduct.

" To Captain Thorn, of His Majesty's twenty-fifth dragoons, my Brigade Major, who, I can venture to say, has hardly slept since we landed, it is difficult to express my value of his services; they are great; but I am sorry to say he has met with two contusions. I should not thus have entered into a detail of the individual services of so many officers, had I not ocular demonstration of their fully deserving such notice, and should feel myself remiss were I to be silent

" I have the honour to be,

(Signed)   " R. R. GILLESPIE, Colonel."

" *P. S.* Subjoined is a list of the killed and wounded. The gallant soldiers who have fallen I much lament, in particular Lieutenant Monro of the seventy-eighth regiment.

" The loss of the enemy must have been severe. It is difficult to estimate it exactly, their dead and wounded being carried off the ground, as fast as possible, in light carts and litters, and conveyed to Cornelis. Amongst them were several officers of distinction. Besides capturing the enemy's guns that were opposed to us in the action, upwards of three hundred pieces of ordnance have been abandoned by them in their arsenal at Weltervreeden, and a quantity of military stores, ammunition gun-carriages, &c. &c. have been taken.

RETURN OF KILLED AND WOUNDED

Of the Advance commanded by Colonel R. R. Gillespie, in the Action of the 10th of August, 1811, near Weltervreeden.

	KILLED.						WOUNDED.						Missing, rank and file.	Total killed, wounded, and missing.	HORSES.			
	Captains.	Lieutenants.	Ensigns.	Sergeants.	Rank and file.	Total.	Captains.	Lieutenants.	Ensigns.	Sergeants.	Rank and file.	Total.			Killed.	Wounded.	Missing.	Total.
Brigade Staff.............................	..	..	..	..	..	..	1	..	..	..	..	1	..	1	1	..	..	1
Horse Artillery	..	..	..	..	..	..	..	1	..	..	4	5	..	5	2	2	..	4
Detachment 22d dragoons.................	..	..	..	..	..	..	..	..	..	..	..	..	..	..	..	2	..	2
Body Guard	..	..	..	..	..	..	..	..	..	..	..	..	..	..	..	..	..	..
Right Flank Battalion { Detachment 14th regiment	..	..	..	..	..	..	..	1	..	..	3	4	..	4	..	..	..	..
Right Flank Battalion { Ditto 59th ditto.............	..	..	..	..	..	..	..	..	..	..	3	3	..	3	..	..	..	..
Right Flank Battalion { Grenadier company 5th vol. bat.	..	..	..	..	..	..	..	..	..	..	..	..	..	..	..	..	..	..
Left Flank Battalion { Light infant. comp. 69th regt...	..	..	..	..	..	..	..	..	..	..	3	3	..	3	..	..	..	..
Left Flank Battalion { Detachment 78th ditto..	..	1	..	..	7	8	1	..	..	2	13	16	..	24	..	..	..	..
Left Flank Battalion { Grenadier company 6th vol. bat.	..	..	..	..	..	..	..	..	..	..	3	3	1	4	..	..	..	..
Detachment H. M. 89th regiment............	..	..	..	..	9	9	1	2	..	2	33	38	..	47	..	..	..	..
Ditto Bengal light infantry battalion.........	..	..	..	..	..	..	..	..	..	..	..	..	..	..	..	..	..	..
Total........	..	1	..	..	16	17	3	3	1	4	62	73	1	91	3	4	..	7

OFFICERS NAMES.

KILLED.—Lieutenant Monro, H. M. 78th Regiment.

WOUNDED.—Captain Thorn, 25th dragoons, Brigade Major to the advance.

Lieutenant and Adjutant Driffield, horse artillery, died of his wounds.

Ensign Nickison, 14th regiment.

Captain Cameron, 78th ditto.

Captain Ramsay, 89th ditto, severely.

Lieutenant French, 89th ditto.

Lieutenant and Adjutant Young, 89th ditto.

Lieutenant Robinson, 69th ditto.

From information just received, one General Officer, a Brigadier, and several Field Officers and Subalterns, are amongst the killed and wounded of the enemy.

Extract of the General Orders by the Commander in Chief,

Head-Quarters at Weltervreeden, 11th August, 1811.

" The Commander in Chief takes the earliest opportunity of express-ing his public thanks to Colonel Gillespie for his conduct yesterday.

" He entirely approves the gallant manner in which that officer profited by the permission given him to exercise his discretion in pushing the enemy some distance towards Cornelis, should he see an opportunity, after possessing himself of the cantonment of Welter-vreeden.

" The gallantry of all the corps of the advance has been reported to the Commander in Chief, as highly honourable to their characters as soldiers; but he thinks it proper to name the detachment of the 89th regiment as particularly distinguished by the energy of their attack on the strong position occupied by the enemy, and the capture of their guns. The prompt advance of the corps of the line under Major General Wetherall to support the advance, and the spirit they dis-played to come into action with the enemy, gave the greatest plea-sure to the Commander in Chief, in the conviction that a short time will enable him to gratify their wishes.

(Signed)   " P. AGNEW, Adj. Gen."

SECTION III.

Bombardment and Battle of Cornelis.

PREPARATIONS were now made for driving the enemy out of their strong-hold of Cornelis, an entrenched camp defended by two rivers, one on the east, the other on the west, with a number of redoubts and batteries guarding each of the fatal passes. The circumference of these fortified lines comprised nearly five miles, defended by two hundred and eighty pieces of cannon.

Here the whole of the French force was concentrated under the command of General Janssens, Governor General, and General Jumel, Senior Military Officer. This force had been augmented by the troops lately brought out from France, of whom a great number were voltigeurs. But to provide against all exigencies, in the case of any reverse, the French Commander in Chief addressed the following circular to the several General Officers and Brigadiers after the action of the 10th of August, 1811.

TRANSLATION.

" SIR,

   " The position of Cornelis, the works that have been constructed, the number of our troops in it, and the quantity of ordnance with which it is provided, renders it capable of a most desperate defence against the enemy. If the troops perform their duty,

G

and the officers commanding corps execute the orders which have been given to them, it cannot be carried by a coup-de-main. However, as it is possible that by a sudden surprise by night, or the neglect of some portion of our troops, the enemy might introduce himself into the place, and maintain himself there ; I have thought proper to communicate to you the measures expedient to be adopted for the security of our troops.

" In case of accidents, four openings remain for us to retreat by—First, the passage near the redoubt No. 3, at the Slokan, a small rivulet.—Second, the bridge opposite to the redoubt No. 5 ; this road leads to Pondockghede, and the road to Buitenzorg.—Third, the bridge on the rear face.—Fourth, the passage of Campong Malayo, which leads also to Buitenzorg by Bonjonghede, and the road called the Western Road.

" Should the enemy attempt an open attack by force, and succeed, he will make his greatest efforts on the front face, and on that of the Slokan, near about the redoubt No. 5. In this case the retreat will be made by the rear face ; and if that road is shut against us, a retreat can be made either through Campong Malayo, or the road to Bonjonghede.

" If the enemy should penetrate through the face of the great river, or the Campong Malayo, the retreat will be by the road of the redoubt No. 5, and that of the redoubt No. 3, both which lead (as has been said) to Pondockghede, so that whichever way the enemy may penetrate, there will always be a retreat for the troops.

" At whatever point the enemy may attack, the troops placed near that point will receive orders to fight to the last man, and wait in their post for support from the reserve. If these are not sufficient to renew the combat with advantage, and that his Excellency, or the General commanding the troops, should deem it necessary to order a retreat, you will in that event order the guns to be spiked of the redoubt entrusted to your care, and you will retire rapidly but in good order as mentioned above. The retreat will be protected by the cavalry and light artillery. You will exert every means to form your troops in column, and keep up the street-firing, which is the best for checking the pursuit of an enemy. It must be tried to induce the soldiers to charge with bayonets.

" In order to make the retreat as orderly as possible, the troops that are retreating will rally always near the Castle, and the Bazar of Cornelis ;—whether the enemy shall have penetrated by the Campong Malayo and the Great River, and that it is necessary to retire by the Slokan ; or whether he shall have made his way by the Slokan itself, or the front face ; and that consequently it will be necessary to retire by the rear face, and Campong Malayo ;

the park of artillery to file off first with an escort of cavalry, and the first corps of infantry that is formed upon the rallying point, the light artillery, and the rest of the infantry, beginning by those corps that may have suffered most in the action.

"All the grenadiers who can be assembled, the company of the imperial corps, the regiment of chasseurs, the dragoons, and two light pieces of artillery, the whole commanded by Brigadier Lutzow, will form the corps charged with the protection of the retreat. The troops will march in regular order, and observe silence; the last retreating corps will set fire to the bridges.

"At the distance of three palls from camp, the column will halt to take breath, and collect stragglers. Should any corps have been datached in advance an attempt must be made to reunite it by marching again upon a new position at Tanjong.

" In the beginning of the action, the baggage will have taken the route to Tanjong, taking care to move as quickly as possible, so as not to encumber the road, by which the march of the troops would be impeded.

" 1. The principal dispositions are, first to defend ourselves desperately against any attack of the enemy, without quitting our posts.

" 2. To renew our efforts, with the reserve, to throw the enemy into the ditch.

" 3. Not to retreat without orders; but when such shall be given, to spike the guns, and to repair quickly, and in good order, upon the square fronting the Castle, assemble there, protect the retreat of the artillery, and retire by the side opposite to that by which the enemy shall have penetrated.

" 4. To set fire to the bridges in retreating.

" In operations of this nature a number of events must unavoidably occur, which cannot be foreseen; but when the general dispositions are known, a brave, zealous, and active officer will easily find the means of saving the troops, and surmount every obstacle which may be thrown in his way.

" His Excellency relies upon your zeal on the present occasion for the services of the Emperor.

" I have the honor to be,

" Sir, &c. &c.

" To General de Brigade, commandant les Troupes."

(Signed) " JUMEL."

G 2

The success that had hitherto attended our operations, was altogether unexpected.   The nature of the country from Chillingching to
Batavia, and from thence to Weltervreeden, opposed serious obstacles
at every step.   The passage of the Anjole river might have impeded
the army many days, and consequently must in that case have been
attended with some loss; and though the fortifications of Batavia
were injudiciously destroyed, an enemy might still have suffered severely, before he could have penetrated into the town.   Again, had
the houses on the Weltervreeden road been occupied, and all the bridges
between the cantonment and Batavia destroyed, it would have been
very difficult to have advanced.   But every thing appears to have
given way in the estimation of the enemy to the confident idea, that
their lines could not be carried, of which indeed, according to account,
they were perfectly convinced.   The plan of defence resorted to by
General Daendels, was certainly judicious in part.   A position in the
country, and in a healthy situation, was no doubt preferable to a
defence at Batavia; but the place chosen in this instance was too near
the Capital, and an enemy had the advantage of water carriage within
two miles of it.   Instead of this the situation, especially where the
selection of places was at his command, ought to have been twenty
or thirty miles inland, and all the stores and magazines, should have
been removed thither.   These, on the contrary, were left either at
Batavia or Weltervreeden.   It has been observed that the fortifications
of Batavia were injudiciously destroyed.   Enough should have been
left to have obliged the invader to open batteries against the place.   The
garrison indeed might have been small, but select; and in so extensive
a place, a retreat was at all times certain.   If three weeks or a month

had been gained by these impediments, the face of affairs might have been materially altered ;—instead of which, in the course of a week, an enemy was permitted to pervade a strong country, to pass an un-fordable river, to occupy the Capital without loss, to possess himself of warlike stores, provisions, and carriages of every kind, with comfortable barracks for the whole of his forces, within two miles of their lines, and to drive them into their works, after a struggle, severe indeed for a short time, but which was never for a moment doubtful, and which must have impressed them with the highest ideas of British valour and discipline. The only active measure pursued, that of the destruction of the magazines in Batavia, was an act of wanton mischief without answering any military purpose. The immense store-houses in the citadel, filled with valuables, were all committed to the flames. Those in the city could not with safety be set on fire ; but the doors were thrown open, the roofs were untiled, and the floors were torn up, in order that as little might be left as possible. On Colonel Gillespie's entrance into the city, the immense population was employed in carrying off the contents of the public stores, and the streets were completely strewed with coffee and sugar.

It was natural that the army should be so elated by their suc-cess, as to be impelled by an ardent desire to decide the contest, in an immediate attack on the enemy's works, but prudence dictated precautionary measures. The position, though it could only be par-tially reconnoitred, appeared very formidable ; and when so much had been gained, it would have been rashness to risk the ad-vantage by any precipitate attempt. Sir Samuel Auchmuty there-fore determined to gain further information, and to make him-self better acquainted with the position, before he attacked it ;

and in the mean time every exertion was made to facilitate operations. by the landing of the battering guns, and collecting materials for the erection of batteries. Though from the nature of the defences the General was aware that our guns would not open the position, he trusted that they would make the situation of the enemy uneasy, divert their attention to one point, and reconcile our troops to the loss which must inevitably be the result of an attempt to carry that by assault, which their own conviction must assure them was impracticable by any other plan of attack. It was expected that a very few days would be sufficient for these purposes, but obstacles occurred which greatly retarded the operations.

An advanced position had already been taken up after the action of the tenth, and our picquets were posted within eight hundred yards of the enemy's works. A battering train was landed from the ships, and every exertion was made for its speedy equipment, under the superintendance of the commissary of stores, Captain Limond of the Madras artillery.

When the enemy were driven into Cornelis, it was not thought necessary or safe to keep a corps at Chillingching. The reserve therefore fell back on Batavia, and joined the army; the communication beyond Anjole river being abandoned, and the bridge taken away.

During the interval a correspondence had taken place with General Janssens. He sent in his Aid-de-Camp, with the Master of the Admiral's ship, and some seamen taken on one of the Eastern Islands, requesting that they might be exchanged for the prisoners taken on the tenth. The Aid-de-Camp was sent back with Sir Samuel

Auchmuty's answer: but a Colonel of Militia, who accompanied the flag as interpreter, was detained, and General Janssens informed, that it was in retaliation for the detention of a Lieutenant of Burghers, who had accompanied a flag as an interpreter, on our part, on the eighth. The consequence was, that a mutual release of these persons was immediately effected.

The fifteenth of August, being the birth-day of Buonaparte, was ushered in by the enemy with a thundering discharge of cannon from their numerous batteries, on which occasion also their whole line was drawn out and inspected by General Janssens.

On the nineteenth, the enemy endeavoured to fill the ditch of their entrenchments between the Slokan and Great River; but observing the damage it was doing to their ramparts, they turned off the water towards our advanced posts. It was night when the inundation was discovered. Two trenches, which were dug to aid our communications, and shelter the troops intended to guard the batteries, were filled with water, and serious apprehensions were entertained of the extent of the mischief; but before-day-break the cause being discovered, a remedy was instantly applied.

Materials having been collected, the army broke ground on the night of the twentieth, within six hundred yards of the enemy's works. A battery of twelve eighteen-pounders was intended to play upon the left of their entrenchments, and on a redoubt that overlooked them. A second battery of eight eighteen-pounders on its left, was intended to play into their works, and annoy their position. A third battery of nine howitzers and mortars was constructed on the same line, but more to the left.

The troops of the advance guarded the trenches under the orders of Colonel Gillespie, and every precaution was taken for the security of the working parties, who continued their labours unmolested the whole night. The batteries, however, were far from finished on the morning of the twenty-first. The enemy had kept up a fire from their works every day since the army had taken post in their front, but in general they were silent during the night. Fortunately they did not discover the men at work till the dawn of the twenty-first, when they opened a severe fire, which somewhat damaged the unfinished batteries, and greatly annoyed the troops in their operations of relief, the advance being that morning replaced by the left brigade of the line, commanded by Colonel Adams of the 78th regiment, in the duties of the trenches, under the superintendance of Major General Wetherall.

The batteries being nearly completed the night following, the guns were brought up by the seamen and mounted early in the morning of the twenty-second of August, when the enemy made a sortie and attacked our works. A body of their troops had lain concealed in the low jungle in front of our batteries; whilst a strong column, with four pieces of horse artillery guns, made a circuitous march to come round upon our left on the side of Weltervreeden. The firing from this body was the signal agreed on for those concealed in front to attack the batteries. But the right column of the enemy lost its way in the dark, and the day beginning now to dawn, their left, which lay in the jungle, impatient of delay, rushed on a sudden upon our batteries, and gained a momentary possession of one of them, whilst the working parties and seamen ran to their arms. The enemy, who had not time to injure the guns, were immediately driven back by a part of the fifty-ninth and seventy-eighth regiments; while their other column, after marching and countermarching all night, found themselves at day-break nearly in the same place from whence they set out; but they resolved to make an effort, and not being able to turn our left as was intended, they attacked in front.

Lieutenant-Colonel Clarges, of the sixty-ninth, instantly advanced against them, from the lines at Struiswyk, with a part of his regiment; but the enemy having no inclination to stand his charge, soon retired, after firing a few rounds from their horse artillery, by which that gallant officer was mortally wounded.

Colonel Gibbs's brigade, which was quartered in a village, between the advanced posts and Weltervreeden, was immediately pushed forward by the Commander in Chief, who had hastened to the spot on the first alarm, and gallantly supported the troops in the trenches.

The enemy having been thus completely foiled in their combined attacks, and in their attempts to render our guns and batteries unserviceable, began to open a tremendous fire from their redoubts. About forty pieces of their heaviest cannon, consisting of twenty-four and thirty-two pounders, bore upon our front, and kept up an incessant cannonade. The working parties, seamen, and soldiers, employed in carrying cartridges to our batteries, were much exposed to the enemy's shot, and several officers were killed and wounded[*].

---

[*] *Total Soldiers killed and wounded on the 22d of August, 1811.*

| Europeans | - | - | - | 67 |
| Natives | - | - | - | 29 |

H

On the twenty-third, the enemy were busily employed in making parapets to their nearest works, and in erecting other batteries. They did not fire, nor did we disturb them during these operations, as Sir Samuel Auchmuty was desirous of having every thing completed for opening with effect the next day.

At eight in the morning of the twenty-fourth, a salute announced his intentions, which was returned in the most spirited manner, and a very severe cannonade continued the greatest part of the day. But it was soon apparent, that though the enemy were superior in number of guns, they were inferior in the management of them. Their nearest redoubt was repeatedly silenced, and before the close of the day most of their batteries were damaged, and many of their guns were dismounted. During the night preparations were made on both sides for a renewal of the attack. Our batteries had been originally manned by a company of His Majesty's artillery, two companies of Bengal artillery, and five hundred seamen, which latter were commanded by Captain Sayer,

Officers killed and wounded on the 22d of August, 1811.

Captain Stopford, R. N. lost his arm.

Lieutenant Farnaby, Bengal Artillery, killed.

Lieutenant Munro, Madras Horse Artillery, lost his arm.

Lieutenant Colebrooke, Royal Artillery, wounded.

Lieutenant Shephard, Madras Pioneers, killed.

Lieutenant Colonel Clarges, 69th Regiment, mortally wounded.

Ensign M'Leod, Madras Pioneers, mortally wounded.

Lieutenant Mitchell, 69th Foot, wounded.

Captain Shaw, 6th Battalion N. 1. Bengal, wounded, since dead.

Ensign Pringle - - - Ditto, - - - - ditto.

of the Leda*. As from the casualties of the day, and the fatigues necessarily incidental to the service, in weather excessively sultry, the numbers were much reduced, every man in the several regiments accustomed to the exercise, was sent into the batteries during the night.
The firing having recommenced with great vigour, the avenue from
Struiswyk was so completely enfiladed by the enemy's shot, that the

---

* The following distribution of the Artillery and Seamen was ordered for the service of
the several Batteries, under the superintendance of Lieutenant-Colonel CALDWELL, Bengal
Artillery.

Captain NAPIER, Royal Artillery, Commanding the Batteries.

No. I.

12 Iron 18 Pounder Battery.

Captain Richards.

———— Dundas.

Lieutenant Colebrook.

———— Ralfe.

Bengal Artillery, - 36 men.

Royal ditto, - - 36

Seamen, - - - 96

Madras Lascars, - 18

Bengal - - - 18

No. II.

8 Iron 18 Pounder Battery.

Captain Smith, Commanding.

Lieut. Munro, Madras Artillery.

———— Farrington.

Royal Artillery, - 18 men.

Bengal ditto, - - 30

Seamen, - - - 64

Madras Lascars, - 12

Bengal ditto, - - 12

No. III.

8 Inch Howitzer Battery.

Captain Faithful, Commanding.

Lieutenant Scott.

Bengal Artillery, - 18 men.

Seamen, - - - 18

Bengal Lascars, - 12

No. IV.

8 Inch Mortar Battery.

Captain Byers, Commanding.

Lieutenant Paston.

Royal Artillery, - 19 men.

Seamen, - - - 24

Madras Lascars, - 16

No. V.

2 Howitzer Batteries on the rear of the right
hand Battery, to fire across the river.

Lieut. Harris, Commanding.

Bengal Golandauze, 12 men.

Seamen, - - - 20

Total men to work the Guns 479.

havock made among the trees, will long remind the passenger of the awful scene. The accustomed retreat to the cool shade under the rich foliage and spreading branches of these beautiful productions of nature, in a climate where their protecting shelter is so needful, was destroyed; and a new path-way cut through the middle of extensive betel plantations, through which our communication with the advanced posts was next established, had also very soon the fire of the enemy's batteries directed on it, which obliged us at last to move along the winding banks of the great river.

Though the enemy suffered very much both in men and guns, it was evident that to make a practicable breach, our approaches and batteries must be considerably advanced, which however from the exhausted state of the troops, the fatigue they had to endure, and the heat to which they were exposed, were measures that could not be adopted *. In the mean time the enemy continued their entrenchments, extending a double ditch along their front, and erecting intermediate fleches, thus strengthening their position daily, and using every means to render it impregnable.

The period therefore had now arrived beyond which an assault could no longer be delayed. It had been evident from the first view of the enemy's works, that this must be eventually the mode of our attack,

* *Casualties which occurred on the twenty-fourth of August.*

Lieutenant Paston, Royal Artillery, killed.
Captain Richards, Royal Artillery, wounded.
Captain Smith, Engineers, ditto.
Ensign Sim, Madras Engineers, ditto.

and to this end indeed all the operations of our army were effectually conducted. It had been found impossible to gain any satisfactory information of the enemy's strength, or the precise state of his position ; such precaution having been taken by General Daendels and his successor, that the inhabitants of Batavia were totally ignorant on these points. The nature of their situation rendered it extremely difficult to approach near enough to reconnoitre, and a very imperfect knowledge was obtained by repeated efforts which were made for that purpose. From observations thus obtained, and the incomplete information which some deserters could furnish, it was evident, that uncommon pains had been taken to render the front towards Batavia as strong as possible ; that the entrenchments could not be forced without great loss, and that when gained, the redoubts within them, supported by the whole of the enemy's power, would remain still to be carried. Under all these circumstances therefore a front attack might be considered as unadvisable. A project for turning the enemy's left by a path which led round the entrenchments by the Great River was given in, and a deserter offered himself as a guide ; but on investigation it appeared, that this path would only admit of a file abreast, and to attack thirteen thousand men, strongly entrenched, by so narrow an aperture, appeared highly imprudent. This plan of attack however was not altogether abandoned, but was judiciously combined by the Commander in Chief with other movements.

From the nature of the ground, and the design of the works, it was natural to conclude that the enemy would be equally well-secured towards their rear as on their front face ; and in fact it turned out that this was the strongest side. An assault on their left flank was equally objectionable, as the Great River which covered it was unford-able, with steep high banks and almost impenetrable jungle. Their position on this front was totally hid from view, and secure from attack. The only bridge across the river, within their lines, was at Campo Malayo, close to the rear face, but it was covered with strong works, and combustibles were ready for its destruction on the least alarm.

The only remaining front to be noticed, that of their right on the Slokan, was unquestionably the weakest. The country was more open, and it could be more closely examined. It was believed that one of their redoubts was beyond that stream, and might be seized by surprise. This might have been ascertained by moving a strong corps on that flank, and pushing forward parties at night, but the suspicion which this movement must produce would greatly have counteracted the advantages Sir Samuel Achmuty hoped to derive from keeping the enemy wholly ignorant of his intentions. With these views he discouraged any reconnoitring on that flank except by a few officers on whose judgement he placed entire reliance.

This desirable point, upon which so much depended was at last clearly settled by an intelligent serjeant, who deserted from that very part on the twenty-fourth. He described its position and strength, the bridge that connected the redoubt with the other works, and the defence by which it was protected.

On this information the principal attack was planned; and the day that was to fix the destiny of Java arrived. The memorable twenty-sixth of August was that on which the formidable lines of Cornelis were stormed.

Colonel Gillespie commanded the principal attack. The troops under his orders consisted of the infantry part of the advance, which formed the leading column, and a part of the right brigade of the line, with Colonel Gibbs at their head, as in the following order:

Sharp Shooters, 14th Regiment, Lieutenant Coghlan.

Pioneers, Madras, Captain Smithwayte.

Grenadier company, 78th Regiment, Captain M'Leod.

RIGHT FLANK BATTALION, MAJOR MILLER, CONSISTING OF

Light company, 14th Regiment, Captain Stanus.

Light company, 59th Regiment, Captain Bowen.

Grenadier company, 5th Volunteer Battalion, Captain Evans.

Rifle company, 59th Regiment, Lieutenant M'Pherson.

LEFT FLANK BATTALION, CAPTAIN FORBES, 78th REGIMENT, CONSISTING OF

Light company, 69th Regiment, Captain Lindsay.

Light company, 78th.

Grenadier company, 6th Volunteer Battalion, Captain M'Pherson.

Rifle company, 78th Regiment, Captain Cameron.

Detachment 89th Regiment, five companies, Major Butler.

Royal Marines, Captain Bunce.

Dismounted Dragoons, 22d Regiment, Lieutenant Dudley.

Governor General's Body Guard, dismounted, Captain Gall.

Detachment of Volunteers, Light Infantry Battalion, Captain Frazer.

Ditto, 4th Volunteer Battalion, Major Grant.

COLONEL GIBBS'S, COLUMN, CONSISTING OF

Grenadier company, 14th Regiment, Captain Kennedy.

Ditto,   59th,   Captain Olphert.

Ditto,   69th,   Captain Ross.

His Majesty's 1st Battalion, 59th, Lieutenant Colonel A. M'Leod.

Detachment of Volunteers, Light Infantry Battalion, Major Dalton,

Ditto, 4th Volunteer Battalion.

These troops moved off soon after midnight on the morning of the 26th of August, and took the route by which the deserter, who now acted as our guide, had escaped. We had to make a detour of many miles, through a very difficult country, intersected with ravines, enclosures, and betel plantations, resembling hop-grounds, many parts of which could only be passed in single file, and though the head of the column moved at a snail's pace, the great darkness of the night caused the troops in the rear to separate from them and miss their way.

On arriving at a place where several roads met, our guide was perplexed which to pursue; but Captain Dickson, of the Madras Cavalry, Aid-de-Camp to Sir Samuel Auchmuty, having been reconnoitering in this direction some days before, very fortunately recollected the right one, which was pursued accordingly, and our guide soon confirmed the choice, by recognizing objects which he had marked in his escape, and being now convinced that it was the right road, he went forward with full confidence at the head of the column, accompanied by Serjeant Smith of the 22d Dragoons, and both behaved with great intrepidity and cool steady courage.

The head of the column had arrived very near the enemy's works when a report was brought to Colonel Gillespie of the rear not being up. He halted. It was an awful moment! One of those pauses of distressful anxiety, which can be better conceived than described; and can be felt only in all its force by a soul engaged in a great undertaking, on the success or failure of which depend the lives of thousands, and the honor and credit of a whole army. Too near to the enemy's works to escape being descried by their scouts and patroling parties, it became necessary to make a retrograde movement, and after taking a few paces to the rear, we again faced towards the enemy, waiting in anxious expectation for the return of the messengers who had been sent to the rear to close up the column. The day was now fast approaching; to delay longer therefore for the rear would have exposed us to a discovery; while a retreat would have been pregnant with incalculable mischief, for as all the secondary attacks were to be guided by our's, these must of necessity have miscarried if the main column had retired.

These considerations determined Colonel Gillespie to venture on the attack with what troops were already up; trusting for timely support to Colonel Gibbs, whose gallantry and military ardour he knew would bring him to the scene of action, the instant the report of the firing should serve to point out the direction of the route. With full confidence, then our leader placed himself at the head of his little band, and we moved on in silent expectation.

A deep cut across the road close to the enemy's lines, obliged us to advance slowly, to afford time for the men to form up after they had passed over.

The morning dawn now shewed us the videttes of the enemy, who were posted outside, on the left of the road. They challenged us twice, and were answered " Patrole." We passed on. An officer's picquet, stationed close to one of their principal redoubts, (number three), situated without the river Slokan, challenged us next, when Colonel Gillespie gave the word " Forward," and so rapidly was the advance conducted, that the enemy's picquet had not time to effect their retreat, but every man was either killed or taken.

A general blaze now suddenly arose; blue lights and rockets being

I

sent forth by the enemy to discover our approach, whilst the artillery on the redoubts, (numbers three and four,) discharged their grape and round shot, which, however, past chiefly over our heads. The foe in the nearest redoubt, (number three,) had not time to reload, for our soldiers instantly assailed it at the point of the bayonet, and carried it with such celerity, that not a man escaped.

Colonel Gillespie continued to press forward in order to secure the passage over the Slokan, leading into the enemy's lines; and which was defended by four guns, horse artillery, directly facing the bridge, and flanked by all their batteries. This therefore was a severe struggle, but the passage being secured, the Colonel next turned to the left, and attacked a second redoubt, (number four,) within the body of their works. Here a sharp conflict ensued. The handful of soldiers by which this post was attacked, were opposed by such great numbers of the enemy, as to call forth the most extraordinary efforts of gallantry on the part of the assailants. It was however carried at the point of the bayonet in the same determined manner, notwithstanding the tremendous fire kept up by the enemy both of grape and musquetry. Several officers here lost their valuable lives in the very bosom of victory, and many gallant soldiers were killed and wounded.

These two captured redoubts mounted each twenty eighteen pounders, and several twenty-four and thirty-two pounders, while the ditches were filled with musqueteers.

Another large redoubt, (number two,) on the right of our entrance was now to be assailed, and Colonel Gibbs just arriving at this time at the head of the grenadiers of the fourteenth, fifty-ninth, and sixty-ninth regiments, Colonel Gillespie directed him to carry it, which was done in the same gallant and successful manner as the preceding had been, and under a severe fire of grape and musquetry. A dreadful explosion took place in this redoubt by the blowing up of the powder magazine, which occasioned the loss of many lives. A great number of shells and rockets were fired by this means, and a sulphureous blast of mingled ashes, smoke, and fragments of every kind, broke upon us like a volcano, stunning all around, both friends and foes. This catastrophe was followed for a minute by an awful silence. The Captains of each of the grenadier companies of the above regiments, and many others, all found a death, but few a grave! Numbers of the enemy also were destroyed, and the ground was strewed with the mangled bodies and scattered limbs of friends and foes, blended together in a horrible state of fraternity. Colonel Gibbs, and several other officers were thrown by the shock to a considerable distance, but fortunately without sustaining any material injury. This magazine is reported to have been fired by two Captains in the French service, named Muller and Osman, both of whom perished in the explosion. Here Brigadier Jauffret was taken prisoner, by Colonel Gillespie in person.

The enemy now renewed their fire upon our troops with increased fury from their park guns and batteries in the rear, and upon the little bridge across the Slokan, over which they had to pass.—While Colonel Gibbs proceeded on to the right, Colonel Gillespie continued his operations on the left, and towards the enemy's rear. All the batteries in succession were stormed and taken ; and being now joined by the fifty-ninth regiment under Lieutenant Colonel Alexander M'Leod; Colonel Gillespie directed the attack of the enemy's park of artillery and reserve. The enemy's cavalry formed upon the left of the line, threatened to charge, but were repulsed by the well directed fire of a party of the fifty-ninth, which were sent against them. The same gallant corps then moved on in column along the face of the redoubt, number four, and gained the saliant angle of the enemy's line of reserve, drawn up in the rear of their park guns and horse artillery, with a double front nearly at right angles, their rear and flanks being covered by the barracks and the small fort of Cornelis.

The attack was carried into effect with the greatest promptitude, and though the assailants were saluted with a shower of grape, the enemy was driven from all his guns. An attempt was then made to effect a stand in front of Fort Cornelis, sheltered by the barracks from whence a sharp fire of musquetry was maintained ; but being soon driven from this last ground, and the small fort itself at Cornelis having been carried by our troops, the enemy broke and dispersed in all directions.

Whilst these operations were going on by the force under the orders of Colonel Gillespie, two other attacks were made ; one on the opposite side of the Great River, by the column under Major Yule at Campong Malayo, but finding the bridge in flames and almost burnt down, the troops here employed were obliged to content themselves with firing their two six-pounders of horse artillery across the river, by which the enemy were excessively annoyed in their retreat. The other attack under Lieutenant Colonel William M'Leod of His Majesty's sixty-ninth regiment, was made on the opposite side from the main assault and had for its object the redoubt (number one) which was gallantly carried; though unfortunately with the death of the brave officer by whom that column was conducted.

The remainder of the army, with the Commander in Chief at their head, and Major General Wetherall, Colonel Wood commanding the reserve, and Colonel Adams commanding the left brigade of the line, threatened the enemy's lines in front, where our batteries were placed; joined by a body of seamen armed with pikes under Captain Sayer of the Royal Navy.

With the view of disconcerting the enemy as much as possible, Sir Samuel Auchmuty had directed a small party to be placed behind a rising ground about two hundred paces in front of the right of the enemy's lines, with orders to open a fire as soon as Colonel Gillespie's attack should commence. This injunction was punctually obeyed, and the enemy concluding it to be a front attack, opened a heavy fire along the whole face which produced the effect that had been expected, for the enemy being persuaded that their front was the object of attack could not draw any supplies from thence to resist that which was really made, and it exhausted their fire before our troops on that side were exposed to it.

The main attack having been so successfully accomplished, all the other parties rushed in from their respective points, and together joined in pursuit of the flying enemy.

The Dragoons now coming up Colonel Gillespie* placed himself at

---

* Colonel Gillespie, weakened by a slow fever, and quite overcome with fatigue, from his extraordinary exertions which were all on foot, as the nature of the country did not permit the use of horses at the onset, and from a blow or contusion he had just received in the attack on the enemy's park, fainted in the arms of Captains Dickson and Thorn, by whom he was supported; soon, however, recovering, and seeing the cavalry come up, he accompanied them on a horse cut from the enemy's guns, till his own charger arrived, which he instantly mounted and headed the fine charge made by our cavalry in the pursuit.

their head followed by a detachment of horse artillery, and by a rapid pursuit of the enemy for ten miles, cut off nearly the whole of them. They rallied several times, but though their generals and other superior officers made every exertion in their power to effect a retreat under cover of the woods, all their efforts were in vain. Our infantry, (the 14th Regiment,) under Lieutenant-Colonel Watson, and a party of Bengal Sepoys, directed by Colonel Gibbs, drove them from their fastnesses, and forced them from the woods upon the road, where they were charged by the dragoons.

At Campong Macassar, the flying foe again rallied, and attempted to make a stand behind broken-down carts and thick hedges, supported by four horse artillery guns, which they had saved from the wreck of their army. But our cavalry, led on by Colonel Gillespie, charged in sections through the different avenues, notwithstanding the enemy's fire of grape and musquetry, with such impetuosity, as to bear down every thing in their way. They now dispersed, and tried to save themselves by flight. Arms, caps, accoutrements, and pouches, were flung away, and marked the direction of their course. Our cavalry rapidly pursued, and took upwards of six thousand prisoners. The pursuit was continued with such activity beyond Tanjong Oost, nearly half-way to Buitenzorg, (distant from Batavia thirty-five miles, and a post of great strength,) that nearly every fugitive was secured, and few succeeded in reaching that place. Had the French been able to effect a retreat on the new-erected batteries at Buitenzorg, the fate of Java might still have remained doubtful. But now it was decided. Those who escaped among the marshes and jungle were very few, and dispersed over the country.

The carnage amongst the enemy was very great. Six thousand prisoners fell into our hands, among whom were two Generals, two of

General Janssens' Aids-de-Camp, the Chief of Engineers, the Commissary General, and Heads of all the Departments, five Colonels, four Majors, twenty-one Lieutenant-Colonels, seventy Captains, one hundred and thirty-four Lieutenants, seven Amboynese Lieutenants, three Native Lieutenants, five Sub-Adjutants, and one Cadet. Two hundred and eighty pieces of ordnance, mostly fine brass cannon, were captured in the works of Cornelis, and several stands of colours*.

Thus the whole of Janssens' assembled forces, who were here concentrated, were either taken or destroyed, amounting to upwards of thirteen thousand regular and well disciplined troops, a large portion of whom consisted of Europeans, and troops fresh from France; among which, an entire and very fine regiment of Voltigeurs, laid down their arms.

Only a small party of horse, under Major Le Blanc, succeeded in getting off with Generals Janssens and Jumel. The two latter escaped by mixing with the foot soldiers in the jungle, and thus were passed by our dragoons without being known.

Our loss was indeed great; though from the nature of the service, it was much less than what might have been expected. This fell chiefly

---

* The new French eagles had not been delivered out to the army at the time of this action. They had been preparing before our arrival at Batavia, and Buonaparte's birth day was to have witnessed the formal presentation of them to the troops; but our taking possession of the city on the eighth of August, frightened them so much, that the eagles were never hatched, at least nothing was ever seen or heard of them. Our intrusive visit spoiled altogether the gaiety and sport of Napoleon's intended fête on the fifteenth of August, for which great preparations had been already made at Goonong Sarie, the residence of General Janssens, and which were afterwards found very convenient, and turned to good account at a banquet given by the British officers to Lord Minto and Sir Samuel Auchmuty, previous to their departure.

on the troops engaged in the principal attack. In the two columns
upwards of five hundred men were killed and wounded, among whom
were forty-eight officers *.

General Janssens first fled to Buitenzorg. He had been twice

* B. O. by Colonel Gillespie, 27th August, 1811.

" Colonel Gillespie feels extremely happy in again having the satisfaction of expressing
his thanks to the troops of the advance, whom he has the honour to command, for their
bravery and gallantry displayed in the action of yesterday, at Cornelis.

" The high sense and admiration he entertained of their conduct in the action of the
10th instant, was fully upheld in that of yesterday. He has made a faithful report of their
heroic conduct to his Excellency the Commander in Chief.—Where all have behaved
with such distinguished bravery, and praise is equally due, it is difficult to mention individuals. Colonel Gillespie therefore requests every Officer commanding Corps and Detachments belonging to the Advance, and Captain Bunce, Marines, and Captain M'Leod, Grenadiers, 78th Regiment, who were attached, to accept his warmest acknowledgements for
the zeal and gallantry, which has been displayed by them all, and they are desired to communicate to the officers and men under their respective command, the grateful sense he entertains of their merits. Colonel Gillespie begs they will accept as a soldier's tribute, the
expression of his sincerest applause and heartfelt gratitude!

(Signed)   " WM. THORN, Maj. Brig."

Official Report from Colonel Gillespie, Commanding the Principal Attack, to Colonel Agnew, Adjutant General.

" August 27th, 1811.

" SIR,

" I have the honor to state to you, for the information of the Commander in Chief, that
agreeably to the instructions received from his Excellency, I moved soon after midnight on
the morning of the 26th instant, to the attack of the enemy's batteries at Cornelis. The
infantry part of the advance, including the dismounted cavalry, formed the leading column,
followed by Colonel Gibbs's brigade. We had to go through a very difficult country, many

summoned to surrender by Lord Minto ; the first time when our troops
obtained possession of Batavia ; and again after the action of the tenth

parts of which could only be passed in single file, and the night being exceeding dark, part
of the troops in the rear were for a time separated from the rest; the day now beginning
to dawn, and the head of the column being challenged by the enemy's sentries, no time was
to be lost. I accordingly pushed rapidly forward, the Rifle Company of the 14th Regiment
leading, supported by the Grenadiers of His Majesty's 78th Regiment, followed by the
remainder of the Right Flank Battalion, and the rest of the Advance.

" We arrived within pistol-shot of number three battery, when the enemy discharged a
round of grape and musquetry, but the work was carried at the point of the bayonet, and
every man in it was either killed or taken prisoner.

" We continued pressing forward, and got possession of the bridge over the Slokan, upon
which the enemy kept a tremendous fire from almost all their batteries; but we immediately
proceeded to the attack of number four redoubt, on our left, which was also carried at the
point of the bayonet, under a shower of grape and musquetry.

" The remainder of the column having now arrived, I directed Colonel Gibbs to the right,
to attack number two redoubt, which was effected in the same gallant manner, by the Grenadiers of His Majesty's 14th, 59th, and 69th Regiments. A dreadful explosion here took
place, which has deprived the service of several valuable lives.

" Whilst Colonel Gibbs continued pushing forward to the right, and driving the enemy
from their works in that quarter, I attacked and carried the remaining redoubts on my left,
and towards the enemy's rear, and being now joined by a part of the 59th Regiment, under
Lieutenant-Col. Alexander M'Leod, proceeded to the attack of the enemy's park of artillery,
which was effected by Lieutenant-Colonel M'Leod, in a most masterly manner. A body of
the enemy's cavalry who had drawn up the moment before, were put to flight by a few sections of the 59th Regiment. A long and sharp fire of musquetry was now kept up by a
strong body of the enemy, who had taken post in the lines, in front of the fort of Cornelis,
but being at last driven from this also, the fort was taken possession of, and the enemy dispersed in all directions.

" Colonel Gibbs, at the head of the 14th Regiment, and a party of Sepoys, followed up
the fugitives through Campong Malayo, driving them along the road and through the woods,

of August.   Captain **Robinson**, Lord Minto's Aid-de-Camp, was now sent to him a third time; but General **Janssens** obstinately refused to

" A body of seamen, under Captain Sayer, of the Royal Navy, joined in the general pursuit of the enemy.

" Part of His Majesty's 22d Dragoons, under Major Travers, arrived very opportunely, and at their head, followed by the Horse Artillery, under Captain Noble, I continued the pursuit, cutting up the enemy, and taking an immense number of prisoners, amongst whom are a great many of the first distinction.

" It is needless to enter into further details; His Excellency was an eye witness of the total defeat of the enemy, from the extent and strength of whose works, and the number and heavy metal of their cannon, he can fully appreciate the merits and gallantry of the troops who conquered on this occasion.

" The gallant manner in which Colonel Gibbs conducted the attack on the right, and the various services performed by him during the day, will, I trust, obtain the approbation of His Excellency, which they so richly deserve.

" To Lieutenant-Colonel M'Leod, of His Majesty's 59th Regiment, who so ably conducted the attack already noticed, my warmest thanks are due; as also to Major Miller, who commanded the Right Flank Battalion, which headed the Advance Column, and who, I am sorry to say, was severely wounded. To Major Grant, of the 4th Bengal Volunteer Battalion, and Captain Forbes, of His Majesty's 78th, who commanded the Left Flank Battalion; and Major Dalton, and Captain Fraser, of the Bengal Light Infantry Volunteer Battalion, my particular thanks are due for their able support. To Lieutenant Dudley and the Officers and Men of the dismounted detachment of His Majesty's 22d Dragoons; to Major Travers and the Officers and Men of the mounted detachment of the same regiment, my acknowledgements are due; as also to Lieutenant-Colonel Watson, who headed the 14th Regiment; and Captain Gall, of the Body Guard; in short, to every man engaged in this active service.

" The Officers of my Staff, and those of His Excellency attached to me, all behaved with their wonted gallantry, and deserve my warmest acknowledgements.

" I lament the fall of many a valuable officer and soldier, but severely as our loss is felt, it is much less, than what might have been expected, when the strength of the enemy's posi-

yield, relying on the resources which he vainly imagined were yet at his disposal, and by which he might still hope to turn the tide of fortune in his favour.

tion is considered. The carnage in the different batteries has been immense, and from the great number of prisoners brought in, both Europeans and Natives, very few can have escaped.

"I have the honor to be, &c. &c.

(Signed) "R. R. GILLESPIE, Colonel."

List of Killed, Wounded, and Missing, of the Columns commanded by Colonel R. R. Gillespie, in the Attack on the Enemy's Works at Cornelis, 26th August, 1811.

		EUROPEANS.													NATIVES.						HORSES.			
		Killed.						Wounded.							Killed.		Wounded.		Missing.			Killed.		Wounded.	
		Majors.	Captains.	Subalterns.	Serjeants.	Drummers.	Rank and File.	Total.	Majors.	Captains.	Subalterns.	Serjeants.	Drummers.	Rank and File.	Total.	Missing.	Officers.	Havildars.	Rank and File.	Officers.	Havildars.	Rank and File.	Officers.	Havildars.	Rank and File.	General Total.	Regimental. Officers.	Officers.	Regimental. Total.
	Staff									1				1	2										2			
	Horse Artillery			2	2									2	2										4	5	1	6
	Mounted Detacht, 22d Drag.	1			1									12	12										13	6	17	23
	Dismounted ditto			1	1						1	1		6	8										9			
	Gov.-General's Body Guard			1	1									5	5										6			
	Detachment Royal Marines			3	3						2	3		22	27										30			
Right	Do, 14th Rgt, Lt. Co. & Rifles			4	4	1	1		1	1				19	23										27			
Flank	Ditto 59th ditto ditto		2		3	5				1				10	11	3									19			
Batt.	5th Vol Batt. Gren, Comp.									1					1		1	1				5			8			
Left	Detachmt. 69th Rgt. Lt. Com.									1				4	5										5			
Flank	Do, 78th Light Com, & Rifle			7	7									12	12										19			
Batt,	Do, 6th Vol. Batt. Gr, Comp									1	1			2	1			2	3	8		1		17			
	78th Grenadier Company			5	5						1	2		19	22										27			
	Detachment 89th Regt,			4	4	1					5	3		22	31	3									38			
	Light Infty. Vol, Battalion									1	1			2	1		4	1	3	11				21			
	4th Bengal Vol, Battalion				1		1			1	2			3	1	9	1		26		1		43				
Right	Detachment 14th Regt,	1		1		2	4			1	6		55	62										68			
Brigade	H. M, 59th ditto	1	2	2		12	17	1	1	8	3	2	05	120										137			
of the Line,	Grenadier Company 69th	1	1	1		4	7			2			119	21										28			
		3	6	5		48	62	3	5	29	19	2	313	371	8	2	13	4	7	50			521		11		9

On the day following, finding that of the remnants of his army, only a few horse had joined him, he proceeded immediately with them for the

Names of Officers Killed and Wounded in the principal attack; in reference to the following Return.

KILLED.

22d Dragoons, Lieutenant Hutchins

14th Regiment, Captain Kennedy

59th ———, Captain Olphert

————, Lieutenant Waring

————, Lieutenant Lloyd

————, Lieutenant Litton

59th Regiment, Ensign Wolfe

69th ———, Captain Ross

————, Lieutenant Hipkins

5th Vol. Batt. Jamidar Ransing

6th Ditto do. Subadar Cassa Rain

WOUNDED.

Staff, Lieut. Hanson, A. Q. M. G.

22d Dragoons, Lieut. Dudley, severely

14th Regiment, Major Miller, severely

————, Captain Stanus

————, Lt. Coghlan, do. since dead

————, Captain Rawlins, do.

————, Lt. M'Kenzie, ditto

59th ———, Brevet Lt.-Col. Alx. M'Leod

————, Captain Campbell

————, Lt. M'Pherson, since dead

————, Lieutenant Butler

————, Lt. Sampson, since dead

————, Lieutenant Dillon

————, Lieutenant Pennyfeather

————, Lieutenant Gordon

————, Ensign Waters, severely

————, Lt. Lowe, Madras service

————, Lieutenant Jourdan, do. do.

69th ———, Lieutenant Lowry

————, Lieutenant M'Pherson

78th Regiment, Ensign Pennycaugh

————, Lieutenant Hart, severely

89th ———, Major Butler

————, Lieutenant Rowe

————, Lieutenant Coates

————, Lt. and Adjt. Young

————, Lieutenant Daniel

56th ———, Lt. Cairns (attached to 89th)

5th Vol. Batt. Lt. M'Donald, since dead

6th ———, Captain M'Pherson

————, Lieut. Murrall, since dead

Light Inf. Vol. Batt. Captain Fraser

————, Lieutenant Pearson

4th Bengal V. B. Captain Knight

————, Captain Campbell

————, Lieutenant Hunter

————, Ensign Anstice

Royal Marines, Lieutenant Haswell

————, Lieutenant Elliot, ditto

eastward, accompanied by General Jumel ; and our troops under the command of Col. Gibbs, reached Buitenzorg the day after. This place would have been soon converted into a much stronger hold than even that of Cornelis, if we had given the French time to finish the nume-

General Return of Killed, Wounded, and Missing, in the British Army, from the 10th to the 26th August, 1811, both inclusive.

	KILLED												WOUNDED														MISSING	TOTAL KILLED WOUNDED AND MISSING		HORSES				
	Europeans								Natives				Europeans									Natives									Killed		Regt.		
	Lieut.-Colonels	Majors	Captains	Lieutenants	Ensigns	Staff Sergeants	Sergeants	Rank and File	Subidars	Jemidars	Havildars	Rank and File	Lieut. Colonels	Majors	Captains	Lieutenants	Ensigns	Staff Sergeants	Sergeants	Drummers	Rank and File	Subidars	Jumidars	Havildars	Drummers	Rank and File	Europeans	Natives		Europeans	Natives	Officers	Regimental	Wounded	Missing	Total
10 August, 1811.			1					16							3	4	1		4		66					3		1	95	4		2	4		7
12																					3								3						
15																					1								1						
20																					1								1						
22			1	1			1	16	1			6	1		2	3	3		2		37	1	1		1	19			67	29					
24			1					2				1			1						8					4			13	5					
25																										1				1					
26	1	3	6	1	1		5	59	1	1	2	16	2	2	8	29	3	1	26	2	397	1	3	9		80	10	1	556	114	1	11	1	3	31
	1	3	9	2	1		6	93	1	2	2	23	3	2	14	36	7	1	32	2	513	2	4	9	1	107	11	2 736	153	1	13	21	3	38	

Names of Officers Killed and Wounded in addition to those already named.

Lieutenant-Colonel M'Leod, His Majesty's 69th Regiment, killed.

Lieutenant-Colonel Campbell, 78th, wounded, since dead.

Lieutenant Ferguson, Madras Native Infantry, killed.

Captain M'Kenzie, 78th, wounded.

Captain J. M'Pherson, ditto, ditto.

Lieutenant M'Donald, 5th Battalion Bengal Native infantry, wounded.

Lieutenant W. H. Burroughs, 69th, wounded.

Lieutenant Wm. Matthewson, 78th, ditto.

rous batteries which they had here begun to construct. It has been already shewn that the intention of the enemy was to have retreated to this post in the event of being forced out of Cornelis; but this design was completely frustrated by the vigorous exertions of the British cavalry, who followed up the victory with such energy in the pursuit, and dispersion of the defeated foe, that Buitenzorg was occupied without opposition by our troops, who found in the batteries forty-three pieces of cannon, with a considerable supply of powder, shot, and other stores.

The following were the public expressions of approbation which immediately rewarded those who had been engaged in this arduous conflict:

General Orders.—By the Commander-in-Chief.

Head-Quarters, Weltervreeden, 29th August, 1811.

PAROLE.—MADRAS.

" The Commander in Chief having received the reports of the Officers commanding the several divisions employed in the late attack of the

---

Seamen and Marines Killed and Wounded, from the 4th to the 26th August, on shore.

Total, Seamen 11—Marines 4, killed. Six officers—Twenty-nine Seamen—Twenty Marines, wounded. Three seamen missing. Total 73.

Names of Officers Wounded.

Captain Stopford, severely.

Lieutenant Noble, of the Scipion, slightly.

John D. Worthy, Master's Mate, ditto.

Robert Dunlop, ditto ditto.

Lieutenants Haswell and Elliott, of the Marines, wounded, already mentioned.

enemy's assembled forces, performs a pleasing part of his duty in expressing to the gallant army he has the honour to command, and to
the officers and seamen of the Royal Navy, and battalion of Royal
Marines, who, by the kindness of the Hon. Rear-Admiral Stopford, were
placed under his orders, his highest approbation and admiration of
the ardent zeal and irresistible bravery which marked their conduct,
during the whole of the recent operations, and particularly in the decisive assault, by which, on the morning of the 26th instant, the strongly
fortified position of the enemy, at Cornelis, was carried, and their army
completely dispersed, their Commander in Chief, with a few cavalry,
saving himself by precipitate flight, while a large proportion of his
generals, staff-officers, and troops, were made prisoners in the action
and pursuit.

" Where ardent gallantry was universally displayed, both by the
European and Native troops, the Commander in Chief can only particularize those whose rank and situations of particular trust, in the
course of the attack, rendered their conduct pre-eminent.

" To Colonel Gillespie, who commanded the principal attack, and
to Colonel Gibbs, who headed the second column under that officer's
orders, it is impossible to say too much ; but the Commander in Chief
will confine himself to the public declaration, that those officers fully
performed every service which he had expected to derive from their
well-known gallantry and conduct, displayed throughout the attack
that heroic spirit of enterprise, which proved them worthy to command
the gallant troops they led.

" To Major-General Wetherall, the Commander in Chief offers his
cordial thanks for the great assistance he has constantly derived from

his zealous exertions, as well on the last attack on the enemy's position at Cornelis, as on the various operations by which it was preceded.

" The full success of the several attacks, led by Colonel Wood, of the Bengal Native Infantry, by Lieut.-Col. M'Leod, of H. M. 69th Regiment, who fell in conducting his column, with that distinguished gallantry, which had ever marked his long career of active military service, and by Major Yule, of the 20th Regiment Bengal Native Infantry—attacks expected only to distract and divide the attention of the enemy, is the best proof of the ability and energy with which those officers conducted the divisions entrusted to their direction.

" The prominent and meritorious exertions of Lieut.-Col. Adams, H. M. 78th Regiment, commanding the left Brigade of the line, of Lieutenant-Colonel Alexander M'Leod, of His Majesty's 59th Regiment, Lieutenant-Colonel Watson, of the 14th Regiment, Lieutenant-Colonel Campbell, of the 78th, Major Miller, of the 14th, Commanding the Right Flank Battalion, Major Butler, of His Majesty's 89th, Major Grant, of the 4th Bengal Volunteer Battalion, Major Dalton, Bengal Light Infantry Volunteer Battalion, Captain Forbes of His Majesty's 78th Regiment, Commanding the Left Flank Battalion, Captain Fraser, Commanding Detachment Light Infantry Battalion, Lieutenant Dudley, Commanding dismounted Party 22d Dragoons, and Captain Gall, the Governor General's Body Guard, have been reported to the Commander in Chief, in terms of strong applause, and the conduct of Major Travers of His Majesty's 22d Dragoons, and Captain Noble, of the Horse Artillery, with the detachments under their command, in their eager and animated pursuit, and dispersion of the enemy, when the roads were cleared for their advance, merits every commendation.

" The Commander in Chief thinks it proper to express his satisfaction at the support he has received from all the Officers of the Staff, but he deems it particularly incumbent on him to mark his fullest approbation of the active energy and gallantry of Captain Dickson, and Lieutenant Blakiston, his Aids-de-Camp, whom he had permitted to act with Colonel Gillespie, on the morning of the attack.

" Colonel Gillespie has also reported the conduct of Captain Taylor, Captain Thorn, and the Officers particularly attached to his Staff, as highly meritorious.

" The Commander in Chief requests Captain Sayer, the senior officer of the detachment, and all the officers and seamen of the Royal Navy, under his command, to accept his thanks, for the able and active assistance rendered by the naval detachment, from the moment of their disembarkation to join the army, and assist in the batteries. The eager exertions of the corps of seamen, when permitted at their request, to leave the batteries, and join in the pursuit of the enemy, gave the most satisfactory proof, that British sailors, though not acting on the element peculiarly their own, are in every situation ready, able, and happy, to oppose with vigour and effect, the enemies of their King and Country.

" The Commander in Chief laments in common with the whole army, the many brave men who fell in the late arduous attack ; but it is ever a pleasing consolation to the surviving friends and relatives of a gallant soldier, when he meets that fate, which sooner or later, is

L.

common to all men, in the execution of his noblest duties—dies with honour—as these brave men whom he now laments have done, gloriously supporting the cause of their beloved Sovereign and their Country.

(Signed)

" P. AGNEW, Adj. Gen."

Review of the Battle of the 26th August, 1811.

————————

W<small>HILE</small> the immediate fate of Europe, and remotely that of the whole civilized world, appeared to be suspended, as it were, by a single thread, it was natural for the public attention to be so absorbed in the momentous events of the peninsular war, as to regard with comparative indifference the arduous conflicts which were maintained for the same cause in remoter regions. Thus, the splendour of the action which has been just described, became obscured by the distance of the scene, and the pressing interest excited by nearer atchievements. Yet, without forming the slightest wish to lower the estimation of those exploits, by which an unprincipled Despot was driven to seal his disgrace in the snows of Russia, it is but justice to those who had to contend with the enemy on the burning plains of Java, to say, that a harder fought or more sanguinary combat, considering the force of the British as contrasted with that to which they were opposed, is not to be found in modern times. When, in addition to this disparity of numbers, we take into account the peculiar circumstances by which this battle was characterized; the almost impregnable position held by the enemy; the skill and vigour with which it was defended; the difficulty and danger attending all approaches to it; the innumerable *Trous de Loup* and *Chausse Trappes* every where interspersed about the line of march, together with abbatis formed by the levelling of the forests, stumps of trees, and various other impediments that rendered the movement singularly appalling and intricate, some idea, though even then but an inadequate one, may be formed of the exertions of our troops on this service.

The loss of the rear of the column, by missing its way for a time, when the head was within musket shot of the enemy's lines, at which moment only the fact was reported to the commanding officer, added to the perils by which we were surrounded. The fast approach of day, however, left no time for deliberation.—An attack of such a body of works, with a handfull of men, was, indeed, most hazardous; but then the rapid opening of the dawn rendered retreat equally fatal, as the guns on most of the batteries and redoubts would have been instantly brought to bear on the only road by which that retreat could be effected.

As in such a state nothing was more to be deprecated than delay, the Advance were under the necessity of coming to a prompt decision; since to have waited for a junction with the rear might have been the destruction of all, and the ruin of the expedition. It was, therefore, instantly resolved to push on to the attack, knowing that a speedy support from Colonel Gibbs was to be relied on;—nor was that confidence erroneous; for, the moment the firing commenced, it served as a beacon to those who had left the road; and the gallant and rapid assistance which was afforded by that excellent officer, effectually contributed to our success.

The overbearing and determined rapidity of the head of the column, who, by the positive orders of the commanding officer, trusted solely to their bayonets, ensured the victory; the pic-quets were destroyed in a moment; the outward redoubt, (number three,) was carried, whilst with a part of the seventy-eighth grenadiers, Colonel Gillespie took possession of the narrow bridge over the Slokan, which was indeed the key to the main object of the attack. This bridge, which was the only point of entrance, was so constructed with bamboos, that six men could have destroyed it in a minute.

It was natural to believe that the enemy were aware of the import-ance of this pass, and the commanding officer was not mistaken in the supposition that it would be strongly and vigorously defended, as he found the principal part of the field train, and many of the guns on the works bearing upon it. The fire was here concentrated to a focus. To preserve this post therefore, was most difficult; but to abandon it defeat. By undaunted perseverance the former was done, till a sufficient force could be collected, to make an attack on the guns, and at the same in-stant, to diverge outwards on the batteries. These different objects were at once gained, though with great loss, the operation, however, in which they were combined, constituted the leading and prominent feature of the day. When most of the redoubts and batteries had been carried, and the light became sufficiently clear to render objects visible, the enemy's line was seen composed of several battalions; upwards of twenty pieces of horse artillery, four-pounders, besides many heavy guns, with a large body of cavalry on their left, the whole forming nearly two faces of a square, were drawn up on the plain, in front of the small fort of Cornelis, by the fire of which we were commanded.

The whole of the column under Colonel Gillespie being now within the works, at once rushed from different points on this formidable reserve, and with the rapidity of lightning, overthrew every thing that impeded their passage. The powerful sweep of that characteristic British arm, the bayonet, was never more vigorously displayed than at this awful moment; and though wielded only by a handful of troops, deeds of gallantry were wrought which cannot be forgotten, even in the distant quarter where they were accomplished.

The main struggle being now decided, and the cavalry soon after joining the advance, poured destruction and defeat on the enemy.

The attack directed against their retreat, was remarkably fine. The French superior officers and sharp shooters all remained in the rear, using every means to get their people off, who retired between two rivers, along a broad road, equally divided by a hedge. Across the approach, in many places, heavy carts, carriages, and baggage-waggons, were formed, and behind them were planted several light artillery guns. When the dragoons advanced, a severe fire both of grape and musquetry opened upon them, but the charge of our cavalry, though directed to a disadvantage, by being obliged to act in sections, in order to force their way through such passages as presented themselves, was made with such rapidity, that the rout was rendered complete, without any material loss on the part of the victors. An excellent officer, however, Lieutenant Hutchins, of the 22d Dragoons, was killed by a grapeshot, by the side of Colonel Gillespie; and so close was the combat in general, that every officer was engaged at times hand to hand. Colonel Gillespie took one General in the batteries, another in the charge, and a Colonel; besides having a personal affair, in which another Colonel fell by his arm.

This gallant officer had very nearly been added to the melancholy list of lamented heroes; for soon after his return from this field, he was attacked by a violent fever, which brought him to the brink of the grave. But when medical skill appeared to be almost baffled in its exertions, and became hopeless, nature happily prevailed in restoring him to the service of his country, and to renewed exertions in the career of glory.

Sir Samuel Auchmuty's Dispatch to Lord Minto.

" Head-quarters, Weltervreeden, August 31st, 1811.

" MY LORD,

" AFTER a short but arduous campaign, the troops you did me the honor to place under my orders, have taken the Capital of Java, have assaulted and carried the enemy's formidable works at Cornelis, have defeated and dispersed their collected force, and have driven them from the Kingdoms of Bantam and Jacatra. This brilliant success, over a well appointed and disciplined force, greatly superior in numbers, and in every respect well equipped, is the result of the great zeal, gallantry, and discipline of the troops; qualities which they have possessed in a degree certainly never surpassed. It is my duty to lay before your Lordship the details of their success, but it is not in my power to do them the justice they deserve, or to express how much their country is indebted to them for their great exertions. Your Lordship is acquainted with the reasons that induced me to attempt a landing in the neighbourhood of Batavia. It was effected without opposition, at the village of Chillingching, twelve miles East of the City, on the fourth instant. My intention was to proceed from thence by the direct road to Cornelis, where the enemy's force was said to be assembled, a strongly fortified position, and to place the City of Batavia in my rear, from whence alone I could expect to derive supplies equal to the arduous contest we were engaged in. As some time was required to make preparations for an inland movement, I judged it proper to reconnoitre the road by the coast leading to Batavia, and observe how far it would be practicable to penetrate by that route. I was aware that it was extremely strong, and, if well defended, nearly impracticable. Advancing with part of the army, I had the satisfaction to find that it was not disputed with us, and the only obstacle to our progress was occasioned by the destruction of the bridge over the Anjole River. I approached the river on the 6th, and observing during that evening a large fire in Batavia, I concluded it was the intention of the enemy to evacuate the city, and, with this impression, I directed the advance of the army under Colonel Gillespie, to pass the river in boats, on the succeeding night. They lodged themselves in the suburbs of the city, and a temporary bridge was hastily constructed in the morning of the 8th, capable of supporting light artillery. On that day, the Burghers of Batavia applied for protection, and surrendered the city without opposition, the garrison having retreated to Weltervreeden.

The possession of Batavia was of the utmost importance, though large store-houses of public property were burned by the enemy, previous to their retreat, and every effort was made to destroy the remainder, we were fortunate in preserving some valuable granaries and other stores.

The city, although abandoned by the principal inhabitants, was filled with an industrious race of people, who could be particularly useful to the army. Provisions were in abundance, and an easy communication preserved with the fleet.

In the night of the 8th, a feeble attempt was made by the enemy, to

M

cut off a small guard I had sent for the security of the place; but the troops of the Advance had, unknown to them, reinforced the party early in the evening, and the attack was repulsed. The Advance, under Colonel Gillespie, occupied the city on the 8th.

" Very early on the morning of the 10th, I directed Colonel Gillespie, with his corps, to move from Batavia towards the enemy's cantonment at Weltervreeden, supported by two Brigades of Infantry, that marched before break of day through the city, and followed his route. The cantonment was abandoned, but the enemy were in force a little beyond it, and about two miles in advance of their works at Cornelis. Their position was strong, and defended by an abbattis, occupied by three thousand of their best troops, and four guns horse artillery. Colonel Gillespie attacked it with spirit and judgment; and after an obstinate resistance, carried it at the point of the bayonet, completely routed their force, and took their guns. A strong column from their works advanced to their support; but our Line being arrived, they were instantly pursued, and driven under shelter of their batteries.

" In this affair, so creditable to Colonel Gillespie, and all the corps of the Advance, the grenadier company of the 78th, and the detachment of the 89th regiment, particularly distinguished themselves, by charging and capturing the enemy's artillery. Our loss was trifling compared with the enemy's, which may be estimated at about 500 men, with Brigadier-General Alberti dangerously wounded.

" Though we had hitherto been successful beyond my most sanguine expectations, our further progress became extremely difficult and somewhat doubtful.

" The enemy, greatly superior in numbers, was strongly intrenched

in a position between the great river Jacatra and the Slokan, an artificial water course, neither of which were fordable. This position was
shut up by a deep trench, strongly pallisaded; seven redoubts, and
many batteries mounted with heavy cannon, occupied the most commanding ground within the lines; the fort of Cornelis was in the
centre; and the whole of the works were defended by a numerous and
well organized artillery. The season was too far advanced, the heat
too violent, and our numbers insufficient, to admit of regular approaches. To carry the works by assault was the alternative, and on
that I decided. In aid of this measure, I erected some batteries to dis-
able the principal redoubts; and for two days kept up a heavy fire
from twenty 18-pounders, and eight mortars and howitzers. Their
execution was great; and I had the pleasure to find, that though answered at the commencement of each day by a far more numerous
artillery, we daily silenced their nearest batteries, considerably disturbed every part of their position, and were evidently superior in our
fire.

" At dawn of day on the 26th, the assault was made: the principal
attack was entrusted to that gallant and experienced officer, Colonel
Gillespie. He had the infantry of the Advance, and the grenadiers of
the Line with him; and was supported by Colonel Gibbs, with the
59th regiment, and the fourth battalion Bengal volunteers. They were
intended, if possible, to surprise the redoubt, No. 3, constructed by the
enemy beyond the Slokan, to endeavour to cross the bridge over that
stream with the fugitives, and then to assault the redoubts within the
lines, Colonel Gillespie attacking those to the left, and Colonel Gibbs
to the right. Lieutenant-Colonel M'Leod, with six companies of the

69th, was directed to follow a path on the banks of the great river; and when the attack had commenced on the Slokan, to endeavour to possess himself of the enemy's left redoubt, No. 1. Major Yule, with the flank corps of the Reserve, reinforced by two troops of cavalry, four guns of horse artillery, two companies of the 69th, and the grenadiers of the Reserve, was directed to attack the corps at Campong Malayo, on the west of the great river, and endeavour to cross the bridge at that post.

" The remainder of the Army, under Major-General Wetherall, was at the batteries, where a column, under Colonel Wood, consisting of the 78th regiment, and the 5th volunteer battalion, was directed to advance against the enemy in front ; and at a favourable moment, when aided by the other attacks, to force his way, if practicable, and open the position for the line.

" The enemy was under arms, and prepared for the combat; and General Janssens, the Commander in Chief, was in the redoubt when it commenced. Colonel Gillespie, after a long detour through a close and intricate country, came on their Advance, routed it in an instant; and with a rapidity never surpassed, under a heavy fire of grape and musquetry, possessed himself of the advance redoubt, No. 3. He passed the bridge with the fugitives under as tremendous a fire, and assaulted and carried with the bayonet the redoubt, No. 4, after a most obstinate resistance.

" Here the two divisions of the column separated: Colonel Gibbs turned to the right, and with the 59th and part of the 78th, who had now forced their way in front, carried the redoubt, No. 2. A tremendous explosion of the magazine of this work (whether accidental or designed is not ascertained) took place at the instant of its capture, and destroyed a number of gallant officers and men, who at the moment were crowded on its ramparts, which the enemy had abandoned. The redoubt, No. 1, against which Lieutenant-Colonel M'Leod's attack was directed, was carried in as gallant a style; and I lament to state, that most valiant and experienced officer fell at the moment of victory. The front of the position was now open, and the troops rushed in from every quarter.

" During the operations on the right, Colonel Gillespie pursued his advantage to the left, carrying the enemy's redoubts towards the rear; and being joined by Lieutenant-Colonel Alexander M'Leod, of the 59th, with part of that corps, he directed him to attack the park of artillery, which that officer carried in a most masterly manner, putting to flight a body of the enemy's cavalry that formed, and attempted to defend it. A sharp fire of musquetry was now kept up by a strong body of the enemy, who had taken post in the lines in front of fort Cornelis; but were driven from them, the fort taken, and the enemy completely dispersed. They were pursued by Colonel Gillespie, with the 14th regiment, a party of Sepoys, and the seamen from the batteries, under Captain Sayer, of the Royal Navy. By this time, the cavalry and horse artillery had effected a passage through the lines, the former commanded by Major Travers, and the latter by Captain Noble; and with the gallant Colonel at their head, the pursuit was continued, till the whole of the enemy's army was killed, taken, or dispersed.

" Major Yule's attack was equally spirited, but after routing the enemy's force at Campong Malayo, and killing many of them, he found the bridge on fire, and was unable to penetrate further.

" I have the honour to enclose a return of the loss sustained, from our landing on the fourth, to the twenty-sixth inclusive ; sincerely I lament its extent, and the many valuable and able officers that have unfortunately fallen ; but when the prepared state of the enemy, their numbers., and the strength of their positions are considered, I trust it will not be deemed heavier than might be expected. Their's has greatly exceeded it. In the action of the twenty-sixth, the numbers killed were immense, but it has been impossible to form any accurate statement of the amount.

" About one thousand have been buried in the works. Multitudes were cut down in the retreat, the rivers are choaked up with dead, and the huts and woods were filled with the wounded, who have since expired. We have taken near five thousand prisoners ; among whom are three General Officers, thirty-four Field Officers, seventy Captains, and one hundred and fifty Subaltern Officers. General Janssens made his escape with difficulty during the action, and reached Buitenzorg, a distance of thirty miles, with a few cavalry, the sole remains of an army of ten thousand men. This place he has since evacuated, and fled to the Eastward. A detachment of our troops is in possession of it.

" The superior discipline and invincible courage which have so highly distinguished the British army, were never more fully displayed, and I have the heartfelt pleasure to add, that they have not been clouded by any acts of insubordination.

" I have the honor to enclose a copy of the orders I have directed to be issued, thanking the troops in general for their services, and particularizing some of the officers, who from their rank or situations, were more fortunate than their equally gallant companions, in opportunities of distinguishing themselves, and serving their Sovereign and their country. But I must not omit noticing to your Lordship the very particular merit of Colonel Gillespie, to whose assistance in planning the principal attack, and to whose gallantry, energy, and judgement in executing it, the success is greatly to be attributed.

" To the general Staff of the army, as well as my own Staff, I feel myself particularly indebted: the professional knowledge, zeal, and activity of Colonel Eden, Quarter Master General, have been essentially useful to me ; but I cannot express how much I have benefited by the able assistance and laborious exertions of Colonel Agnew, the Adjutant General, an officer whose activity and meritorious services have frequently attracted the notice, and received the thanks of the Governments in India.

" It is with particular pleasure I assure your Lordship, that I have received the most cordial support from the Honourable Rear Admiral Stopford, and Commodore Broughton, during the period of their commanding the squadron. The former was pleased to allow a body of five hundred seamen, under that valuable officer Captain Sayer, of the Leda, to assist at our batteries. Their services were particularly useful, and I have the satisfaction to assure you, that both the artillery and engineers were actuated by the same zeal in performing their respective duties, that has been so conspicuous in all ranks and departments, though from the deficiency of the means at their disposal, their operations were unavoidably embarrassed with uncommon difficulties.

" I have the honor to be, &c.

(Signed)   " S. AUCHMUTY, Lieut. Gen."

Letter from Lord Minto to the Earl of Liverpool, Secretary of State for the War Department.

" Batavia, September 2d, 1811.

" My Lord,

" I have the honor to submit to your Lordship a copy of my letter to the Honourable the Court of Directors, of the first of September, inclosing his Excellency Sir Samuel Auchmuty's report of military proceedings, in Java, to the 31st of August.

" Your Lordship will observe, with satisfaction, that the conquest of Java is already substantially accomplished, although the operations of the army have not hitherto been directed to the eastern parts of the island. But a powerful force is now embarking against Sourabaya, where, with the exception of the crews of two French frigates, the enemy has only a small body of native troops.

" The Armament, which is now proceeding under the personal command of his Excellency the Commander in Chief, and which may reach its destination in ten days, cannot fail of overpowering any resistance the enemy may make, if any should be attempted, and finally terminating the contest in Java.

" An Empire, which for two centuries has contributed greatly to the power, prosperity, and grandeur of one of the principal and most respected States of Europe, has been thus wrested from the short usurpation of the French Government, added to the dominion of the British Crown; and converted from a seat of hostile machination and commercial competition, into an augmentation of British power and prosperity.

" For this signal, and as your Lordship will collect from the inclosed Documents, this most splendid and illustrious service, Great Britain is indebted to the truly British intrepidity of as brave an army as ever did honour to our country; to the professional skill and spirit of their officers; and to the wisdom, decision, and firmness of the eminent Man who directed their courage, and led them to victory.

" Your Lordship will, I am sure, share with me the gratifying reflection, that by the successive reduction of the French Islands and Java, the British nation has neither an enemy nor a rival left from the Cape of Good Hope to Cape Horn.

" I have the honour to be, &c.

(Signed)   " MINTO."

SECTION IV

Conclusion of Lieutenant General Sir Samuel Auchmuty's Campaign in Java.

THE two French frigates La Nymphe and La Medusa, under the command of Commodore Reval, who were blockaded in Sourabaya Harbour, succeeded in making their escape the moment they received the news of the destruction of their army. In these ships several Officers, Aids-de-Camp to General Janssens, with Dibbatz, Chef de Battalion, Major Godders, Larienty, Auditor to the Council of State, and Monsieur Panat, went passengers, carrying home with them to France, the General's own account of the defeat which he had sustained, and the consequent fall of this valuable settlement.

In this " afflicting report" to the Minister of Marine and the Colonies, who is instructed by Janssens to lay it before " His Majesty the Emperor," he states that his army was considerably weakened by disease and that he never could muster eight thousand effective men under arms *.

* The French have been always very apt to attribute their defeat to a superiority of numbers, on the part of their opponents. An instance of this occurred in the enquiry into General De Caen's conduct, on the occasion of the capture of the Isle of France, by Sir John Aber-

Having thus depreciated his own force, and aggravated that of his adversaries, he proceeds to express his intention of repairing to Samarang, with the view of seeking some resources among the Javanese and Madurese, it being his determination to maintain himself on the Island as long as possible, though he candidly adds, " I must not conceal from your Excellency, that I cannot expect the Indians will resist regular European troops, or that they can stand against the discipline of the British."

When Sir Samuel Auchmuty was informed of the flight of General Janssens to the Eastward, he immediately dispatched by sea, a detachment to Cheribon, which place, from its situation, was now become of considerable importance. The mountains which separate the northern

cromby. The British force is there estimated at above twenty thousand men, whereas the total number of troops landed on that service, amounted to nine thousand nine hundred and ninety-nine men.

From the reports and other official papers found at Cornelis, the French army concentrated there, could not have been less than thirteen thousand men, on the morning of the twenty-sixth of August; while the British army, from the number of sick in the hospitals, &c. could not have mustered eight thousand effectives on that day; and the number of combatants actually engaged, was much more widely disproportionate, compared with the enemy's force opposed to us, without mentioning the strength of their position, their numerous and well-served artillery, and other important advantages.

General Janssens' dispatch is also incorrect in the article of dates, for he states that the landing of the British did not take place till the fifth, whereas it happened on the fourth; that the batteries were erected on the night of the nineteenth, instead of the twentieth; that they opened on the twentieth, when, with the exception of a few shot on the morning of the twenty-second, it was the twenty-fourth before they commenced a regular cannonade. The General also asserts, that his sortie took place on the twenty-fourth, when it actually happened on the twenty-second of August.

N 2

from the southern coasts, approach the former so closely near Cheribon, that the occupation of this place not only commanded the great road, but tended most effectually to impede, if not to cut off entirely all communication with the eastern part of the Island. A squadron of frigates, therefore, with the marines, commanded by Captain Beaver, of the Nisus, and a battalion of Sepoys, under Colonel Wood, were employed on this service. The frigates sailed from Batavia on the thirty-first of August, and when they appeared off Cheribon, that fort instantly surrendered at the first summons. General Janssens had passed through this place on his route to the eastward, only two days preceding; and soon after the possession of it by our marines, General Jumel, the second in command, also arrived there, without knowing of the change that had happened, in consequence of which he was taken, with the Chef de Battalion Knotzer, Aid-de-Camp to General Janssens. Jumel had assumed the command of the troops on quitting Buitenzorg, but after witnessing a mutiny among the Malays, who had murdered one of their officers, and then disbanded, he abandoned the remainder, to follow the footsteps and the fortune of his chief.

The enemy's remaining force, principally cavalry, consisting of about fifty Officers, two hundred Europeans, and five hundred Native troops, who had followed General Janssens by the eastern route, finding themselves cut off in consequence of our possession of Cheribon, surrendered by capitulation, and returned to Buitenzorg as prisoners of war, together with Major Le Blanc, their commandant. Carang Sambong was also occupied by a party of seamen and marines, under Captain Welchman, R. M. on the 6th of September, and the public stores were there placed in safety. Many of the straggling parties found here, on their way to the Eastward, surrendered themselves prisoners of war ; and thus not a man in arms was left to the Westward of Cheribon.

The fort of Taggal, situated between Cheribon and Samarang, surrendered to Captain Hillyar, of his Majesty's ship the Phœbe.

Soon after the capture of Batavia, a communication had been opened with the Rajah of Madura, and a detachment from the naval force, consisting of his Majesty's ships the Sir Francis Drake, Captain Harris, and the Phaëton, Captain Fleetwood Pellew, with their marines, and a part of the fourteenth regiment of foot, acting in the latter capacity, was now despatched to make an attempt upon that island. This attack, through the judicious arrangement of Captain Harris, with the able assistance of Captain Pellew, and the efficient gallantry of the men employed, was crowned with complete success.

After taking the fort of Samanap, Captain Harris completely defeated a desperate attempt which was made to recapture that place. Some Dutchmen who headed the natives on this occasion, were made prisoners, and of such decisive importance was the affair, that the Chiefs of Madura immediately declared themselves in favour of the English, and seized the several garrisons that were still remaining on the island.

A force under the command of Sir Samuel Auchmuty in person having been prepared for the purpose of following Janssens to the eastward, the General left Batavia on the fifth of September, the troops being directed to make the best of their way to Zedayo, which was the appointed rendezvous.

Here Sir Samuel intended to land, having concluded that General

Janssens would proceed to Sourabaya, and endeavour to defend both that place and Fort Ludowyck. The General, on touching at Cheribon, there found, from intercepted letters, that the object of his pursuit was at Samarang, with the intention of making a stand there, and of eventually retiring upon Solo, the capital of the Emperor. This intelligence determined Sir Samuel to meet Janssens at Samarang; and after forcing him back upon Solo, to leave him for the present, while possession was taken of the eastern part of the Island, a measure which the Admiral conceived to be absolutely necessary for the safety of the shipping before the change of the monsoon.

In pursuance of this plan of operations, vessels were dispatched with orders for all the transports to repair to Samarang; and the General fortunately meeting Commodore Broughton with the squadron, having troops on board, requested him to hasten to those roads. On the ninth, the General reached that place, where he was joined the same evening by Admiral Stopford, and the Commodore arrived the next day.

Though the relative situation of the two armies by no means rendered such a measure essentially necessary as that of inviting Janssens to a surrender, yet there were circumstances which rendered the proceeding advisable. Immediately after the assault at Cornelis, a verbal message was sent to Buitenzorg, with an offer of terms; which General Janssens rejected, on the plea that his resources were by no means as yet exhausted. Notwithstanding this refusal and boast, a considerable object was obtained by this step, as it was ascertained that no troops were on the road; and consequently, that no part of the army had eluded pursuit. By the present flag, the accounts of his being at Samarang were fully confirmed, and it was observed also, that he was attended by a numerous Staff, besides which it was also discovered that there was an encampment in the neighbourhood. The following invitation was sent on this last occasion:

General Sir Samuel Auchmuty and Rear-Admiral Stopford, to General Janssens.

" September 10, 1811.

" SIR,

" After the proposals made to your Excellency at Buitenzorg, we might be excused again offering favourable terms of surrender. But your Excellency was not then perhaps aware, that the whole of your efficient force was killed, taken, or dispersed in the action of the 26th. You had not, perhaps, reflected on the miseries to which the European inhabitants of the Colony must be exposed from a protracted warfare. You must be now sensible that the Colony is lost to France; and though by intriguing with the Native Powers, its possession may be rendered for some time inquiet, the unfortunate Colonists alone will be the sufferers.

" Enough, Sir, has been sacrificed to reputation: think now of the interests of those placed under your protection. By submitting to a destiny that cannot be avoided, you immediately arrest the hand of the armed ruffian, that now riots in the blood of the Colonists. The British troops will then be employed in the grateful office of giving them protection. But if, Sir, you continue deaf to the cries of a distressed people,—if blood must be unnecessarily shed,—if the Natives must be let loose to plunder and massacre the European inhabitants of Java, we shall hold you, Sir, and those who continue to support you, as answerable for the consequences. It is our earnest intention to pre-

vent those horrors.   Your perseverance in a hopeless cause, will counteract our efforts.

" We have directed Colonel Agnew, of the Army, and the Honourable Captain Elliott, of the Navy, to wait on you with this Letter;
and we beg to refer you to them for particulars.

" We have the honour to be, &c. &c. &c.

(Signed)   " S. AUCHMUTY.

                            " P. STOPFORD."

———

THE ANSWER.

(TRANSLATION.)

" Samarang, the 10th September, 1811.

" *The Governor-General, to His Excellency Lieutenant-General Sir
Samuel Auchmuty, Commander in Chief of the Army, and Rear-
Admiral Stopford, Commander in Chief of His Britannic Majes-
ty's Naval Forces.*

" GENERALS,

" Colonel Agnew, and the Honourable Captain Elliott, have delivered to me the Letter your Excellencies did me the honour to address
to me.   Notwithstanding the losses of the 26th of last month, there yet
remain resources in the Colony.   The faithful Vassals of the Government have the same cause to defend with ourselves; and I owe to them
the same protection as to the Europeans, the direct subjects of His
Majesty the Emperor and King.   I am not insensible to the evils
which the inhabitants of the Colony suffer; but it is not I that am the
cause of their sufferings.   I have the highest opinion of the personal
qualities of your Excellencies not to be persuaded, that in the same

manner that you combat those who carry arms, you will protect the peaceable Colonists and Natives who inhabit the territory occupied by the troops of his Britannic Majesty, and prevent those horrors which are not the necessary consequences of a state of war.

" I have the honour to be, with perfect consideration, &c. &c.

(Signed) " JANSSENS."

As General Janssens refused to treat, and the number of troops judged necessary to attack Samarang were not yet arrived, the Admiral determined, in the mean time, to cut out some boats which flanked the approaches to the town. This plan was carried into execution, on the night of the tenth, by the armed boats of the squadron, under the orders of Captain Maxwell, of his Majesty's sloop the Procris. Six of those that were anchored west of the town, with French colours flying, were taken possession of; but the crews had abandoned them, and the guns were taken out. Those to the eastward of the town had been already carried up the river.

In the mean time, the General waited in hourly expectation, and with some impatience, for the arrival of the transports.

On the 12th, it was fully ascertained, that the formidable works which commanded the landing were dismantled; and therefore preparations were made to land that night with the little force which the General had at his disposal. It was discovered, however, in the afternoon, that the town was evacuated, on which Colonel Gibbs took quiet possession of it the same evening.

As it was now ascertained that General Janssens had collected a considerable force, principally from the Native Princes ; among whom was Prince Prangwedona, with fifteen hundred men, chiefly horse, and that having been joined by a regular battalion from Soura-baya, he had taken up a fortified position within a few miles of the town, Sir Samuel Auchmuty determined to attack the place, and force him further into the interior before he began his own operations to the eastward.

The troops were accordingly landed on the 13th, but at so late an hour that the attack could not take place, as it had been intended, till the next morning. During that day many ships appeared in the offing, and the General again delayed his design, in the expectation of a rein-forcement, which was very desirable. One transport only, with Se-poys, however, came in, and the others continued their course towards Zedayo, owing to a mistake in the delivery of orders. The Admiral himself sailed on the 15th, to make arrangements for the attack on Fort Ludowyck ; and the slender reinforcement which the General had obtained, enabled him to march the same night with about 1200 firelocks and six guns, to attack the enemy.

This force, under the command of Colonel Gibbs, moved at two o'clock on the morning of the 16th from Samarang ; and after a march of six miles over a hilly and difficult country, descried the enemy's forces at Jattoo. The Colonel halted in front of the position before the dawn, in order to reconnoitre, which was essentially necessary pre-vious to an assault, as no information, on which any reliance was to be placed, could be obtained at Samarang.

The enemy were posted on some very high and rugged hills, which extend for many miles to the back of Samarang ; and the high road to Solo intersected their line. This road, which had been cut at a vast expense, was now shut up in many places by chevaux de frise. The flanks of the position were protected by the extreme difficulty of the approach, and could not be turned in any other way than by a circuit of many miles through an intricate country. About thirty pieces of cannon, regularly placed on platforms, covered the front; and a valley, of about twelve hundred yards in breadth, separated the two armies.

At the first dawn of day, the enemy's position appeared to be so formidable, that the general opinion was against a front attack ; which, however, was the measure that the General had determined upon, though he was neither insensible of the difficulty of the attempt, nor regardless of the loss which he might sustain. But then it was to be considered that his hopes of a reinforcement were at an end, as all the other transports had sailed to Zedayo. His weakness would have been exposed by delay, and confidence thereby given to the enemy, whose flanks he knew were not to be approached. To these imperious reasons, for the resolution which the General had formed, was to be added the entire trust he placed in his troops; together with his conviction, that the enemy, on the contrary, could have no dependence on themselves.

A detachment with two guns, was sent to occupy a hill, which appeared to overlook the left of the enemy's line ; and the remaining guns were brought to throw shot at a great elevation across the valley into their position. As soon as these pieces opened, the Advance, with Colonel Gibbs at their head, rushed across the valley, and up to the great road, till they nearly reached the summit of the hill. Here they halted to take breath, and to allow the main body to advance. The enemy being taken by surprise, did not open their fire till our troops were under shelter. Some of their guns then attempted to reach them, while, at the same time, others fired at the Line as it was crossing the valley. But the confusion attending an unexpected attack, the fire from our artillery, the vicinity of the Advance, and the imposing appearance of the column, will account for the little execution done by their numerous artillery. With the loss of two men killed, and a few wounded, the Line crossed the valley ; and as soon as they had taken breath, the whole advanced on the enemy; who were already vanquished, and retreating in all directions, leaving their guns behind them, with the exception of a few light field-pieces attached to the cavalry. Colonel Gibbs followed as fast as possible ; but though many European officers and some men were taken, it was soon evident, that as their principal force was mounted, pursuit would be fruitless. It was, however, determined to assault the fort of Onarang, a small square brick-work, about twelve miles from Samarang, on the Solo road ; and as a force appeared to be collecting there, the troops advanced without halting. The enemy fired from their works on the Advance ; but perceiving that movements were making to surround the fort, they evacuated it, though not without committing many enormities; then throwing away their arms and clothing, they disbanded in all directions.

This was the last effort of General Janssens, who fled to the Fort of Salatiga ; but finding himself totally deserted by his men, he sent the same night a request to the General for a cessation of arms, and an offer to treat for a capitulation. This proposition was the more acceptable, as the British Commander had given up all intentions of advancing further into the interior, until the operations to the Eastward should be completed, which he had promised the Admiral immediately to commence.

There were, however, some difficulties to be surmounted in this negociation ; one of the principal of which lay in the proposal of General Janssens, to treat with Lord Minto, who was then at Batavia, three hundred and fifty miles distant from the scene of action, and therefore an acquiescence with this request would have been attended with serious delay, at the precise period when it was of the utmost importance to take advantage of the impression which had been made by our success. Sir Samuel Auchmuty was persuaded, that the Admiral would attempt fort Ludowyck, with his ships, if he saw any chance of reducing it; but there was reason to apprehend, that a failure in this point, and he knew that fort Ludowyck was very formidable, would give an unfortunate turn to the campaign : added to all this, General Janssens might, when the panic of his troops subsided, be joined by a number sufficient to induce him to fall back on Solo, or by marching towards Sourabaya, it was probable that he would be enabled still to prolong the contest, while, from the knowledge which he could not fail to obtain, of the actual force with the British General, and of its inefficiency to the task of penetrating into the interior, he might be induced to hold out, trusting for some change in his favour, to the approaching Monsoon, and the nature of the climate. With these impressions on his mind, Sir Samuel Auchmuty informed General Janssens, he must treat with him alone, and that immediately. In consequence of this prompt decision, a cessation of arms for twenty-four hours was agreed upon, to arrange the terms.

Sir Samuel Auchmuty being aware that the responsibility of the eaty would rest solely with himself, was extremely cautious in the management of this important business taking care that nothing should be conceded, which could be liable to objection. He therefore determined on settling, as a basis, that the treaty should embrace all the dependencies of Java; that all the military should be prisoners of war; and that government should be left unfettered on the three essential points of the future government of the island; the guarantee of the public debt, and the liquidation of the paper money.

The articles were framed at the head-quarters at Onarang, and sent for confirmation to General Janssens, who objected strongly to the clauses which related to the public debts, and requested an interview with Sir Samuel Auchmuty. This the latter declined, and intimated his fixed resolution, not to consent to any alteration in the proposed terms. As the armistice must necessarily expire, before a final answer could be received, Sir Samuel determined to advance towards Salatiga; and he had actually marched some miles, when a ratified copy of the capitulation was received, though General Janssens was by no means satisfied with the manner in which the capitulation was forced upon him, and his feelings on this occasion may be judged of from the following paper:

" When I applied to treat for a capitulation, it was because all my resources were exhausted ; as long as I had any left me, I would never have submitted : I could not pretend then, in this situation, to prescribe the articles.

" I was affected at your Excellency's refusal to have an interview. It would not have bound you to any thing. The prolongation or the suspension of the armistice, were matters equally indifferent, not having one soldier left me, the possibility of making resistance no longer existed.   I am perfectly convinced, that if your Excellency had granted an interview, you would have consented, without having surrendered any of the advantages to be derived to your Government, to give terms to the capitulation, less hard and humiliating to me.

" I submitted because I preferred putting an end to the miseries of the colonists, my countrymen, to my private interests.   In this moment, it is impossible, either to ameliorate my fate, or to render it worse, and I have only to ask orders for my future destination, about which I am perfectly indifferent.   I shall only entreat your Excellency, to soften as much as it is in your power, the condition of the officers, who had the misfortune to serve under my orders."

With every allowance for the feelings of General Janssens, which at this time were naturally irritated by his misfortunes, it is certain that he had no reason whatever to complain of any harsh treatment on the part of his conquerors.   On the contrary, a review of his own conduct ought to have satisfied him, that he had laid himself open to have harder measures exacted from him, and that the victor had, in fact, manifested a forbearance which afforded a striking contrast to his own example.   The only justification that can be offered for General Janssens, arises from the circumstance of his being in the service of a Despot, whose words to him, when he took leave, on being appointed to this command, were calculated to produce a deep impression on his mind ; " Souvenez vous Monsieur, qu'un General François ne se laisse pas prendre une seconde fois."   This observation was an allusion to the surrender of the Cape of Good Hope to Sir David Baird, and the whole was a pretty broad hint, that no unfortunate occurrence would again meet with forgiveness. The remembrance of this charge, and the apprehension of what might befal him on his return to France, no doubt occasioned the temerity with which this post was defended, even when it was obvious, that farther resistance was fruitless, and that hope was at an end. But though much may be allowed to a brave man, who is tenacious of his military reputation; it will be difficult to furnish an apology for the obstinacy, which indicated a total disregard of human life, and which, without any adequate cause, or probable consequence, exposed the peaceable inhabitants, not only to the ordinary evils of war, but to the ravages of a Malay banditti.

Another particular, which deprived General Janssens of any right to complain, was the wanton destruction of the spice stores, in the castle of Batavia, all of which were burned by his orders immediately on our arrival. In the same spirit, he caused the rich magazines of spices at Rustenberg, to be set on fire, after his defeat at Cornelis. These acts of useless devastation, though they were calculated to recommend the author of them to the ruler whose commission he bore, ill became the character of a warrior, much less that of one who had under his protection the property of numbers, and which thus became exposed to the most extensive retaliation. British valour and generosity, however, proved on this occasion, a more effectual security to the natives and settlers of Java, than the energy or justice of their own Government. But warranted as the conquerors would have been by the laws of nations, in retaliating with severity, and prosecuting hostilities to the extremity of an unconditional surrender, without condescending to stipulate for any term; humanity dictated a more magnanimous course. The blood which had already been spilt, rendered it an imperious duty on the part of the Commander in Chief to stop any further effusion; and this could only be done by pressing the conclusion of the treaty.

An express was immediately forwarded to the Admiral, for the purpose of suspending hostilities in that quarter, as the General was anxious to prevent, if possible, an assault on fort Ludowyck, nor was he quite easy with regard to the situation of the troops, who had been, as already stated, hurried away to the rendezvous at Zedayo, and he was apprehensive that they might be ordered to land, and act with a force which he knew was advancing from Madura. He was not mistaken in this conjecture.

The Admiral arrived at Zedayo on the seventeenth, and on the eighteenth, which was the same day that the capitulation of Onarang was signed, he directed Major Farquhar, the senior officer of the army, on board the transports, to land the troops at that place, and to act in conjunction with Captain Harris, who was there with a body of Madurese. This force amounted to about five hundred men, one half of whom were Europeans, with some artillery.

The troops having landed on the nineteenth, occupied Gressie the next day, and on the twenty-second, Sourabaya surrendered without opposition, as the news of the capitulation of General Janssens, had already reached that station.

The Admiral having reconnoitered fort Ludowyck, and finding it too strong to be taken by a *Coup de Main*, fixed upon a spot for a

P

mortar battery ; but as the nearest point of land was fifteen hundred yards from the works, there appeared no reasonable expectation of its being quickly reduced by a bombardment. On the contrary, such was the apparent strength of the place, with a hundred pieces of capital ordnance, mounted on traversing carriages, that there was reason to fear it would remain in the possession of the enemy, as long as the garrison, which was a strong one, could be supplied with provisions. In the midst of this doubtful uncertainty, the capitulation of Onarang took place, which gave us possession of this formidable station, thereby completing the reduction of all the posts which the enemy held in the island of Java. As in this general surrender were comprehended Macassar, Timor, and all the other dependencies on the Government of Batavia, these places were subsequently occupied by the British forces without any further opposition.

Thus happily terminated a campaign, which, from the peculiar hardships of the service, and the importance of its object, independent of the atchievements, by which it was distinguished, has never been surpassed, and will indeed be found to have but few parallels, when we consider the small number of combatants that were opposed to the best disciplined troops of the enemy, Europeans and Natives, and who had all the advantages arising from local knowledge, the choice of positions, and the erection of batteries, which nature had made strong, and art had almost rendered impregnable. Yet, in defiance of the most formidable obstacles, and under the pressure of continual fatigue, an inferior force succeeded, by the combination of skill, bravery, and perseverance, in overcoming an army of seventeen thousand regularly organized troops; and in making seven Generals, with upwards of three hundred field and inferior officers prisoners of war; added to which, fifteen hundred pieces of cannon were taken, with all the appurtenances of military stores.

Most truly may it be said, that in no instance has British military discipline shone with greater lustre, than what appeared throughout this interesting expedition and brilliant conquest; during the whole of which, scarcely a single instance of marauding or plunder occurred. The mind of every soldier was deeply impressed with a sense of the honourable duties that were expected of him, and which the public admonitions of the Commander in Chief, tended strongly to enforce. These injunctions, which were drawn up with great perspicuity by Colonel Agnew, Adjutant General, were ordered to be frequently read during the passage, and thus, by being stamped on the memory of the men, contributed very powerfully to the regularity of their conduct, and the success which they richly merited. The expedition indeed, was so completely arranged in all its various and complicated parts, under the immediate direction of Sir Samuel Auchmuty, whose judicious measures were carried into effect by the active management of the Adjutant and Quarter-Master General, that while the order which was thereby maintained commanded admiration, the vigilance it provided, facilitated the conquest, and added value to the acquisition. That this is neither exaggerated praise, nor the ebullition of vanity, will be evident from the following testimony, which was borne to the exertions of the officers on the Staff of the Army, by the most competent judge of their services.

Extract of the General Orders by the Commander in Chief.

" 1st October, 1811.

" The surrender by capitulation of the Island of Java and its Dependencies, having completed the object for which the army was equipped, it is the intention of the Commander in Chief to return to the Coast of Coromandel, and to order to their respective Presidencies, by the earliest opportunity, such corps of the army formed for the expedition, which has so happily terminated, as are not required for the security of the captured countries.

" As the separate destination of the officers on the staff of the army may prevent the Commander in Chief from having another occasion to express to them collectively, the obligation he feels for their attention to the duties of their several offices and departments on the recent service ; he requests that the Officers of the General and Brigade Staff of the Army, and Heads of Departments, will accept his thanks for their conduct, during the important service on which they have been employed, under his immediate command.

(Signed)　　　　　" P. AGNEW, Adj. Gen."

Nor should the estimation in which this conquest was held, by the highest authorities both in India and in England be omitted, since it marks that attention to great actions which will always prove a powerful incentive to honourable exertion and virtuous imitation. The expression of feeling which pervades the first of these documents, is to be ascribed to that lively sensibility which must have animated Lord Minto, in the remembrance of the personal share which he had in this expedition. That Nobleman, on the arrival of the fleet in the bay of Batavia, volunteered his services on shore as a private individual, and was one of the first of the British advance, in occupying the village of Chillingching. Having happily witnessed the conquest of Java, and completed the necessary arrangements for the local government, his Lordship returned to Calcutta, where he gave orders for erecting, at his own expence, a monument to the memory of the heroes who fell on this occasion.

Letter from the Supreme Government of India, to the Honourable Sir G. H. Barlow, K. B. Governor in Council, Fort St. George.

" Fort William, 26th December, 1811.

" HONOURABLE SIR,

" We have the honour to acknowledge the receipt, on the 23d instant, of your letter, under date the 23d ultimo, communicating the satisfactory intelligence, of the arrival of his Excellency Lieutenant General Sir Samuel Auchmuty, at Cannanore, and his Excellency's resumption of the immediate command of the army of Fort St. George; and we request you will be pleased to convey to his Excellency our congratulations on this occasion.

" We have awaited the receipt of the intelligence of Sir Samuel Auchmuty's return to India, to convey to his Excellency, through the channel of your Honourable Board, the tribute of those acknowledg-

ments, which are so eminently due for the invaluable services rendered by his Excellency to our Sovereign, our Country, and our
immediate Superiors, in the exercise of the great and important
command, of which our previous sense of his Excellency's high character and distinguished abilities induced us to request his acceptance.

" In whatever degree the late glorious success of the British arms
on the Island of Java, are proximately to be ascribed to the exemplary
skill and resistless gallantry of the officers and men under his Excellency's command, who were engaged in the operations of the field ; we
must primarily refer the glory of the late atchievements, and the final
issue of the contest, to the genius which combined the complicated arrangements of the campaign, which framed the plan of each successive
attack on the enemy's posts, and directed and animated the exertions
of the troops.

" With that reserve which ever accompanies transcendent merit, his
Excellency has abstained in his report of the operations of the field,
from drawing the public attention to any circumstances calculated to
place in a conspicuous point of view, the honour which attaches personally to him. It is our duty to supply this defect, by recording our
high and grateful sense of his Excellency's merits and services in the
conduct of the military branch of the late arduous and brilliant expedition.

" We request that these sentiments may be communicated to Lieutenant-General Sir Samuel Auchmuty, with the expression of our
thanks for his Excellency's most able conduct and eminent services, in
the chief command of the military branch of the Expedition ; by the

success of which, a valuable and important Colony has been added to the British dominions; and the last remnant of the enemy's power and influence in the East, has been permanently extinguished.

" We further request that this address may be published for general information.

" We have the honour to be, &c. &c. &c.

(Signed)   {   " MINTO.
                " J. LUMSDEN.
                " H. COLEBROOKE."

General Orders by the Right Honourable the Governor-General in Council.

" Fort William, 11th February, 1812.

" The success of the late measures for the reduction of the French power in Java, and the splendid atchievements of the army employed on that enterprize, were in substance communicated to the public, by order of His Excellency General Hewitt, the late Vice-President in Council, at two several periods, when the official relations had not yet been received, and the sense entertained by his Excellency in Council of events so favourable to the public interest, so grateful to this Government, and so glorious to the troops, was published under the same circumstances to the army of this Presidency.

" The Governor-General in Council, penetrated with admiration of the scarcely paralleled exertions, by which the gallant troops under the direction of their distinguished Commander, accomplished so signal a service, cannot but be anxious to deliver in his own name, sentiments so deeply impressed upon his mind.

" His Excellency Sir Samuel Auchmuty, has conveyed in his General Orders and in his Official Reports, the applause which is due to the officers and troops who have conquered under his command; and that authentic testimony derives a value from his high authority, which it could have obtained from no other quarter.

" There is one defect, however, in the praise of these great actions, which modesty, the companion of exalted merit, could alone have left to others the gratifying privilege of supplying.

" His Lordship in Council, therefore, seizes with the highest satisfaction the opportunity afforded him of rendering the homage which is due to the illustrious person, under whose superintending judgment, firmness, energy, and prudence, the conquest of Java was atchieved with rapidity indeed, but with as much exertion of wisdom, decision, enterprize, and valour, as have sufficed for the lustre of much more protracted periods of warfare. His Lordship in Council does not fear the reproach of partial exaggeration in saying, that greater glory was never acquired by the same number of men, in the same short space of time.

" The Governor-General in Council would scarcely think himself justified in reciting in his own name, however grateful it would be to himself, the merited notice which his Excellency Sir Samuel Auchmuty, the Commander in Chief of the Expedition, has taken of individual officers and corps who have justly obtained his commendation;

but in recording, in full concurrence with his Excellency, his Lordship's cordial and lively sense of the glory which has been won by the whole army in this signal service, the Governor-General in Council cannot omit, from the seat of his more immediate authority, congratulating the army of Bengal, on the distinguished honour which has fallen upon the Native troops of this Presidency, serving in Java. Opposed as they have rarely been to an European enemy, they attracted the unanimous applause of the whole army; and by steady as well as ardent valour, displayed in the most trying scenes of war, proved themselves fit comrades of our brave and illustrious countrymen, whose triumph and glory they shared. But verbal applause alone to this army would be a feeble and imperfect acknowledgment of services so important, and merits so transcendant.

" The Governor-General, before his departure from Java, has announced his resolution to propose the commemoration of this conquest, and of the noble efforts of valour and discipline to which the country owes so great a benefit, by Medals to be distributed to the troops ; and his Lordship had the gratification of finding, on his return to Bengal, that his wishes had been anticipated, and that the measure was already in progress, by the orders of his Excellency the Vice-President in Council.

" To his authentic act of public approbation, the Governor-General has indulged the earnest desire of adding a testimony of his personal sentiments by resolving to erect at his own expence a Monument to the memory of those brave men, who in the short but arduous war of Java, purchased the triumph of their country, and perfected their own title to immortal fame, by illustrious death in the very bosom of victory.   Q

" As just objects of similar honours, merited in the strenuous discharge of duties, closely connected with the same system of national services, his Lordship proposes to consecrate this memorial to the names also of those gallant and lamented officers and men, who, animated with the same spirit, fell gloriously in the conquests of Bourbon and Mauritius.

" The time that has been required for maturing the latter proposition has occasioned some delay; and his Lordship in Council is pleased to direct the immediate publication of this order to the army of Bengal, to be transmitted afterwards to the Presidencies of Fort St. George and Bombay, and to the island of Ceylon, the Government and armies of which have so honourably co-operated in those eminent services.

(Signed)

> " MINTO.
>
> " G. NUGENT.
>
> " J. LUMSDEN.
>
> " H. COLEBROOKE."

General Orders. By the Commander in Chief in India, Lieutenant-General Sir George Nugent.

" Head-Quarters, Calcutta, June, 1812.

" The Commander in Chief in India, feels the highest gratification in publishing to the army on this Establishment, and to the troops of His Majesty, and the Honourable Company's, serving in Java, the following dispatch, received from his Excellency Lieutenant General

Sir Samuel Auchmuty, announcing the gracious sentiments of approbation and applause with which His Royal Highness the Prince Regent has viewed the brilliant services of the army, which under the
able direction of the above distinguished Commander, so gloriously
atchieved the conquest of the last remaining Colony of France.

" Lieutenant-General Sir George Nugent, cordially unites in the
sentiments which his Excellency Sir Samuel Auchmuty has expressed
in his General Orders to the troops he so recently led to victory ; and
feels convinced with his Excellency, that they will justly appreciate
the special marks of favour and approbation so graciously bestowed on
them by His Royal Highness."

———————

General Orders.   By His Excellency Lieutenant-General Sir Samuel
Auchmuty, Commander in Chief.

" Madras, May 12, 1812.

" Lieutenant-General Sir Samuel Auchmuty has it in command
from His Royal Highness the Prince Regent, to convey in public
orders, and in the strongest terms to the troops who atchieved the conquest of Java, His Royal Highness's approbation of the distinguished
gallantry and spirit displayed by them during a succession of the most
brilliant operations, and in particular on the 26th of August, when the
enemy's entrenchments were assaulted and carried, and their army defeated and destroyed.

" In communicating so gratifying an acknowledgment of their valuable services, the Lieutenant-General is convinced that the army it was

his good fortune to command, will justly appreciate the distinguished honour conferred on them, by His Royal Highness's gracious appro-bation.

" The marks of royal approbation bestowed on their leaders, are a source of pride and gratification to every rank in well constituted ar-mies; with this impression, the Lieutenant-General cannot refuse the assailants at Cornelis, the satisfaction of knowing, that His Royal Highness the Prince Regent has graciously announced his intention of bestowing Medals on the Superior Officers of His Majesty's and the Honourable Company's Forces, who distinguished themselves on that memorable service.

(Signed)   " S. AUCHMUTY."

By order of H. E. the Commander in Chief in India,

(Signed)   G. H. FAGAN, Adj. Gen.

Letter from Lord Liverpool, Secretary of State for the War Depart-ment, to Lieutenant-General Sir Samuel Auchmuty, &c. &c.

" Downing-street, December, 1811.

" SIR,

" Your dispatch of the 31st August, and Lord Minto's of the 2d September, with its inclosures, have been received, and laid before His Royal Highness the Prince Regent.

" The important result of an expedition which has wrested from the enemy the only remaining Settlement which they possessed in the

East, and has left them without a Colony in any part of the world, has afforded the greatest satisfaction to His Royal Highness.

" Whilst he fully appreciates the wisdom and prudence with which this most important enterprize has been planned, he is sensible that the splendid success which has attended it, and has brought to so complete and speedy an issue, is principally to be ascribed to the distinguished gallantry and spirit displayed by the army under your command, in a succession of the most brilliant operations, and to the judgement and decision so conspicuously manifested by you during their progress, from the first landing of the troops on the 4th August, to the day on which the works at Cornelis were carried, and the whole of the French army finally dispersed.

" His Royal Highness has commanded me to convey to you in the strongest terms, his approbation of your conduct, and that of the brave army under your command ; and he designs that the high sense which he entertains of their services on this most important occasion, may by you be made known to them in public orders.

" As it is His Royal Highness the Prince Regent's intention to confer Medals upon the Officers employed on this service, in conformity to the principle which has of late been adopted with respect to the Campaigns in Spain and Portugal, I am to desire that you will furnish me with the names of those Officers of His Majesty's land forces, and those of the East India Company, who have particularly distinguished themselves, subject to the limitations explained in the enclosed papers.

" I have, &c. &c.

(Signed)   " LIVERPOOL "

" 1st. Medals are only to be bestowed upon occasions of great importance, or of peculiar brilliancy.

" 2d. Medals of a larger size are conferred upon General Officers, including Brigadiers, who wear them suspended by a ribband round
the neck.   Medals of a smaller size are bestowed upon Colonels,
and Officers of the senior ranks.

" 3d. No General or other Officer is considered to be entitled to receive
a Medal, except he has been personally and particularly engaged
upon the occasion, in commemoration of which this distinction is
bestowed, and has been selected by the Commander of the Forces
upon the spot, and has been reported by him to have merited the
distinction, by very conspicuous services.

" 4th. The Commander of the Forces, (after he shall have been informed of the intention of Government to bestow Medals,) shall transmit
to the Secretary of State for the War Department, and to the Commander in Chief, returns signed by himself, specifying the names
and ranks of those Officers whom he shall have selected as particularly deserving.

" 5th. The Commander of the Forces, in making this selection of the
most deserving officers, will consider his choice restricted to the
under-mentioned ranks, as it is found to be absolutely necessary
that some limitation should be put upon the grant of this honour.

----

*Rank and Situations which must be held by Officers, to render them
eligible for the distinction of Medals.*

" General Officers.—Commanding Officers of Brigades ; Commanding Officers of Artillery, or Engineers ; Adjutant-General, and Quarter-

Master-General; Deputies of ditto and ditto, having the **Rank of Field Officers**; Assistants of ditto and ditto, having the **Rank** as before, and being at the head of the Staff with a detached corps or distinct division of the Army; Military Secretary, having the **Rank of Field Officers**; Commanding Officers of Battalions, Corps equivalent thereto, and Officers who have succeeded to the actual command, during the engagement, in consequence of the death or removal of the original Commanding Officer.

(A true Copy.)

(Signed)   " S. AUCHMUTY."

PART III.

SUBSEQUENT OPERATIONS OF THE BRITISH FORCES.

SECTION I.

Disturbed State of Java.

The Empire of Java having been thus wrested out of the hands of France, such troops as were not deemed requisite for the defence of the island, returned to their several stations in India. But the temporary repose enjoyed by the victors who remained in the country, was of short duration. The treachery of the Native Powers, soon called forth fresh exertions on the part of the British troops, whose feats of gallantry exceeded their former exploits; and who displayed an energy and heroism commensurate with the magnitude of the dangers which accumulating around the settlement, threatened its utter destruction.

The Sultan of Djoejocarta, the most turbulent and intriguing of these Princes, having long entertained a rooted animosity against the Europeans settled in the island of Java, now indulged the hope, and meditated the design of accomplishing their entire expulsion. Under the former Government, he had evinced a degree of hostility which

R

compelled Marshal Daendels to march an army against him, and to proceed in person to his capital. The plans of the Sultan not being then sufficiently matured on the one hand, and Daendels fearing the arrival of the British Expedition on the other, a compromise was entered into between them, by which the former agreed to pay the sum of two hundred thousand Spanish dollars; which he the more readily acceded to, as he cherished the idea of being soon enabled to carry into full effect his vengeful purposes.

The turbulent spirit of this Chief broke out again soon after the establishment of the British in the island; in consequence of which, Mr. Raffles, who had been appointed Lieutenant-Governor of Java by Lord Minto, judged it necessary to proceed in person to the Sultan's Court, in the month of December, 1811, with the intention of fixing definitively the relations between the two Governments by a Treaty, which it was vainly imagined would prove as binding on the one side as it would be strictly observed on the other. But the event soon proved how fallacious are all professions of amity in the Native Princes, who are neither to be kept within the bounds of good faith by a sense of honour, nor by the most sacred obligations, when they cease to be overawed by the presence of a strong military power.

A treaty, however, was concluded on terms which were considered at the time as equally advantageous to the British interests, and beneficial to the prosperity of the country which remained under the administration of the Sultan. In this treaty, the sovereignty of the British over the island of Java was acknowledged by the Sultan, who confirmed to the English East India Company all the privileges, advantages, and prerogatives, which had been possessed by the Dutch and French Governments. To the Company also were transferred the sole regulation of the duties, and the collection of tribute within the dominions of the Sultan, as well as the general administration of justice in cases where the British interests might be concerned.

As the Sultan on this occasion expressed his contrition for the atrocities which had been committed under his authority, and also manifested much apparent sincerity in his professions of friendship, some confidence was entertained that the conditions of this treaty would be punctually observed, and tranquillity maintained. But the power which remained in the hands of this sovereign, who made such an ill use of it, was valued by him only in the degree by which it enabled him to violate his engagements, and to exercise the most savage tyranny. Experience had, indeed, already proved the necessity of modifying and dividing this power, by associating the Prince Royal in the government with the Sultan. But though this measure appeared to be the best calculated for the internal benefit of the kingdom, and had long been considered as most advisable for the general good, it was deemed prudent, on the present occasion, to forbear the suggestion of a proposition, which, however desirable it might be on all accounts, had a natural tendency to provoke the personal resentment of the tyrant.

The small British escort who accompanied Mr. Raffles, consisting only of a part of the fourteenth regiment, a troop of the twenty-second light dragoons, and the ordinary garrison of Bengal Sepoys in the Fort and at the Residency House, were not in a condition to enforce terms any way obnoxious to the personal feelings of the Sultan. The whole retinue, indeed, of the Governor were in imminent danger of being murdered. Crisses were actually unsheathed by several of the Sultan's own suite in the Audience Hall, where Mr. Raffles received that Prince, who was accompanied by several thousands of armed followers, expressing in their behaviour such an infuriated spirit of insolence, as plainly to indicate that they only waited for the signal to perpetrate the work of destruction, in which case not a man of our brave soldiers, from the manner in which they were surrendered, could have escaped.

Though at this time no act of treacherous hostility took place, the crafty and sanguinary Sultan drew from the circumstances which he observed a confidence in his own strength ; and being thus persuaded that the expulsion of the Europeans from the island of Java was become more feasible, he resolved at once to adopt means for accomplishing this favourite object of his ambition.

In the mean time, the attention of the British Government was drawn to the noted Rebel, Bagoos-Rangin, who had assembled in the hilly tracts of Indramayo a large force of insurgents, many of whom were deserters and fugitive soldiers from the late French army, who, after the battle of Cornelis, escaped across the marshes and jungle.

This cunning Chieftain, who, during six years had eluded all pursuit, and defeated every attempt made to seize his person by the Dutch Government, imposed himself on the credulous multitude as a Prophet and High Priest, securing the attachment of his followers so completely, that whenever he was hard pressed he found a sure retreat in the mountains. Such, indeed, was the fanaticism of the people, and their veneration of the assumed high functions of this deceiver, that all the temptations arising from the rewards which were offered for his apprehension, could not prevail on any of his adherents to seize or betray him. At this time, he had possessed himself of a number of villages, the inhabitants of which he compelled to join his standard; and thus, flushed with success, he proceeded so far as to threaten the town and fort of Indramayo. On this, a detachment of Bengal Sepoys under Captain Pool, was immediately despatched from Batavia to strengthen that garrison; and another detachment of Europeans and Natives, under Captain Ralph, of His Majesty's 59th regiment, followed soon after, with orders to attack the rebels, and endeavour to destroy a torrent which had already become formidable. Captain Ralph and his detachment came at last by surprise upon a large body of the insurgents, whom he immediately attacked. Upwards of two thousand musqueteers, regularly drawn up in line behind a bank, opened their fire upon the British, whilst they were wading through the rice fields in order to close with the enemy; but when they came within reach, the resistless charge of the bayonet soon broke through the whole multitude, of whom considerable numbers were killed and wounded, and the rest dispersed. Our loss in this affair was very trifling; consisting of one rank and file, of the fifty-ninth, killed; and Captain Jones, of the Bengal service, with several rank and file wounded. Though Bagoos-Rangin himself effected his escape, the check which his troops had received was decisive; for as the notion of the invincibility of their Chief no longer swayed the misguided minds of his followers, they abandoned his standard in great numbers.

But unsettled as the internal state of the country was at this period, we must for the present take our leave of Java, and turn our view to the island of Sumatra, where cruelties of the blackest description had been committed by an unfeeling tyrant, in the massacre of the peace-able European and Native inhabitants belonging to the Dutch factory. These unfortunate victims of lawless power, who had resided many years at Palimbang without giving any offence by their conduct, or exciting any justifiable apprehensions by their appearance, number, or connections, were put to death in cold blood by the mandate of the Sultan.

SECTION II.

Expedition to Palimbang.

WHEN the account of this shocking catastrophe at Palimbang arrived at Batavia, it became a duty incumbent on the Government there, to punish as it deserved this flagrant outrage of justice and humanity, that had been perpetrated on the inhabitants of a settlement, which being dependent on Java, was consequently under British protection. The cruelty of the Sultan was heightened in atrocity, if possible, by the basest ingratitude, since the unoffending objects of his vengeance, were the agents and representatives of that very government, by whose influence the family of the murderer had been raised to the throne, in the person of Ratu Ahmet Badruddin, in the year 1780.

To punish this act of perfidy, an expedition was immediately fitted out and sailed from Batavia, on the 20th March, 1812, under the orders of Colonel Gillespie, who was entrusted with the execution of the views of Government, and had the whole management confided to his individual judgment and direction. The fleet consisted of

His Majesty's Ship Cornelia, Captain Owen.
———————— Bucephalus, Captain Drury.
————— Sloop Procris, Captain Freeman.
The Hon. Company's Cruizer, Teignmouth, Captain Howitson.
———————————— Mercury, Captain Conyers.

Gun-boats—Schooner Wellington, Captain Cromy.
—————————— Young Barracouta, Captain Lynch.
Transports—Samdany, Minerva, Matilda, Mary Ann.

Captain Bowen, of his Majesty's ship Phœnix, meeting us at sea, took the command of the fleet as senior officer.

TROOPS EMBARKED.

Detachment H. M. 59th Regt. 3 Companies, Rifle and Flank Companies.
Ditto,   ——— 89th,   —— 5 Companies.
Ditto, Madras Horse Artillery, and Hussars dismounted.
Ditto, Bengal Artillery, detail and detachment of Sepoys 5th and 6th Battalions.
Ditto, Amboynese.

A considerable number of guns and military stores, intended for the new settlement of Banea, were put on board the transports.

Contrary winds and currents, which, during the Western Monsoon, are violent and unchangeable, still maintained their influence at this advanced season, and considerably retarded our progress.

On the third of April, the fleet reached Nanka Island, where we continued a week at anchor. Tents were pitched on shore, and all the artificers were employed in the completion of the boats intended for the passage up the Palimbang River, by constructing platforms for the field-pieces, and making coverings to shelter the troops, as much as possible, from the burning violence of the solar heat, and the inclemency of the nocturnal air. On the night of the ninth of April, a severe gale of wind occasioned the loss of several of these boats, and damaged many others.

The fleet supplied themselves with water, of a very good quality, at this island, which is covered with wood, and inhabited by bears, monkies, and wild hogs. Fish is here in great abundance, and pirates frequently visit the place to take in water and fuel.

The fleet got under weigh on the tenth of April, and came to an anchor on the fifteenth at noon, opposite the West Channel of Palimbang River.

The two succeeding days were employed in getting the Procris, Barracouta, Wellington, Teignmouth, and Mercury, over the bar; and the greater part of the troops destined to proceed up the river, were removed in the evening of the seventeenth, from the large ships and transports, on board the armed brigs and small craft; but a very violent storm coming on this night, with heavy rain, considerably damaged the boats, and destroyed the coverings which had been made with so much labour and difficulty. The few serviceable flat boats that could afford any kind of shelter to the men, were appropriated to the field artillery, and to the reception of such troops as could be accommodated in them.

A number of armed prows having been seen at the mouth of the river, a party of seamen, and thirty riflemen of the fifty-ninth, were sent up in boats towards the close of the evening. One was captured and brought in, but the others escaped up the river. Of the former, the alarmed crew leaped overboard, and got away into the jungle; and the village of Soosang, also at the mouth of the river, was deserted.

On the eighteenth, in the evening, the remaining troops proceeded towards the entrance of the river, at the flow of the tide, to their respective vessels, after which, the whole having got under weigh, were carried about ten miles up the stream, and towards midnight came to an anchor.   The breadth of the river thus far, runs from six to seven hundred yards, and the depth by soundings throughout our progress, was generally between six and seven fathoms.

Major Raban, of the Bengal Service, was detached with the Native Troops, consisting of two hundred Sepoys, and the same number of Amboynese, to effect a landing at the point which projects from Monapin Hill, near Minto, on the Island of Banca, where he established himself without opposition.

The great distance at which Palimbang is situated up the river, and that in a country so little known to Europeans, rendered the utmost care and observation indispensible ; while the numerous means which the Sultan possessed of annoying and impeding our advance, with the peril to which our flotilla was exposed by his fire-rafts, called for extreme vigilance and unwearied exertions.   The formidable resistance also, which the batteries at Borang, from their judicious situation, enabled the enemy to oppose to us, aided besides by numerous armed prows and floating batteries, all placed in the best order of defence, and made ready for action ; by increasing our difficulties gave an impulse to energy, and yet reduced us to the necessity of proceeding with particular caution, as will appear from

The following directions for the Line of Battle a-head and the Order of Sailing.

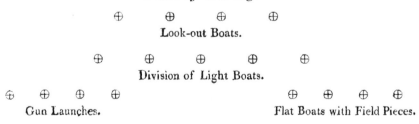

Look-out Boats.

Division of Light Boats.

Gun Launches.   Flat Boats with Field Pieces.

Procris.

Young Barracouta Schooner, G. B.

Mercury.

Flats and other Boats.

Wellington.

Teignmouth.

When the signal is made to anchor, it will be accompanied with a red pendant over.—If the squadron are to anchor in line a-head, with the same pendant under.—If a line a-breast, or athwart the river, the division of Light Boats under Lieutenant Monday, will always anchor in line a-breast, about half-a-mile a-head of the leader of the line of battle. The other boats will anchor in their stations. The Gun Boats, Flats, and Launches, rather a-head of the leader of the line, and on each bow.

The line of battle abreast, will be formed by the division of Light Boats in advance, anchored in a line a-breast.

The Gun Boats, Flats, and Launches, in the next line, Mercury, Wellington, Procris, Young Barracouta, and Teignmouth. In this order, if it should become necessary to bring the broadsides of the ships to bear up the river—the signal will be made for the boats 1st and 2d line, to retire through the intervals of the 3d line, and form in the rear, in two lines as before. The light boats are to keep a strict look-out and have the fire grapplings and dogs constantly ready.

The Look-out Boats of the Light Division, are never to be more than one mile from the headmost ship or vessel of the squadron, unless otherwise directed by signal; and no boat whatever, except the Commander of the Forces be in her, to pass a-head of the headmost look-out boat without permission. The boats of the Light Division are never to lose sight of the squadron, even though the winding of the river should enable them to do so without exceeding their prescribed distance.

On the approach of armed Boats of the Natives, the Look-out Boats are to retreat in silence and good order to the body of their Division, which is also to fall back to the Procris, where they will receive further orders. And no boats are, on any account, to fire a shot, or to attempt a dash, though the circumstances be ever so favourable; nor in short, commit any act of hostility without orders.

s 2

The squadron are to observe and obey the signals of the Barracouta, where the Commander of the Forces is embarked. The Barracouta wears a Union Jack, while the Commander of the Forces remains on board.

Here follow various signals for forming the line of battle according to circumstances.

———————

The unavoidable delay which the fleet experienced by encountering contrary winds and currents in the Straits, afforded ample time to the guilty Sultan, to prepare either for resistance or flight. With a view to the latter course he had, as we afterwards learned, removed his treasure and women, at a very early period, into the interior; whilst himself and his ministers, putting on the air of duplicity, sent message after message to the British Commander, filled with expressions of respect, and framed with apparent candour; but hypocritical in their language, and treacherous in their object.

The continuance of the ebb tide during the whole of the nineteenth of April, obliged us to remain stationary till about four in the afternoon, when a gentle sea breeze favouring our progress, enabled the flotilla to move, though it was only for a short distance, as the wind soon failed, and the flood tide being very slack, some of the vessels got entangled among the branches of the trees and bushes, which, therefore, it was necessary to cut away. At the turn of the tide, which was about six on the following morning, we came to an anchor.

In the early part of this day, Pangarang Sheriff, arrived from the Sultan of Palimbang, begging to know the intention of the British Commander, in thus advancing with such a force: to which Colonel Gillespie returned for answer, that he must acquaint the Sultan in person, with the propositions he was entrusted with on the part of his Government, and the messenger returned immediately.

At five in the evening we proceeded on our passage; but the tide becoming slacker every day in proportion to our distance from the sea, and the wind being against us, we did not gain above six miles all night. The ebb tide, at six the next morning, or the twenty-first of April, obliged us to come to an anchor, near the junction of False River.

Another messenger, Pangarang Pranah, arrived this morning from Palimbang, bringing with him a letter from the Sultan, to whom he was related. In this epistle, the crafty Monarch congratulated our Commander on his arrival in the River Soosang, and professing at the same time to be the friend of the English, with other expressions of duplicity, the design of which was too obvious to impose upon those who were acquainted with the writer's character. Colonel Gillespie replied, that he meant to be at Palimbang in two days, where he expected to see the Sultan, having matters to disclose to him in person, of the greatest consequence; and, at the same time, assuring the inhabitants of Palimbang, of the protection of the British Government. Before the ambassador could receive this reply in writing, another arrived with a similar letter from the Sultan, requesting an immediate explanation. Both messengers therefore returned together about five in the evening; and as soon as the tide permitted, at seven the flotilla got again under weigh. At sun-rise on the twenty-second of April, we descried the batteries at Borang; but about the same time, the Procris, to our great disappointment, got aground, and the tide failing, we were obliged to come to an anchor before the village of Slot Jarrong, distant about five miles from the batteries.

In the course of the forenoon, Captain Owen, of the Royal Navy, with Major Thorn, Deputy Quarter-Master-General, reconnoitred the batteries and armed prows stationed here, and which had been joined by a large Arab ship, armed for the occasion, sent down from Palimbang by the Sultan to add to the defence of this post. These vessels, with the floating batteries, were moored across the river in echellon, raking with their guns the whole length of the passage, whilst the numerous artillery on the three fixed batteries, bore across on the channel by which we had to advance, thus enabling them to bring the fire of their guns almost to a ray on any point in the line of our course. Numerous fire-rafts were placed on the front and flank of the batteries, ready to be set adrift to fire our shipping. Piles of wood, driven into the river, defended the approach to the batteries in boats, whilst a strong palisade protected the rear and flanks. A great deal of bustle and activity was observable within the several defences, which appeared to be fully manned and prepared for resistance.

The violent rain which lasted all the afternoon, and continued during the night, proved of considerable annoyance, particularly to the men who were embarked in boats. Great, indeed, and scarcely to be conceived, was the fatigue which the sailors and soldiers had to undergo in a region, where, during the day, they were exposed, while employed in laborious rowing, to the rays of a burning sun, directly under the equator, and deprived in the night of the refreshment of sleep.

But notwithstanding the excessive hardships which all ranks and descriptions of persons in the service were called to bear, and the privations they had to endure, nothing could shake their resolution or abate their ardour in the performance of their duty.

In the evening another messenger, named Pangarang Martoo, arrived, with a letter from the Sultan, importing that he should be happy to see his friend, the Commander of the Expedition, at Palimbang; but requesting that he would dispense with so large an armed force, and visit the capital unattended, being fearful, as he pretended, that the appearance of so many troops would occasion serious disturbances among the inhabitants at Palimbang

It was easy enough to perceive the insidious drift of this proposition; but the treachery of the Sultan had already been too notorious to allow such fallacious declarations and hollow professions the slightest respect, or even a moment's attention.

The Sultan had grossly insulted Government by his arrogant and offensive treatment of the British mission, which was sent to him in the preceding November. He afterwards carried his insolence still farther, by sending to Java, in January, Tumangung Lanang, who had executed his orders, in the massacre of the Dutch. This man, who had been appointed to reside at Batavia as the Ambassador of the Sultan, and to present to the British Government there, a false statement of the iniquitous transactions in which he had acted so distinguished a part, was now in the fleet, and was one of the principal Tumangungs; but though deserving of the gallows, his person was respected in consideration of his public character.

Colonel Gillespie demanded of the messenger who last arrived, an unmolested passage up the river, and also a hostage as a security for their good behaviour; to which Pangarang Martoo instantly assented, offering at the same time to give us possession of the batteries, and to leave them entirely at our disposal, as also the ship which was lying there, to be made use of as the British Commander might please to direct. As a pledge of their sincerity, a person bearing the title of Commandant of the batteries, and who accompanied the messenger, remained behind for the purpose of conducting us to Borang.

The Procris had been fortunately got afloat again; but being far astern, it took her the whole night and the following day to come up with us. On the twenty-third, Captain Owen and Major Butler, with several boats of the advance, proceeded in the afternoon to inspect the ship lying in the river, and which, as already mentioned, was offered to be given up; but on their approach, they were met by several boats from the batteries, and advised not to go any farther. At this time also, the armed prows made a show of resistance, attended with great shouting from the batteries, and other demonstrations of hostility, on which the boats of the advance returned, in conformity to their orders.

Where the chiefs of a nation act with so much treachery, and where the breach of faith uniformly marks their character, it is a most unpleasant and difficult task for a generous mind to counteract and oppose their proceedings. To avoid bloodshed, as far as possible, and to prevent those calamities attendant on war, which were incurred by the crimes of the Sultan, from falling on the innocent part of the community, was a duty equally imposed by justice and agreeable to the feelings of humanity. It was not so much against the state of Palimbang generally, as the Government of the Sultan and his adherents, that measures of hostility were requisite to be directed on the principle of retaliation, and for the maintenance of public faith, in order that enormities such as those of which we had to complain might not be repeated.

The proper arrangements being made to carry these objects on the following night, Captain Meares, Malay interpreter to the Commander of the Forces, was directed to proceed to Borang, accompanied by the officer who had been left with us as a hostage, and to demand a decisive answer whether or not they would let the batteries be taken possession of amicably, or whether they would resist the passage of the flotilla. No time was allowed for equivocation, on the part of the Chief Pangarang; and Colonel Gillespie followed close after, at the head of the small but formidable array of the British advance, composed of detachments of the 59th and 89th regiments, in light boats, supported by the gun-launches and field artillery, in the flat boats. On their arrival at the dawn of day, within half gun shot distance of the batteries, the Pangarang came off with Captain Meares, and offered to deliver up the works with all the other defences, which, in consequence, were immediately occupied by the British troops. The garrison, terrified at our sudden approach, and unmindful of the positive orders of the Sultan to defend the passage to the last, took themselves to flight, and escaped in some prows that had been kept concealed round the eastern part of Borang island, and on the western side of Binting isle. All the guns taken, to the number of one hundred and two, were ready charged and primed. The large ship afforded quarters for a great portion of our soldiers, but the remainder were placed in huts and floating batteries which had coverings.

In the evening, the troops were all reimbarked, and we proceeded on to a little distance. Fires now appeared in all directions, and several of the rafts were set in flames by the enemy, with the view of effecting, if possible, the destruction of our shipping, which had not as

T

yet passed the batteries; but though they were coming up at this time
(8 P. M.) fortunately, the exertions of Captain Owen, with the crews
of the light boats, were successful in cutting the rafts asunder before
they were thoroughly in flames, by which means, a general conflagration was seasonably prevented*. Several shots were fired from one
of the Cornelia's boats at the Malays, who were seen setting fire to the
rafts, which had the effect of instantly dispersing them.

This strong hold, about forty miles from the coast, seems peculiarly
well calculated for a haunt of pirates, who have of late resorted to it
for shelter, the fastnesses in the wood always affording them a secure
retreat, where all search and pursuit would be useless. The batteries
are built upon artificial ground, raised on a stone foundation, in the
water, inclosed with wooden piles. The sides of the ramparts are
faced with strong bamboos and tar trees, the space within being filled
up with earth to the thickness of from twenty to thirty feet. The elasticity of the bamboos on the exterior side, and of the stockades of
cocoa-nut or tar trees, by which the ramparts are surrounded, prevents
any great impression being made on them by gun-shots. But though
the position of the batteries is judicious, the construction of them is
wretched in the extreme. The embrazures are covered in, close down
to the muzzles of the guns, like the port-holes of a ship. These works

---

* These fire-rafts are large magazines, filled with combustibles of every kind, and as
many are fastened together as will reach across the whole breadth of the river, where,
floating with the tide or current, they are extremely dangerous, when once in a blaze, to
ships coming in the opposite direction. The heat produced is so great, that no boats can
venture to approach sufficiently near to throw graplings into them for the purpose of drag-
ging them aside and fastening them to the shore.

however, are very difficult of access; for being entirely surrounded by water, and fenced on the flanks and rear by strong stockades, whilst in front, massy wooden piles are fixed, which, like *chevaux de frise*, run out one hundred and fifty or two hundred yards into the river, they effectually prevent the approach of boats, and the landing of troops.

Early on the following morning, the twenty-fifth of April, an Arab arrived, who stated himself to be the owner of the ship before mentioned, and begging that she might be restored, which request was granted. He brought information that the Sultan immediately fled from Palimbang, on hearing that the defences at Borang, which had been considered such a formidable barrier, no longer obstructed the farther progress of the British troops.

Colonel Gillespie, on hearing this, determined to push forward with the light boats; and whilst making this arrangement another Arab arrived, the Pangarang Sheriff, who confirmed the account of the Sultan's flight, adding the afflicting intelligence, that the greatest confusion, plunder, and assassination prevailed, not only within the interior of the fort and palace, but in many parts of the city. Upon this, Colonel Gillespie resolved to lose not a moment, but to hasten by the quickest possible manner, to put a stop to this scene of horror, and by his immediate presence, prevent the execution of the massacre, which it was reported the Sultan's adherents meditated to perpetrate the very next night, upon the wealthy Chinese and other inhabitants, whose property was to become the prize of the assassins.

The Colonel, therefore, proceeded instantly with the Arab Chief in his canoe, accompanied by Captain Meares and Mr. Villneruby, a Spanish gentleman, who acted as Malay interpreters. In that and another small canoe, which accompanied them, were distributed seven grenadiers of the fifty-ninth regiment; and these were followed by Captain Bowen, of the Royal Navy, Major Butler, Deputy Adjutant-General, and Major Thorn, Deputy Quarter-Master General, in the gig belonging to the Phœnix, and ten more grenadiers of the same regiment, in the barge of the same ship, with Lieutenant Monday, R. N. and Lieutenant Forrest, of the fifty-ninth ; the remaining troops, under Lieutenant-Colonel M'Leod, having orders to follow with all possible speed. The distance was twenty miles, so that it was dark when the party arrived at Old Palimbang. The canoes, in one of which the Colonel was, had gained much on the other two boats ; and were now completely out of sight, when the report of a signal gun, fired by the enemy, not a little alarmed us, and increased our anxiety for our friends; the more so, as every thing around us tended to excite suspicion of some treacherous design being in agitation. A dreadful yell and shrieking in all directions was next heard, and lights and conflagrations were seen throughout the whole extent of this large tract of population, which stretched along both banks of the river for upwards of seven miles. By the redoubled exertions of the crews, the boats in the rear were soon brought up to the support of our friends, and thus happily formed in time an important junction.

To paint the horrors of the scene that presented itself to our view in proper colours, or to attempt an expression of the sensations it was calculated to excite, would be a difficult task. Romance never described any thing half so hideous, nor has the invention of the imagination ever given representations equally appalling, with what here struck us in reality. Nor will the undaunted act which gained us possession of the fort, the palace, and its batteries, scarcely be credited. Undismayed, in the face of numerous bodies of armed men, Colonel Gillespie boldly stepped on shore at eight o'clock at night, and with those who had accompanied him in the canoe, and the seven grenadiers, he marched with a firm step, through a multitude of Arabs and treacherous Malays, whose missile weapons, steeped in poison, glimmered by the light of torches.

Huge battlements, with immense gates leading from one area to another, received our friends, and presented to them the frightful spectacle of human blood, still reeking and flowing on the pavement. The massy gates closed upon our rear, and the blood-stained court-yards through which we were conducted, appeared as if it were the passage to a slaughter-house.

A Malay, who had pressed through the crowd, approached the Colonel, and was walking by his side, when a large double-edged knife was secretly put into his hands by one of his countrymen. It was a dark stormy night, and a ray of lightning at the very instant when the fellow was pushing the knife up his long loose sleeve to conceal it, discovered the weapon. The Colonel's eye caught the object, and instantly turning round, he had the fellow seized, totally regardless of the crowd ; thus fortunately frustrating by his firmness the murderous design. The weapon was found as described ; but the fellow contrived to steal away in the crowd and escaped.

The palace, at our arrival, exhibited a still more melancholy picture of devastation and cruelty. Murder had here been succeeded by rapine ; and while the place was completely ransacked, the pavements and floors were clotted with blood. In every direction spectacles of woe caught our sight, and rendered peculiarly awful by the glare of the surrounding conflagration, and vivid flashes of lightning, amidst loud peals of thunder. The devouring flames which continued to spread destruction, notwithstanding the heavy rain that poured down in torrents, had now reached the outer buildings of the palace, and threatened the part where we had taken up our temporary abode. The crackling of bamboos, resembling the discharge of musquetry—the tumbling in of burning roofs, with a tremendous crash—the near approach of the fire, situated as we were in the midst of an immense hostile multitude and assassins, altogether gave to our situation a most appalling prospect.

Our little band, consisting only of seventeen British grenadiers, with the officers naval and military already mentioned, and a few seamen belonging to the gig and barge, had to secure possession of the fort, and to provide for their safety in the determined resolution of selling their lives dear, should any attack be made before the arrival of reinforcements. Having carefully reconnoitred by the light of torches, the interior of the palace court, and ordered all the entrances except one to be shut and barricadoed, Colonel Gillespie stationed the grenadiers at the principal entrance, and the strictest guard was kept up. Soon after midnight, we had the satisfaction of hailing the welcome arrival of Major Trench, with about sixty men of the 89th Regiment ; and the remaining part of the ordered advance, under Lieutenant-Colonel M'Leod, joined our little garrison early the next morning.

Thus an act of unexampled fortitude and daring enterprize, conceived with judgement, and executed with intrepidity, put us in possession of the fort and batteries, defended by two hundred and forty-two pieces of cannon, without the loss of a man. This formidable position could not have been carried under any other circumstances of attack, but by the sacrifice of many lives, and by hazarding altogether our little armament.

The rapidity of the movement, and the sudden and unexpected arrival of the few British at that late hour in the evening, whose numbers were greatly magnified, by the panic which seized the foe, caused the immediate dispersion of the Sultan's adherents, who fled in confusion, thereby timely preventing their barbarous intent from being carried into execution, and relieving the town from the miseries with which it was threatened, of plunder and destruction. An American, who was the supercargo of a large Chinese junk, then lying at Palimbang, gave us a melancholy recital of the woe by which they were threatened, and which would have burst on them that very night, had our little force not arrived in time to prevent it. This junk, with all on board, had, in fact, been marked out as the first victims.

With that feeling regard for the interests of humanity which always distinguishes the British character in the midst of the fiercest conflicts, and the moment of victory, the most prompt measures were immediately taken to restore order and maintain tranquillity. These were so effectual, that the inhabitants assumed confidence, and many who had fled into the woods returned to their homes. The great body of the people were pleased at the change, and rejoiced in being relieved from the tyranny of the Sultan, which seems to have attained its height.

The eldest son of that Sovereign, Pangarang Rattoo, had been particularly notorious in the wanton exercise of every species of oppression and cruelty. The vile libidinous habits of this Prince, occasioned the late horrid massacre of the Dutch, who fell a deplorable sacrifice to his sanguinary vengeance. The Pangarang, in one of his nocturnal visits, had been disappointed through them, in the indulgence of his criminal designs upon the wife of an industrious native, whose screams brought the patrole from the Dutch factory, near which it happened, to her assistance, and the guard, unconscious of whom they were in pursuit, pressed so hard upon him, that he was obliged to plunge into the river, and with great difficulty reached his boat. That resentment which naturally fills the mind of the wicked against those who have thwarted their malevolent purposes, took full possession of this Prince, who vowed to extirpate the whole Dutch settlement; and this he spoke loud enough to be heard by all around his person. Two days afterwards, the Sultan sent a messenger to invite the Dutch Resident to come over to the palace at Palimbang, with which he imprudently complied, contrary to the salutary advice of his friends; and notwithstanding the strength of the fort, and the means possessed by the garrison of making a long defence. Armed Malays then intruded themselves, one by one, and under various pretences, into the fort, where they suddenly overpowered the guards; seized upon the Garrison, both Europeans and Natives, whom they bound, and hurried them off from their weeping families, on board the prows, prepared for their conveyance down the river, at the mouth of which, near Soosang, they were all put to death. Every cruelty was practised to prolong the sufferings of those unhappy persons, by poignarding them with crisses, and shockingly lacerated them, after which, the prows were set on fire, and all were reduced together to ashes.

An interesting European woman, the wife of an officer, not being able to bear the thoughts of a separation from her husband, followed him on board with her infant child, and shared the same unhappy fate, after being first polluted by the monsters in a manner too shocking to relate. The other unfortunate women with their children, took refuge in the woods, where they lingered out a miserable existence among the wild beasts, naked and forlorn, a prey to hunger and disease. The few who survived were brought, though naturally in a most deplorable state of wretchedness, to the British head-quarters, in consequence of the search that was instituted for the purpose, immediately after our capture of Palimbang.

The exact day on which this melancholy catastrophe took place, could never be correctly ascertained; but, from the circumstance of the Sultan's refusal in November, 1811, to renew his relation with the new Government in Java, and from his forbidding the British detachment, which accompanied Captain Phillips, the appointed Resident, sent for the purpose, to advance to Palimbang, there is reason to believe, it must have happened soon after the news of our conquest had reached that treacherous court. The Sultan, no doubt, thought the invasion of Java a favourable moment for throwing off all dependency on the Government there, and of erecting himself supreme on the ruins of the Dutch establishment. By the entire destruction of their fort, he entertained the hope of becoming an independent power; and he expected also, that, in assuming the lead amongst the Piratical

U

States, he should be able to commit depredations at his pleasure, on the commerce carried on in these seas. In support of this, the following Depositions upon Oath, of Toonko Mahomed, and Syod Abu Bakir, of Pulo Penang, who had been sent as Agents by Mr. Raffles, to Palimbang, bear strong testimony ;

EXTRACT.

" On the 27th of the month Sabon, being equal to the 14th September last, the principal Chiefs of the place were sent by the Sultan to the Fort, in order to inform the Resident of the surrender of Batavia.

" That successively all the Chiefs with their suite, were sent to the Fort, under pretext of consulting with the Resident, which lasted until three or four o'clock in the afternoon, when the Fort was filled with people.

" The Chiefs now informed the Resident, that he and his troops must now quit the Fort, on which the Resident answered, ' Where shall I go ? I have no vessel to depart with : I request to be allowed to remain three days longer, that I may prepare a vessel to convey me from hence.' The Chiefs said they had orders from the Sultan, to direct the Resident to quit the fort immediately, and if he had any request to make, he must address himself to the Sultan. The Chiefs sent a messenger to the Sultan, to inform him of this request. The Sultan granted the Resident an audience, and sent two Chiefs to conduct the Resident to him.

" The Resident and his Assistant, the Commander of the Troops, and Secretary, followed the two Chiefs, who had been sent to conduct them, and within a short distance of the palace, were met by several other Chiefs, who interrogated the Resident what he had to say to the Sultan. The Resident replied, ' I intended to request to be provided with a vessel ; whereupon the Chiefs said, ' It is unnecessary, here are two vessels in readiness for the gentlemen to embark in.' They now took from the Commander his sword, and ordered all the servants of the Company, with the exception of the women, on board a Pantyallang, which was lying there ; this vessel remained there until evening, when she disappeared.

" That shortly after this, some of the Chiefs came to the said Toonko, and said, that they had orders from the Sultan to murder all the Company's servants on board the Pantyallang, and to demolish the fort and buildings.

" That said Toonko, upon hearing this, addressed himself to the Sultan, and requested that the people of the Dutch factory might not be molested, but that they might be allowed to depart to Batavia, and not to demolish the fort, because it was unlawful, as Batavia had surrendered, its dependencies must be considered a conquest likewise ; on which the Sultan replied, ' I am not like other Native Princes, I dread nobody, I fear no Nation, I shall listen to nobody, and let me not hear this a second time.' This he uttered in a violent passion. That three days after this, the said Toonko and Sayed saw the fort and buildings demolished, and enquired of some of the Chiefs why this was done ; they were answered, ' What have we to do with the fort any longer, as all the Dutchmen have been murdered.' It is said, they consisted of twenty-four Europeans, and sixty-three Native soldiers.

" The Sultan's eldest son, Bangarang Ratoo, by order of his father, extorted six days afterwards, a fictitious declaration of those facts (which was forwarded to Java,) from the deponents. The latter were in great danger of their lives. They were forced to swear by order of the Sultan, never to divulge the truth ; that if they did, they should be punished with death, and their family at Palimbang murdered. Suspecting that the Sultan's emissaries were lying in wait to murder them, they made off to Malacca, leaving their family and baggage behind ;—and there made the Deposition, in presence of the Members of the Court of Justice, by order of Major Farquhar.

" The Deposition is signed by,

" J. H. STOCKEN, Sec.

Commissioned Members of the Court of Justice { " A. KOECK.
at Malacca, - - - - - { " C. WALBECHM.

And   ..   .   ..   -   -   " VAN BEUCHEM, Translator."

At noon, the twenty-eighth of April, the British flag was hoisted on the Sultan's Bastion, under a royal salute ; and the same day, Pangarang Adipatti, brother to the Sultan, who had been invited by the British Commander to a conference, returned from his retreat in the country. This Prince had obtained the reputation of being a mild and beneficent character, on which account he was greatly beloved by all descriptions of the people. As a proof of the goodness of his disposition, it was known that he had strongly dissuaded his brother from the barbarous conduct pursued by him towards the Dutch, and that he had warned him of the vengeance which would surely await him from the British Government.

This person being the nearest of kin to the family so justly excluded, the Commander of the Forces determined to place him on the vacant throne. On the 29th of April, the Prince paid his first visit, being received at the landing place by Captain Meares, with other Officers of the General Staff; and Colonel Gillespie met him at the door of the Public Hall, where seats were arranged for all the Company. The Pangarang was saluted at his landing with nineteen guns from the Mercury, and, on his entering the Hall, with the same number from the guns on shore. After sitting some time, he was conducted by Colonel Gillespie to another apartment, where they had a private conference; and, in the afternoon, the Commander of the Forces returned the visit.

On the first of May, various reports were circulated of a body of Malays having resolved upon running a Muck, which is a desperate custom peculiar to this people, who, infuriated with opium, run about the streets in the wildest state of phrenzy, with drawn crisses, stabbing or killing every one they encounter. The reported arrival of Pangarang Ratoo, in the neighbourhood of Palimbang, and the intercourse that was suspected to be kept up between him and some of the principal Chiefs in the town, gave additional weight to these rumours; in consequence of which, orders were given for all to be on the alert. In the middle of the night, a considerable uproar was heard, and large fires were observed on the East side of the town, but the precautionary measures which had been taken, prevented any mischief.

The deceitfulness of the Malay character, which was uniformly displayed in their conduct, became at the present time so remarkably conspicuous, as to render the situation in which Colonel Gillespie was placed extremely embarrassing. To establish an efficient government, under existing circumstances, in order to save from the horrors of anarchy, a nation whose chiefs are distinguished solely by craft and treachery, was a most important but difficult undertaking. The management of the negotiation was indeed of the most delicate nature; in the progress of which, the cunning and intrigue so inseparable from Eastern Courts, obtained full exercise on the part of the Malay Chiefs. Every hour, in fact, produced some fresh evasion to create difficulty, or a new subterfuge to protract the time and impede the business.

The dethronement of the Sultan had already been resolved; but the treasures carried off by him, gave him such weight as to prove a serious object of consideration in the choice of a successor, who might be possessed of the requisite means to maintain his seat and authority against the influence of riches and bribery, which advantages there could be no doubt the deprived Sultan would exert to the great misery of the people as soon as the British armament should have quitted the place. To obviate these evils, an arrangement was formed and almost completed, but, by an unlucky accident, it was well nigh frustrated.

On the third of May, a report was made of a quantity of arms being introduced from a boat into a house, which afterwards proved to be that of Pangarang Adipatti. The Guard, sent to examine into the business, imprudently forced their way into the house, not aware that it was the residence of a Prince who was under our protection. Several Chieftains were assembled here to consult together on the proposed arrangements just alluded to, when this armed party arrived; and, owing to the sudden surprize which their appearance occasioned, one of the Chiefs drew his criss and struck a blow at the Officer who commanded the party; but fortunately he missed his aim, and in return received the cut of a sabre, which was instantly followed by one of the Soldiers run a bayonet through his body. The Chief kept hold of his criss and made efforts of resistance, but was at last disarmed, after giving and receiving several wounds. During this scuffle the Pangarang Adipatti fled from his house, and all who were able went off with him. The Arab Chief who had so gallantly conducted us into the Fort on the 25th of April, was one of those who were present, but luckily sustained no other injury than that of having his criss taken from him by the Soldiers, who did not know him, and to which disgrace he quietly submitted. With manly confidence in our Commander, he came immediately to Head Quarters, where his appearance without a criss, and the terror depicted in his countenance, was the first intimation received of the sad affray. The party, ignorant of any wrong, were now returning from the search, carrying spears richly gilt and crisses set with diamonds, as trophies of their triumph; but they were instantly ordered back, and every article was safely restored to their owners. The wounded Malay Chief was still weltering in his blood, and medical assistance was instantly afforded him, but without effect, for he died a few minutes afterwards.

This melancholy occurrence proved extremely distressing to Colonel Gillespie, as the painful work, the result of several weeks anxious solicitude in the settlement of a permanent government, was rent asunder by a momentary accident which could not have been foreseen, and the consequences of which it was impossible to trace. Proclamations were immediately issued to restore tranquillity among the people, and explaining the affair as an accidental affray, originating in mistake, and deploring the misfortune. The Pangarang Adipatti had a friendly letter sent to him by the Commander of the Forces, assuring him of his protection, upon the receipt of which he returned ; and the following day, in the evening, Colonel Gillespie, attended by his Staff, paid a visit to the Pangarang, at his house, which greatly tended to restore confidence, and gave general satisfaction.

On the fifth of May, Pangarang Adipatti came early in the morning to the palace, and held a long conference with the Colonel upon the business that had been so unluckily suspended. The necessary preliminaries and general heads of a treaty having been agreed upon with the new Sultan, and signed by both parties, the fourteenth of May was fixed for the inauguration, that being the day of the new moon ; which was purposely chosen, that the influence of this planet might give success to the new monarch ; and that the rather, as the old one had proved so unfortunate to his predecessor, of whose miserable condition report gave a dismal account, representing him as being utterly forsaken by his former subjects ; and obliged to roam in the recesses and wildernesses of the interior, whither it would have been in vain to have followed him. His treasure, the only means by which he might be enabled to raise fresh disturbances, he had carefully concealed in haunts known only to himself; and the persons employed in burying it, were put to death by his orders, to prevent the possibility of a discovery.

The new Sultan, however, relied on being able to counteract the mischievous tendency of this measure, by compelling the exile to give up a portion of his treasure, as the purchase of personal security, and in consideration of having a place of retreat granted him in the interior of the country for the remainder of his life.

The day appointed for the Coronation having arrived ; about half-past nine in the morning, the Pangarang Adipatti landed at the stairs in front of the Palace. He was there received by Lieutenant-Colonel Alexander M'Leod, attended by the Officers of the Staff, and conducted to the gate of the inner court; where, being met by Colonel Gillespie, he was led by him to the Public Hall, in which a Throne was erected, under a canopy of Yellow Silk, the distinguishing colour of Royalty at this place. The Colonel conducted him first to a Couch, on the left of the Throne, and covered with Crimson Velvet, where they both seated themselves.

The troops were drawn up so as to form a street from the landing-place, and a square which encompassed the Public Hall. A great concourse of Natives, among whom were several of the Chief Panga-rangs, and two of the brothers of the newly-elected Sultan attended on this occasion. These being seated on the ground, and the European Gentlemen standing on the left side of the Couch, the following Pro-clamation was read in the Malay Language :—

" Whereas the late Sultan Ratu Mahmoud Badruddin, having forfeit-ed his right to the Sovereignty of Palimbang, by various Acts of Rapine,

Treachery, and Barbarity, especially by the Murder of the Members of the late Dutch Factory, the Plunder of their Goods, the Demolition of their Fort, contrary to the Laws of Nations, and his existing Engagements with the Dutch, to whose Right the English Company have succeeded, in virtue of the Cession of Java and its Dependencies; and, moreover, has abdicated the Throne by his shameful flight. The Commander of the British Forces, in virtue of Powers vested in him by the Government of Java, hereby declares the said Mahmoud Badruddin, to be deposed from the Throne of this Kingdom. And the Commander of the Forces, in consideration of the virtues of Pangarang Adipatti, and of the love, esteem, and veneration with which he is regarded by the Natives, Inhabitants of this Country, as well as the Arab and Chinese Colonists, has, in pursuance of his instructions, selected the said Pangarang Adipatti, to fill the vacant Throne of this Kingdom, subject to the confirmation of the Government of Java, and the Supreme Government of India. The said Pangarang is hereby declared true and lawful Sultan of Palimbang and its Dependencies, under the style and title of Sultan Ratoo Ahmed Najmuddin; and all the Inhabitants of this Kingdom, are enjoined to yield him obedience accordingly."

Adipatti was evidently much affected by the notice taken of his brother's crimes, with the reflection of their having been the cause of his own elevation to the throne ; and he was observed to wipe his eyes several times during the recital of this part of the Proclamation.

Particular care was taken to afford every protection to the Chinese, which industrious people, since the destruction of the Dutch Factory, under whose protection they had always been, suffered so much from the rapacity of the Malays, that the idea of the approaching departure of the British, impressed them with the fear of experiencing still greater oppression, in our absence. The new Sultan did indeed possess great personal popularity; yet, as his relations were equally those of the deprived Sovereign, it was to be apprehended, that on their return, they would exercise a power of savage persecution, on the Chinese and other defenceless persons, from a spirit of revenge, or the desire of gain. To guard against such evils, and to secure the safety of the helpless as far as possible, was a concern which occupied much of the attention of the British Commander, who, had recourse to the only precaution that could be adopted, in the formation of a solemn and explicit Treaty, binding the Court to the observance of strict justice to all parties and descriptions of persons therein specified. This preliminary measure being settled, Colonel Gillespie desired Captain Mears to address the crowd, demanding whether " it was their wish that Pangarang Adipatti should reign over them ;" to which they gave a hearty assent, by loud acclamations.

Colonel Gillespie then led Pangarang Adipatti and seated him on the Throne, which was raised three steps above the level of the Hall. When he had taken his Seat, a Royal Salute was fired from our Artillery on shore, and the Colours of the Sultan being displayed from the walls of the Palace, instead of the British, which had been hoisted during the Interregnum ; the new Monarch received the salutations and congratulations of all who were present.

The European Officers passed first in front of the Throne, and having saluted the Sultan, who returned the compliment by taking off his cap, they took their stations on the opposite side. The Natives then came according to their order of precedency up to the Throne, and some kissed the hands, others the knees or feet of the Sultan. When this ceremony was ended, the Natives again seated themselves upon the ground, and silence being proclaimed, the Commander of the Forces, by an Interpreter, addressed the Sultan in the following Speech ;—

" In the name of His Britannic Majesty, and the Honourable the East India Company, I have the honour to place you, Pangarang Adipatti, on the Throne of your brother Mahmud Badruddin, deposed for atrocious and barbarous Murders, and now declare you duly constituted Sultan of Palimbang and its Dependencies, under the title of Sultan Ratu Achmed Najmuddin.

" Long may you live to enjoy the high and exalted rank which the English Nation have conferred on you ! May God watch over your Actions, and direct your Councils ! and may the Punishment inflicted on the late Sultan, (who, by listening to evil Counsellers and wicked Men, has drawn on himself the vengeance of a great and powerful People,) be a warning to you to avoid similar errors.

" May your Reign be prosperous and happy ! May you contribute by your goodness and justice, to the happiness and welfare of your Subjects ! and may they have reason to bless the Nation that have placed you on the Throne of the City of Safety ! *"

* Palimbang, in the Malay Historical Books, is emphatically styled, " The City of Safety."

This Ceremony, which was very striking and impressive, appeared to produce a powerful effect as well on the feelings of the Prince, who was the immediate object of it, as on many among the European and Native part of the audience, exhibiting a brilliant display of that magnanimity for which the British character is celebrated through the whole Eastern world.

The Speech being concluded, the Sultan descended from the Throne, and Colonel Gillespie taking his hand, conducted him to the stairs, where his boat was waiting to receive him. He was attended by all the British Officers, and a great number of Natives to the beach, which presented a very beautiful spectacle. The Brigs of War, and the Sloops in the River, decorated with the Colours of all Nations, fired each a Royal Salute, as the Sultan's boat left the shore, and this circumstance excited the admiration of all the inhabitants.

On the sixteenth, Colonel Gillespie, with a large party of Officers, supped by invitation with the Sultan; and the next day, the troops having embarked, the Sultan took possession of the Palace.

The City of Palimbang, the Emporium of the inland Commerce of the Island of Sumatra, is situated in a flat marshy tract, on the left bank, and a few miles above the Delta of a large river, which rises in the district of Musi, within two or three days journey of Bencoolen, and running to the Eastward, receives many subsidiary streams, till it falls into the Straits of Banca. The mouth of this river lies in lat. 2 deg. 18 min. S. and long. 105 deg. 8 min. E. There is a bar on which the depth is only two fathoms and a quarter at low water; but after passing that, although vessels unacquainted with the channel are apt to get a-ground, it is reckoned to have a sufficiency of depth to carry a frigate as far up as the town. The river is of very considerable breadth, its banks low and woody, very much resembling the Sunderbunds, at the mouth of the Ganges.

The town is, by estimation, about sixty miles from the sea, its lat. being 2 deg. 58 min. 51 seconds S., and long. 104 deg. 54 min. E. The Dutch Factory was on the right bank, which is higher than the left, and where there are consequently more extensive tracts of dry ground. Scarcely a vestige, however, of it now remains, and even the foundations of the walls of the fort, and of the houses have been dug up and carried away. Immediately below the scite of the Factory, is a small branch of the River called Sungi Awar, which gives name to the adjoining Campong, inhabited chiefly by Chinese. But there are also some Malays in this district, all the inhabitants of which, appear to have been formerly under the authority and protection of the Dutch Factory. The Chinese Campong is on the side of the rivulet opposite the Factory, and is divided into two parts, the old and new Campongs. The inhabitants of both amount to about seven hundred families, and these are the principal merchants and artizans in this place.

On the left bank of the river, a little below the Palace, is a colony of about three hundred Arabs, among whom are some merchants of eminence. The remaining inhabitants of Palimbang are Malays, and estimated at between twenty and thirty thousand. The city is intersected by several little branches of the river, which form a number of islands, said to be between twenty and thirty: whence the place has also been called " The City of Twenty Islands." One of these contains the Palaces of the late Sultan, and his son, Pangarang Ratoo; and the house of Pangarang Adipatti, the present Sultan. In front

of the Palaces of the Sultan and Pangarang Ratoo, is an extensive battery, facing the river. It is a rampart of mud, about
twenty feet thick, faced within and without with bamboos, and
pierced with embrazures close above, like the ports of a ship; but,
the outer part of each embrazure being the narrowest, there is little
room to alter the direction of the guns. This lower range of batteries,
which covers the front of both Palaces, is again supported by the
bastions of the inclosed outer wall of the Sultan's Fort, with a number of cannon mounted upon them. Of the iron and brass guns found
in these works, the latter were chiefly Dutch, though some of them
appear, by inscriptions on them, to have been cast at Palimbang.
One of the largest of these, a forty-two pounder, which was sent to
England in the Java, to His Royal Highness the Prince Regent,
in the name of the Captors, has the following in Arabic: " Made
by Sultan Ratoo Ahmed Naj-muddin, in the City of Palimbang,
the Abode of Safety, in the year 1183." This date corresponds
to A.D. 1769. Between the two batteries is seen the Maidan, or
Plain, at the extremity of which appears the Bateron, or Hall, where
the Sultan gives audiences in public. Beyond this, nothing was known
to Europeans before our arrival, as it was death for any one to venture
farther without the Sultan's express permission ; and none but females
were admitted into the interior court of the Palace.

The houses of the Sultan and Pangarang Ratoo, are square areas,
surrounded with very high brick walls. Each of these Palaces contains several detached buildings of the pavilion form, having portions
of ground planted with fruit-trees and ornamental shrubs.

Part of the materials of the demolished factory have been used by the late Sultan, in the construction of a new Haram, which joins the inner Palace; but the buildings are still incomplete. A large reservoir of water, with pleasure-boats in it, occupies the middle of this area; which is surrounded by numerous detached buildings, for the females of the court.

Between the outer walls of the Sultan's Palace and that of Pangarang Ratoo, is a road leading to the principal Mosque, which is a pretty large building, nearly square, and covered with a pavilion roof of tiles. Adjoining to it, is a high octagonal tower, from which the Muezzin calls the people to prayers.

The houses of the common people are made of bamboos, with mats, and thatched. They stand on platforms of bamboos; and some of them are raised on stakes of the same; others, which are constructed on rafts of wood, or bamboo, float on the river, where they rise and fall with the tide, and are fastened to the shore with ropes of rattan. Buildings of this description are often constructed up the country, where the materials are cheap, and are then brought down the stream. Some of these floating rafts are very large, having, in addition to commodious dwelling-houses and out-offices, pleasant gardens, with trees and various plants.

About two miles above Palimbang, the river divides into two large branches; that on the left, leading to a country seat of the Sultan, consisting of several bungalows and gardens, delightfully situated on a cluster of small islands, called, in allusion to their multitude, " Pulo Sariboo," or " The Thousand Islands." We found here, immense heaps of door and window-frames, with other articles belonging to the razed Dutch factory, which the Sultan caused to be transported hither.

for the purpose of building a new country residence. These materials were sent by Colonel Gillespie to Banca, to be used in the construction of quarters for the troops.

The articles of commerce supplied by this country are, pepper, Rattans, Gambir, Silk Cotton (Bombax Ceiba), Damor, Ivory, Cat's Eyes, Sulphur, Salt, Wax, Rice, Benzoin, Indigo, Tobacco, Areca, Buffaloes, and Gold; most of which are brought from a great distance up the country. The forests of Sumatra also abound, among other valuable productions, with the ebony tree. The pepper trade at Palimbang, was formerly exclusively in the hands of the Dutch; and this was so very profitable, that at least two millions of pounds weight were annually exported. A metallic composition named Calin, found here, was also a very lucrative branch of trade; but the most considerable article of commerce, was the Tin of Banca; which the Sultan was obliged to furnish to the Dutch monopolists, at a comparatively very low rate, to what they charged for it in the Chinese market. Much lower still was the price which the Sultan allowed his subjects for that and every other article of trade. These he obtained on his own terms, and almost for nothing; while from the Dutch, with whom he transacted business, he received Spanish Dollars for all that he sold, so that in consequence, an immense influx of specie poured into the Royal Treasury, which, together with the great quantity of Gold Dust collected in the hills, rendered him one of the richest Sovereigns in the East.

At this time, the deposed Sultan was about forty-seven years of age, of which he had reigned about eight when he was expelled for his atrocities by the British power. His brother, the present Sultan, is two years younger, and there are two more brothers, Pangarang Argo, and Pangarang Surgo. The sons of the late Sultan are many, but the three eldest by the Queen are first, Pangarang Ratoo, then aged twenty-one years, whose infamous conduct occasioned the ruin of his family; the second Pangarang Nadi, aged seventeen, respecting whose character accounts were various and contradictory. The third son, Pangarang Rabhu, aged ten years, was reported, as far as could be judged at his tender age, to be of a good and gentle disposition.

The Court of Palimbang has always been considered as taking the lead, and fixing the Court Etiquette among the Malay Princes; The Malay language as here spoken, is esteemed by the other native Courts the standard of perfection.

There are two other tongues, the Rajang and Batta, in use among the inhabitants of the interior of Sumatra; and these are both written in characters totally distinct from each other, as well as from the Malay on the coast. The people in the inland parts of the island are still in a wild uncivilized state; and though all along the coasts the inhabitants are more tractable, they are exceedingly treacherous, and the Dutch have repeatedly fallen victims to their perfidy. Formerly a small Factory was maintained on the River Bongalis, by means of which the Dutch carried on a very profitable trade with the inhabitants of the interior, in Opium, piece goods, and other valuable articles.

Jambi was formerly a considerable place, and the Factory of Siack on the great River of Androgiri, was also once in a flourishing condition, but on account of its extreme unhealthiness it has been deserted.

V

At first, the principal Settlement possessed by the Dutch, on Sumatra, was Padang, which being closely connected with the regency of Achen, was considered as so valuable and lucrative a Government, that the person exercising its functions was changed every two or three years. Gold is here so abundant as to be considered by the people in the interior of little value, and great quantities of the dust are, in consequence, suffered to flow with the rivers into the sea. When the Dutch were in full possession of power, the Mines of Irion and Marincabo used to yield five thousand pounds weight of this metal annually, and considerable fortunes were amassed by the simple operation of spreading nets or blankets across the streams to arrest and receive the floating mud which was mixed with gold-dust.

With all these riches, the Island has many disadvantages. In the interior, an immense Volcano frequently convulses the country with dreadful Earthquakes, and sends forth rivers of burning lava. The stagnation of the waters in the low grounds, and along the coasts, by infecting the atmosphere, generates diseases; whilst the western Monsoons are attended with heavy rains and storms of thunder and lightning exceeding in violence all the powers of description. Mount Ophir, which is situated nearly under the Equator, and is about the height of the Peak of Teneriffe, appears like an obtuse cone by itself, being seperated from the chain of other mountains. It is about eight leagues inland to the eastward of Seacarboa. Bencoolen, nearly opposite to Palimbang, comprizes the Residency of Padang, Achen and many minor places along the South Coast of this vast Island. The Fort and Town of Pedang are situated on the north bank of a river, about a mile up from the sea, with houses and gardens on the opposite side. Provisions for supplying ships are to be had in abundance at a moderate rate; here also is excellent water, which, issuing from the rocks on the south side of the river, is conveyed in spouts to the boats. Gold dust, benzoin, and other articles are bartered here for opium, blue and white cloth, and various piece goods.

Fort Marlborough, which is in lat. 3 deg 48 min. South, and long. 102 deg. 28 min. E. or 4 deg. 25 min. W. from Batavia, is, together with the town of Bencoolen, built on a point of land called Oossong Currang moderately elevated. The land in the country to the north-eastward is high and hilly, but very little known. Could a communication be opened across this tract with Palimbang, which is a measure that would, on trial, be found less difficult to accomplish than is supposed, it must be productive of very great advantages; new channels of trade would be hereby opened, and a secure intercourse established with the inland country of the Lampoons; an object which General Daendals had in view, and endeavoured to effect by means of the river Toulang Boowang which he caused to be surveyed, and ordering batteries to be erected on its banks.

The island of Banca ceded to the British Government by the new Sultan, was formally taken possession of on the twentieth of May, 1812, by Colonel Gillespie, and named " Duke of York Island."

Banca produces Tin, an article of primary consequence in the commerce with China, in greater quantity than any other place; while from Billiton, another island that was then ceded to us, is procured almost all the Steel used by the Malays, in making their arms and tools of various kinds. Besides the benefit derived to commerce from the possession of these islands, another advantage of equal, if not greater importance, consists in the security hereby afforded to trading vessels against pirates, who used to assemble here under the protection of the Sultan of Palimbang, and to commit numerous depredations.

Fort Nugent, constructed by us at Banca, is situated on a rising ground, about two miles to the Westward of the small town of Minto. The beach is sandy, and a fine rivulet of sweet and clear water runs between the fort and the town. The situation had all the appearance of being favourable to health ; but the mortality which has since pre-vailed among the troops of the garrison, and by which several valuable officers, and many private soldiers have found an untimely grave, proves the uncertainty of human expectation.

Minto, the Capital of the Island, is situated near the sea, towards the West, at the foot of the Mountain called Monapin, and nearly opposite to the River of Palimbang, between two points forming the road, of which that to the East is called Tanjong Poeni, and the Western, Sandy Creek, distant from the former fourteen, and from the latter four miles, where there is a Bank or Flat, running in a Western direction, about five miles towards the extreme point, called Tanjong Onlar.

The Campong, or residence of the Governor, named Dato Toma-gong, is surrounded to the East by an irregular entrenchment, which is now falling into decay ; and facing this Fort, on the opposite bank of Minto River, stands a Village, that extends on the hills to the dist-ance of about four hundred, and along the sea six hundred yards, bearing the resemblance of an amphitheatre, one house rising above the other.

Here is good anchorage in from six to twelve fathoms of water, and ships find shelter from the Sandy Point to the N. and W. against the boisterous waves which roll into the Straits from the China Sea, as well as against the North and West winds, which blow very hard along the coast of Sumatra, during the Monsoon.

The point of Tanjong Poeni, affords shelter during the E. and S. E. winds, which blow from the coast of Sumatra, into the Roads; but as they raise no great swell, little danger is to be apprehended from them.

Extract of the General Orders issued by the Honourable the Lieutenant Governor.

" Cheribon, May 27th, 1812.

" The Lieutenant Governor has the highest satisfaction in communicating to the army, during the absence of the Commander of the Forces, and to the public in general, the full and complete accomplishment of the objects which the British Government had in view, in adopting measures of hostility against the Sultan of Palimbang.

" In addition to the Military operations detailed in the following letter from Colonel Gillespie, the Lieutenant Governor is happy to state, that tranquillity and confidence have been established at Palimbang; and that, under the sanction of the higher authority of the Supreme Government, subsequently received, a permanent arrangement has been made for its future Government, to the exclusion of the late Sultan and his adherents.

" To estimate the superior conduct of the forces employed on this delicate and peculiar service, it may be proper to advert to the proceedings of the Sultan, which rendered hostilities indispensable; and a full statement of the occasion and result of this decided interference of the British Government, cannot be less interesting to the Dutch inhabitants of this Island than beneficial to the Native States of the Eastern Seas in general. [Here, after detailing a variety of particulars and documents, the orders proceed as follow :]

" On the importance of the service, and the ardent zeal, superior ability, and discernment, with which it has from its commencement been directed by its gallant Commander, the Lieutenant Governor will refrain from offering his sentiments, until the return of the Commander of the Forces, which may be hourly expected.

" The conduct of the forces employed on this service, and particularly that of the officers, noticed in such high terms by Colonel Gillespie, entitles them to the warmest approbation of Government. The forbearance which has been evinced in effecting the object of the armament without the effusion of blood, is as creditable to their discipline, as honourable to their character.

" The assistance rendered by Captain Owen, of His Majesty's ship Cornelia, in the earlier arrangements, claims the particular acknowledgements of this Government. The sentiments expressed by Colonel Gillespie, in favour of Captain Drury, of His Majesty's ship Bucephalus, are likewise entitled to the same mark of public attention ; and the Lieutenant Governor requests that Colonel Gillespie will convey to Captain Bowen, of His Majesty's ship Phœnix, his thanks for the cordial co-operation and effectual support, rendered by His Majesty's Navy.

" Colonel Gillespie is also requested to inform the Captains of the Honourable Company's Cruizers, that the Lieutenant Governor will have much pleasure in communicating to the Supreme Government, the favourable sentiments which are entertained of the conduct of this branch of the Naval service.

" By order of the Honourable the Lieutenant Governor,

(Signed) " C. G. BLAGRAVE,

" A. Sec. to Gov."

Extract of a Letter from Colonel Gillespie, to the Honourable T. S. Raffles, Lieutenant Governor of Java and its Dependencies, in which, after detailing the several operations, it concludes as follows:

" Dated Palimbang, 28th April, 1812.

" I cannot avoid expressing to you, the high sense I entertain of the cordial co-operation and support that has been afforded to me by every branch of the Naval service, during the progress of our voyage ; particularly the arrangements which were made in the first instance by Captain Owen, of the Cornelia, and conducted subsequently by Capt. Bowen, of the Phœnix, who relieved him in the command. Captain Drury, of the Bucephalus, was necessarily separated from the body of the expedition, where he had previously manifested great anxiety to forward the public interest. Although I am not qualified to give a professional opinion upon the value of their services, I cannot refrain from offering my most grateful acknowledgements to Captain Bowen, and bearing public testimony to the energy, zeal, and exertion displayed by those valuable officers, in executing the important duties of their situation, which tended materially to lessen the difficulties we experienced, and to overcome the obstacles opposed to our success.

" The military reputation and gallantry of Lieut. Colonel M'Leod, of H. M. 59th Reg. are already so well established, that any panegyric of mine would add little to the fame he has so justly earned.—I shall therefore content myself on the present occasion, with returning him my very best thanks, for the activity, anxiety, and attention, he has manifested during the progress of the service.

" Major Trench, and the detachment of the 89th Regiment ; Captain Campbell, and the detachment of the 59th Regiment ; Captain Limond of the Artillery, and all who were embarked at Batavia, are entitled to my warmest approbation. To Major Butler, Deputy Adjutant-General, Major Thorn, Deputy Quarter-Master-General, and the Officers composing General, Personal, and Brigade Staff, I am much indebted, for their assiduity and attention. I am desirous, however, of bringing particularly to your notice, the superior qualifications of Captain Meares, who has been acting both as my Aid-de-Camp and Interpreter, and who has displayed an activity, zeal, and acquirement, that enables him to discharge the delicate and important duties of his situation, with honour to himself, and great advantage to the Public Service.

" I have the honour to be, &c. &c.

(Signed)   " ROBERT ROLLO GILLESPIE,

" Colonel Commanding H. M. Troops."

Return of Ordnance on the Batteries at Borang River, Palimbang, Captured Twenty-fourth of April, 1812, by the British Forces under the Orders of Colonel R. R. Gillespie.

	BRASS. Pounders.			IRON. Pounders.						Total.
	2½	2	1	14	12	9	8	6	4	
Battery on Borang Island, - - - - -	4			1	9	6	5	1		26
Ditto, West-side of the River, - - - - -					1	7	4	1	2	15
Ditto, Binting Island, on the East-side of the River, -	2	1			1	9	3	1		17
Floating Batteries, Nos. 1, 2, 3, 4, 5, 6, - - -					4			2	8	14
War Prows, Nos. 1, 2, 3, 4, 5, - - - -	4	9	2		2	2			8	30
Grand Total,	10	10	2	1	17	24	2	5	18	102

(Signed) **J. LIMOND, Capt. Com. Artil.**

Return of Ordnance on the Works of Palimbang, Captured Twenty-fifth of April, 1812.

	BRASS. Pounders.							IRON. Pounders.					Total.
	42	9	8	6	3	2½	1	24	12	9	8	4	
North West Cavalier on the River, - - -					23								23
Line of Defence along the River, - - -	1					16		1	13	37	17	12	97
North-west Bastion of Palace Square, - -		4		6			1				10		21
South-east ditto, - - - - - -					21								21
Outer Gate of the Palace, - - - -						4				15		4	23
Inner Gate of ditto, - - - - -			2		2								4
Palace Yard, - - - - - - -					5	40	15						60
Grand Total,	1	4	2	6	51	60	16	1	13	52	27	16	249

General Total of Ordnance Captured by the British Forces in the Expedition to Palimbang, **351 Guns.**

(Signed) **J. LIMOND, Capt. Com. Art.**

z

In the seventh article of the treaty concluded with the new Sultan, he engages to protect the Chinese and Arabs who were settled in Palimbang, and all those persons who formerly lived under the protection of the Dutch Factory; to punish such as may commit any act of violence towards them, and to attend to the representations which may be made to him by the agent of the British Government on their behalf.

By the eighth article, the Sultan Ratoo Ahmed Nujm-ud-din engages to use his utmost diligence to obtain possession of the treasure which has been carried away by the late Sultan Mahmoud Budruddin, and to pay to the Commander of the Forces on behalf of the British Government, half of the sum which he may recover, partly to defray the expense of the armament fitted out against the said Sultan, and partly as a fine imposed for his acts of tyranny, cruelty, and perfidy.

In the ninth Article the Sultan Ratoo Ahmed Nujm-ud-din engages to use every exertion to obtain possession of the persons of those who were the principal advisers and instigators of the cruel and rapacious acts of the late Sultan, together with their property wherever it may be found. He promises to inflict on those persons condign punishment for their enormous offences, which are deserving of death, and out of their confiscated property to appropriate a sum to alleviate the distress of the families of the deceased members of the Dutch Factory. He further engages to make search for the remaining men, women, and children of the Dutch, who may still remain alive in this country, and to send them to Java by the first opportunity.

"I, Sultan Ratoo Ahmed Nujm-ud-din of Palimbang, do, of my own free will, as an acknowledgement of the favour conferred on me, by the English Government of Java, in advancing me to the throne of the kingdom of Palimbang, and relying on the liberality of the English Government, for a suitable provision to maintain my Rank and Dignity, cede to His Majesty, the King of Great Britain, and to the Honourable the English East India Company, in full and unlimited sovereignty, the islands of Banca and Billiton, and the islets thereon depending; hereby renouncing on my own behalf, as well as on behalf of my heirs and successors for ever, all claim and title to those islands, with the mines and produce thereof, which, together with all the privileges and prerogatives heretofore exercised there by the Sultans of Palimbang, I acknowledge to be henceforth the sole and exclusive property of His Majesty, the King of Great Britain, and the Honourable East India Company. And I do hereby enjoin all the inhabitants now residing in those islands, as well as those under my authority, who may hereafter be desirous of settling there, and may obtain the permission of the British Government for so doing, to yield to the British Government due submission and obedience. And I do hereby further promise and engage to protect the property and families which may be now or hereafter at Palimbang, belonging to the inhabitants of Banca, Billiton and their dependencies, with perfect freedom of removal to those islands when demanded. In witness whereof, I have hereunto put my hand and seal, together with the hands and seals of my heir apparent and of the principal Pangarangs of this Kingdom.

" Written on the 5th day of the month *Jamad-ul-Anwull*, or Sunday, in the year 1227.

(Signed)   " PANGARANG SURYA.

"PANGARANG ARYA.

(Seal of Sultan Ratoo, Ahmed Nujm-ood-deen of Palimbang.)

" Signed and sealed at Palimbang this 17th day of May, 1812, in presence of,

(Signed)   " WILLIAM HUNTER.

" R. MEARES."

Proclamation of the Commander of the Forces, published at Minto,
the 20th May, 1812.

" The Island of Banca having been ceded in full sovereignty to his Majesty the King of Great Britain, by Sultan Ratoo Ahmed Nujm-ood-din, of Palimbang, I, Robert Rollo Gillespie, Commander of his Britannic Majesty's forces to the eastward, do hereby take possession of the said Island, in the name and on behalf of our gracious Sovereign and the United East India Company of England ; requiring and commanding that all manner and description of persons shall honour and respect the British Flag, hereby established, and yield obedience to the constituted authorities that may now or hereafter be appointed to govern them." (In pursuance of which the following Oath of Allegiance has been administered to all the chiefs and principal inhabitants of the said Island: " I, A. B., do hereby solemnly swear that I will be true and faithful to his gracious Majesty, the King of Great Britain, and neither directly nor indirectly hold communication or intercourse with his enemies; that I will respect and obey the Officers, both civil and military, who many be appointed to govern the said Island; and that I will assist and succour all British subjects, and their Allies, to the best of my ability and power.")

" I do also will and command that this Island shall be henceforward named Duke of York's Island, in honour of his Royal Highness the Commander in Chief of his Britannic Majesty's Forces; that Minto shall be the capital of the said Island, and called Minto, in honour of the Right Honourable the Governor General of all India; that the Fort now building near Minto, shall be named Fort Nugent, in honour of his Excellency Sir George Nugent, Commander in Chief of all the land forces serving in the East Indies; and that Klabut Bayor harbour, on the N. E. side of the Island, shall be called Port Wellington, in honour of General Lord Viscount Wellington, of the British army."

SECTION III

Hostilities with the Sultan of Mataram, and Capture of Djoejocarta

———————

THE objects of the Expedition to Palimbang being accomplished, the Commander of the Forces, and Staff, sailed on the 22d of May, in the Wellington schooner, from Fort Nugent, and, after several narrow escapes from numerous perils, which more than once threatened the destruction of our little vessel, she arrived at Batavia on the 1st of June; and on the 6th, we set out over land for Samarang, where, the same day, were published the following General Orders:

" Samarang, June 6th, 1812.

" The Lieutenant-Governor is happy to congratulate Colonel Gillespie on his return to Java, and on the full accomplishment of the objects of the late Expedition.

" The successful termination of these operations in a manner so highly beneficial to the interests of humanity, and to the security and advantage of the British possessions in those seas, must be entirely attributed to the prompt, judicious, and politic measures adopted under the personal direction of the Commander of the Forces. And although the applause so justly due on this occasion may rather fall within the province of a higher authority, to whom the proceedings will be submitted, it is gratifying to the Lieutenant-Governor that he is not precluded from bearing public testimony to the services which have been rendered, nor of expressing his admiration of the superior talent and character which has been so conspicuous throughout.

" The Lieutenant-Governor requests Colonel Gillespie will accept his best thanks for the zeal, ability, and precision with which the service has been executed; and, in recording his entire approbation, and unreserved confirmation of the whole of the arrangements made for the future security and advantage of the British interests, the Lieutenant-Governor is satisfied that he only anticipates the sentiments of the supreme Government.

" By order of the Honourable the Lieutenant-Governor,

(Signed) " J. ECKFORD, Act. Sec."

The troops of the Expedition, with the exception of the necessary garrison for the security of the new Colony, had directions to proceed to Samarang, where a new field of glory opened for the display of British valour, in the very heart of Java.

An incidental notice has already been taken of the power of the Sultan of Djoejocarta, and of the ambitious views of aggrandizement entertained by that monarch. In addition to that statement, and as illustrative of the conduct pursued by the natives, it may be proper here to give a brief account of the rise of the Court of Mataram, which is of modern date, and owes its origin entirely to the very colony of Europeans which it sought now, by ingratitude and treachery, to annihilate.

When the Dutch had succeeded in despoiling the dominions of their first victim, the Sovereign of Jaccatra, whose capital was destroyed, and his country seized by the victors, they next directed their attention to the Soosoohoon, who, being too formidable to be attacked by arms, was assailed by stratagem. The Dutch flattered the credulous Prince with assurances of succour against one of his own family, who had been secretly instigated to rebellion. The Soosoohoon being deceived by these offers, was induced, by a fatal confidence in the good faith of his pretended friends, to adopt the advice which they gave him, but which was, in fact, the very course he should have avoided. By this management, the infatuated monarch became completely entangled in the toils which superior cunning had laid for him; and when it was found that he was utterly incapable of extricating himself, they, whose arts had brought him into that situation, made an open avowal of their alliance, offensive and defensive, with the rebellious Chief. Still their designs extended no farther than to the weakening of the Sovereign whose confidence they had so egregiously abused; and, therefore, on his submission to the allies, he was allowed to retain a large proportion of his territory, with the ancient capital of Solo, or Soura-carta. On this occasion, the Dutch took as their share of the spoil, the whole of the North coast, as that part only being navigable, this alone could be serviceable to their purposes. The remainder was created into a separate Sovereignty for the rebel who assumed the title of Sultan of Mataram, and whose residence was fixed at Djoejocarta. But with the characteristic bad faith which invariably marks the conduct of those who have been associated together in acts of treachery and plunder, the new Sultan very soon began to manifest his enmity to the very power that had elevated him to the throne ; and these hostile proceedings were the cause of the expedition which General Daendels found it necessary to form, and of which some notice has already been taken. A compromise was entered into by both parties for their mutual convenience ; but the radical hatred of the Sultan continuing unabated, or rather being probably increased by the humiliation which he had been compelled to endure, the state of the colony excited his hopes, that he should be soon enabled to carry into effect his favourite project of completely overturning the European Government in Java.

Having now matured his measures, he considered the present moment as the most favourable for carrying his design into execution ; and that the rather, as he stood at the head of a general confederacy of all the native Courts, constituting, as it were, the Pith, the Sinews, and the Strength of Java. Even the animosity, which had subsisted between the Emperor of Solo and the Sultan, owing to the defection and rebellion of the latter ; and which, it was supposed, would have proved an insurmountable bar to their union, yielded in the present instance to other motives, and all family feuds subsided, the better to enable these princes to combine their forces in effecting our destruction, as well as that of the whole Colony, consisting of a vast multitude of European settlers, extended along a coast of more than seven hundred miles, and who naturally looked to the British Government for protection. The magnitude of the threatened danger, therefore, calling for immediate action, no procrastination could possibly be admitted.

The troops of the Palimbang expedition had not yet returned, except one Company of Grenadiers of the 59th Regiment, in the Phœnix

2 A

Frigate, which came by the direct passage, whilst the remainder of the Fleet had to go round the island of Banca, and to pass over to Borneo, by which their passage was lengthened out to a month. But matters were now come to such a crisis, that to have waited for the arrival of these troops, would have been extremely dangerous. It was therefore resolved, to move such of the military force as could be collected to Djoejocarta, and in the event of hostilities being unavoidable, to break at once that chain of combination, which, if suffered to increase and strengthen, would, in all probability, prove the absolute ruin of the European settlements in this part of the East

On the evening of the 17th of June, the Lieutenant Governor and Commander of the Forces arrived at Djoejocarta; and immediately on their arrival, the Sultan, who had long before prepared for active operations, sent out strong bodies of horse to intercept the communication in our rear, by burning and destroying the bridges, and laying waste the country. Upon receiving this intelligence, Colonel Gillespie went in person, escorted by fifty Dragoons, to reconnoitre the country; and after making several detours, we fell in with a large body of the Sultan's Horse; but as no final determination with respect to offensive measures had yet taken place, the Commander of the Forces, withheld by sentiments of honour, from dispersing those people by force, endeavoured, through Mr. Crawfurd, the Resident, who accompanied him as Interpreter, to induce them, by every amicable means, to return peaceably to the Crattan. To all solicitations, and even threats, however, they paid no regard for a long time; and some stones were actually thrown at us from slings, which they use very dexterously. Still, amidst these provocations, forbearance was observed on our part, and at last they consented to return, but, on a sudden availing themselves of the growing darkness, they threw their spears at our men, by which a serjeant and four dragoons were wounded. Thus they were the first to provoke hostility, which ended in their defeat. This act of treachery was followed by several other attacks during the night upon the cavalry patroles, which obliged our Dragoons to cut their way sword in hand, through the surrounding multitudes, with the loss of one man killed and one wounded.

The following day, the Lieutenant Governor being still anxious to avoid the effusion of blood, and, if possible, to bring matters to an amicable adjustment, sent a messenger with the final resolution of his Government to the Sultan. But the arrogant Chief continued deaf to every proposition that was made to him, and feeling confidence in his accumulating force, and the strength of his fortifications, he scrupled not to add threats to his insult, and dismissed the messenger.

This unfavourable result of the negociation, the particulars of which were instantly communicated by the Governour to the Commander of the forces, shewed clearly that every thing now depended on the issue of a battle; and that any farther delay from a principle of lenity, would only serve to heighten the insolence of the enemy, and consequently to injure the colony.

Though the troops which we had collected at this period were but few in number, they were formidable by their intrepidity. These consisted of a part of the fourteenth Regiment of Foot, part of the Bengal Light Infantry, and the Third Volunteer Battalion; a proportion of Artillery, and two troops of the 22d Dragoons. The remainder of our force, with the principal supply of Ordnance, were coming forward, under the Orders of Lieutenant Colonel Alexander M'Leod, and might be expected to join during the night.

It may be proper here to remark, that when the Dutch had obtained the undisturbed possession of the finest portion of the Island, they entered into such agreements with the native Princes as were calculated to maintain the influence they had so artfully acquired over them and their councils. Among other stipulations, they succeeded in gaining permission to erect forts, which, being built close to the Capitals of the respective Chiefs, gave the Dutch nearly the command of those places where they were so powerfully settled.

Upon the return of the messenger, a fire was instantly opened from our Fort, and which was as soon returned from the Crattan; and thus presenting the singular spectacle of two contiguous forts, belonging to nations situated at opposite extremes of the globe, bombarding each other.

The Crattan or residence of the Sultan of Mataram, and of all his Court, is about three miles in circumference, surrounded by a broad wet ditch with drawbridges; a strong thick high rampart with bastions, and defended by near one hundred pieces of cannon. In the interior, are numerous squares and court-yards, enclosed with high walls, all very strong within themselves, and defensible.—At this time, the principal entrance or Square in front, had a double row of cannon facing the entrance, besides which, it was flanked with new-erected batteries to the right and left. Seventeen thousand regular troops manned the works; whilst an armed population of more than one hundred thousand, surrounded the exterior Campongs for many miles round, and also occupying the walls and fastnesses along the sides of the different roads leading to the Crattan.

The Fort built by the Dutch, which is about eight hundred yards from the nearest face of the Crattan, is but ill calculated for any other use than as a depot for military stores. These were scanty, and the powder, which was of the old Dutch manufactory, proved very bad; so that our firing was only intended to amuse the enemy, whilst our little force was concentrating. One of the depots of powder belonging to the enemy exploded soon after the firing commenced; and a similar accident happened on our side, by which several officers and artillery soldiers were severely burned; among whom were Lieutenant Young, Brigade-Major, and Lieutenant Hunter, of the Bengal Service; Captain Teesdale also, of the Royal Navy, who volunteered his services, was wounded by this occurrence. This explosion set fire to one of the buildings in the Fort; but it was rapidly extinguished, and the cannonade continued. Light parties were detached to scour the Campongs on the right and left, to keep the Sultan's troops in play, and prevent their passing to our rear, and harassing the detachment under Lieutenant-Colonel M'Leod, who were marching from Salatiga to join the forces at this place. Towards evening, the Sultan sent out a flag of truce, attended by a large body of troops, and in the pride of his heart, imagining himself already victorious, he demanded our unconditional surrender; an act of arrogant exultation which could alone proceed from the fullest dependence he placed on his internal strength to resist every attack, and the overwhelming superiority of his force, which, in respect of numbers, was undoubtedly immense.

Major Dalton, with a part of his Battalion of the Bengal Light

Infantry, who occupied part of the Dutch Town, between our Fort
and the Crattan, was spiritedly attacked, during the night, four successive times, but repulsed the enemy with steadiness and good conduct.
On the high-road by which Colonel M'Leod's detachment had to
march to join us, numerous parties were employed in burning or
breaking down the bridges, and throwing every obstacle in the way to
impede their advance.   Frequent skirmishes ensued between those
Parties of the enemy and our Dragoons, who were sent to keep the
communication open ; in which rencontres, some astonishing traits of
gallantry were exhibited, our men being forced to make up for their
extreme inferiority in numbers, by the most strenuous exertions of
their superior activity, valour, and skill.   Late in the evening, a party
of Dragoons, under Lieutenant Hale, of the 22d Regiment were sent
out to force their way to Colonel M'Leod's detachment, of whom no
tidings had been heard for some time ; the messenger, despatched by
the Lieutenant-Colonel, having been murdered on the road.   The
country was so thickly beset by the Sultan's people, that it was almost
impossible to send a report or order by a messenger on foot ; and even
a Native could neither pass undiscovered, nor escape being murdered.
In this dilemma, Colonel M'Leod offered a reward to any man who
would volunteer to carry an order to Captain Byers, then commanding a detachment of Royal Artillery, and who was a day's march in
his rear.   John O'Brien, private in the Madras Horse Artillery, immediately undertook this desperate service.   He galloped through the
midst of the enemy's parties, delivered his orders, and hastened back
again, fortunately without being touched.   The Commander of the
Forces, ever attentive to individual merit, rewarded this brave soldier

with the public expression of his thanks, and bestowed on him a gold medal to commemorate his gallantry.

The party of Dragoons were attacked by a numerous body of the enemy, who fired on them from behind walls, whilst multitudes, drawn up across the road, presented to them a formidable and deep array of spears, through which our men had to cut their way, most gallantly maintaining a running fight the whole way, till they joined the detachment. The officer, Lieutenant Hale, was wounded, and narrowly escaped being speared to the ground; which was the case with six of his party, who were killed, and found the next day, mangled in a most barbarous manner.

In the morning of the nineteenth of June, the whole of the troops under Lieutenant-Colonel M'Leod, reached Head-quarters, consisting of a detachment of Royal Artillery, the Grenadiers of the 59th Regiment, and the Flank Companies and Rifle Company of the 78th Regiment, a small party of Hussars, and a detachment of Madras Horse Artillery. The long marches performed by the troops, and their exposure to a burning sun, rendered some repose necessary. In the mean time, the cannonade was continued on both sides. The enemy, posted behind the walls, outside the Crattan, were burned out and dislodged, by setting fire to their Campongs, which brought on a general conflagration, and prepared the way for the assault.

In the evening, Colonel Gillespie ordered all the troops both cavalry and infantry into the Fort, which produced the desired effect of lulling the enemy into a fatal security, and of removing from their minds all ideas of any serious attack being in contemplation on the Crattan. By these means also, the vanity of the Sultan became more inflated, and he was confirmed in the belief, that we were actually afraid of him, which ridiculous fancy had taken full possession of his imagination, when he sent the flag of truce with the summons to surrender.

Whilst thus humouring the credulity of the enemy, care was taken to fatigue and harrass them. The roaring of cannon, sending forth shot and shells at intervals, from our fort, disturbed their rest all night, till towards three o'clock in the morning of the 20th June, when a perfect silence ensued, which lulled the greater part to sleep;—but it was the sleep of death.

Two hours before dawn, the leaders of columns having received their orders respectively, instantly proceeded to execute them. To assault a place of such magnitude with so small a force, and the knowledge that we had to contend with a vast superiority of numbers, could not fail to give a very serious and appalling aspect to our enterprise. But the stake at issue was nothing less than our very existence ; and the fate of the whole Colony depended on the event.

At Bantam, Cheribon, Sourabaya, and other places, thousands were ready to burst forth against the Colonists at the first signal. The alarm, indeed, had already been given at Sourabaya, where the Sepoys were fired on in their barracks, in the night, and, at the same time, a fire of musketry opened from the Malay part of the town, across the river, into the streets of the European quarter. The affrighted Dutch inhabitants shut themselves up in their houses, expecting every moment to be massacred ; but as the troops got immediately under arms, by the vigilance of the Commanding Officer, Lieutenant-Colonel Fraser, of the 78th Regiment, this rising tumult was fortunately suppressed.

On an enquiry being instituted the next day into the cause of this infant rebellion, it was traced to a priest, who, designedly no doubt, had spread a story that he had seen two Eagles in his dream; one white, the other black; that, after fighting in the air for a long time, with various success, the black Eagle at last conquered the white, and having brought his adversary to the ground, tore him to pieces. The allusion was easily understood, and very readily credited at this critical moment, when every eye was turned towards Djoejocarta, with the most anxious expectation.

It was evident that no safety could be ensured to the colony but in the capture of the Crattan, the dispersion of the forces of the Sultan, and the seizure of his person, who was the soul of that confederacy which it became now an imperious duty to dissolve by every means in our power.

These were the objects to which the comprehensive and active mind of the British Commander was directed at this important moment; and how well his plans were laid for the accomplishment of the great ends he had in view, will appear from the result.

A column under Lieutenant-Colonel Dewar, with a part of the Bengal Light Infantry, and the third Volunteer Battalion, joined by Prince Prangwedona's corps, proceeded at four o'clock in the morning, by a circuitous route, to dislodge a large body of the enemy who were posted outside, to the southward of the Crattan, and afterwards to force their way in at the south gate; whilst, on the north side, a successful diversion was made by an attack at the principal entrance, under Major Grant.

2 B

The column under Lieutenant-Colonel Watson, with a part of the fourteenth Regiment, a part of the Bengal Light Infantry, with Lieutenant-Colonel M'Leod's column of Grenadiers, of the 59th Regiment, Flank Companies, and the Rifle ditto of the 78th Regiment, composed the main attack.

This column had to move round the north-east Bastion, and close under it, to arrive at the point for escalade; but such was the silence observed, and so complete the success of the previous measures, in taking the enemy off his guard, that this column moved on undiscovered. The head of the column had just gained the spot for placing the ladders, when the alarm was given by a sentry in the north-east bastion, the guns of which immediately poured forth a shower of grape, by which several were killed and wounded; but this only increased the activity and emulation of our troops. Led on by Lieutenant Colonel Watson, the column, headed by the brave Grenadiers of the fourteenth, under Captain Johnstone, crossed the broad and deep ditch, and escaladed the ramparts on the north-east face, notwithstanding the shower of grape shot poured upon them by the enemy. This, however, was soon silenced by the irresistible rapidity of the Grenadiers, followed by the remainder of the fourteenth Regiment, supported by a well-directed fire from our sharp shooters, so posted as to send their shot direct into the embrazures, which made it too hot for the enemy to stand long to their guns.

Lieutenant Colonel Watson pushed along the top of the ramparts, for the Prince's gate, on the north face, whilst a party of Sepoys crossed the ditch, at the angle of the bastion first attacked, but which had become defenceless by the explosion of its powder magazine; and passing along the Berm, at the bottom of the rampart, towards the same gate, they let down the drawbridge, for the admission of Lieutenant-Colonel M'Leod's column.

The Prince's gate, being strongly barricaded, was with difficulty blown open; but, in the mean time, the troops, having cleared the ditch over the drawbridge, ascended upon one another's shoulders through the embrazures; and, having reinforced Lieutenant-Colonel Watson's column, they rapidly swept the ramparts. In all this time, a brisk fire of shot and shells was kept up from our fort, upon the interior of the Crattan.

The enemy raked the ramparts with grape shot during the whole of the passage to the south-east Bastion, which was finally taken possession of at the point of the bayonet. From thence the troops rushed on along the south face; and, after a severe conflict with the enemy, who were here in large numbers, and fighting desperately, they succeeded in opening the gate for Lieutenant-Colonel Dewar's column, who arrived just at this moment, after defeating the forces in the suburbs, in which affair their chieftain, the Toomoogong Senoot Deningrat, fell, who was one of the Sultan's principal advisers and chief instigators, in every hostile proceeding against the British Government. The whole column together now pushed on for the west gate; and, in their progress, the captured guns were turned occasionally with such effect upon the enemy, in the surrounding Campongs, as materially contributed to the dispersion of those troops; after which, the pieces were thrown off their carriages, or tumbled into the ditch; since, from the smallness of our force, it would have been impossible to occupy such extensive works, each face of the fort being three-quarters of a mile in length. By these means, the men were kept collected, and in possession of that impelling force, which, like a whirlwind, swept every thing before it.

During these operations, Colonel Gillespie had so disposed the Cavalry and Horse Artillery, in parties supporting each other, and to scour the roads which surrounded the Crattan, as to cut off the fugitives from the Fort in every direction ; and thus preventing any attempt to escape on the part of the Sultan or his principal adherents. To this measure may be attributed the complete success of the enterprize, in ensuring the possession of the Sultan's person, who, finding that he had no chance of escaping, surrendered himself a prisoner ; and thus was prevented that predatory warfare which would probably otherwise have desolated the country for a long time.

The hereditary Prince threw himself under our protection at the West gate ; but the enemy still continued to hold out at the North West bastion, from whence however they were soon driven.

The fortifications being all cleared of the enemy, their last refuge, which they obstinately contested, was a mosque on the outside of the Fort, from whence they kept up a brisk fire over the walls and through the apertures. It was here that Colonel Gillespie unfortunately received a severe wound in his arm, from a blunderbuss, which one of the enemy fired at him through an opening. A small number of Bengal Sepoys, who were the only infantry with this party, which consisted besides of two horse artillery guns and some dragoons, behaved with uncommon intrepidity on the present occasion.

This arduous and unequal conflict having lasted full three hours, terminated in a complete victory, the immediate effect of which, by the possession of the Sultan, was an entire dissolution of the whole formidable confederacy.

Our loss, consisting of one hundred killed and wounded, though much to be regretted, was certainly far below what could reasonably have been expected, considering the desperate nature of the service, and the disparity of force which was throughout actually engaged. To the bravery of the troops and their overbearing rapidity in the attack, alone is this great achievement, accomplished with such a comparatively trifling loss, to be attributed. That on the part of the enemy cannot be correctly stated, but it must have been very great; as besides the killed and wounded on the ramparts and in the bastions, a prodigious number of dead were lying in heaps under every gateway, particularly at the central one.

The conduct of the officers and men employed on this enterprize, cannot fail to excite admiration; for brighter traits of bravery, discipline, and humanity, have never been displayed in any assault. The handful of brave troops engaged, being less than one thousand firelocks, defeating upwards of seventeen thousand men, well appointed, and obstinately bent on defending the Crattan to the last; together with the discipline of the troops in the execution, will render this act conspicuous in the annals of our Military History. The word was, " Death or Victory!" And so impressed were the soldiers with the important truth in this trying moment, when one hundred thousand armed men were ready from all points to pour vengeance upon us, thereby rendering retreat almost impossible, as every direction presented hordes of inveterate foes, that no thoughts but their King and

Country, entered the devoted minds of our warriors. Such was the effect of this elevated sentiment, which pervaded all orders, that not a man attempted to leave his ranks, or to go after plunder. This it was that ensured the victory; in which valour was crowned by that humanity so characteristic of British soldiers, but which, in the present instance, was preeminently conspicuous and admirable, as the conduct of the enemy had been marked by peculiar circumstances of atrocious barbarity. But the forbearance of our troops when flushed with success, was the more honourable, as they had a fresh recollection in their minds, of what their comrades had suffered in being mangled and tortured to death. The females in the inner apartments of the palace were all respected, and the property was protected. So strict indeed was discipline observed on this occasion, that not a single person was molested, nor did any outrage take place.

The old Sultan indeed, was exiled to Prince of Wales's Island, and his son, the Hereditary Prince, was placed on the Throne, by the name and title of HAMANG KUBUANA the Third. The Emperor of Solo, equally intimidated and astonished by the wonderful instance of determined intrepidity which had been displayed in his own immediate neighbourhood, readily acceded to the terms which were offered to him on the part of our Government. This example was followed by the other Native Princes; and thus the British supremacy over the whole Island of Java, was established on a solid basis, and that attended by a splendour unparalleled in the history of this distant region.

Bagoos Rangin, the Rebel Chieftain already mentioned, after having eluded every pursuit for a number of years, was taken on the twenty-eighth of June, together with his nephew named Bagoos Manoch, and his uncle Griessen, otherwise Sidja Djuda. On the twenty-fifth of the same month, a party under the noted Naireem, was also defeated, and thus peace and tranquillity became restored to the whole Island.

Return of Killed and Wounded of the Forces employed in the Capture of Djoejocarta by Assault, 20th June, 1812.

KILLED.

His Majesty's Twenty-second Dragoons, - - 8 Rank and File.
——————— Fourteenth Regiment, - - 8 Do.
——————— Seventy-eighth, - - - 1 Do.
Light Infantry Battalion, - - - 3 Do.
Djyang Sekars, - - - - - 3 Do.

Total killed 23 Rank and File.

WOUNDED.

Staff, Colonel Gillespie, Commander of the Forces.
Horse Artillery, two Rank and File.
Bengal Artillery, Major Butler, slightly.
                    1 Drummer, 11 Rank and File.
Twenty-second Dragoons, Lieutenant Hale, severely.
                    12 Rank and File.
His Majesty's Fourteenth Regiment, Lieutenant M'Lean, severely, since dead.
                    30 Rank and File.
——————— Seventy-eighth Regiment, Lieutenant Robertson, slightly.
                    3 Rank and File.
——————— Eighty-ninth Regiment, Lieutenant Young, Brigade Major.
Light Infantry Battalion, Lieutenant J. H. Paul.
                    7 Rank and File.
Third Bengal Volunteer Battalion, two Rank and File.
Fourth ditto, Lieutenant Hunter.
Amboynese, one Havildar.
Royal Navy, Captain Teesdale.
                    Total wounded, - - 76

                    Grand total, - - - 99

N.B. Of Prince Prangwedona's and Nunky de Sumas' Corps, the killed and wounded are not included.

Horses.	Killed.	Wounded.
Horse Artillery.	1	2
Twenty-second Dragoons,	5	13
Hussars,	1	
Staff,	1	
Total killed, - -	8 Wounded, - 15	

List of Ordnance captured on the Works of Djeojocarta, June 20, 1812.

BRASS.				IRON.								
Pounders.				Pounders.								
Four.	Three.	Two	Swivels.	Eighteen.	Twelve	Nine.	Six.	Four.	Three.	Two	One.	Total
2	3	4	18	8	7	3	15	26	1	3	2	92

With a considerable quantity of powder and ammunition, and some shells.

General Orders, by the Commander of the Forces.

" Head-quarters, Djoejocarta, June 21st, 1812.

" The Commander of the Forces congratulates the troops he had the honour personally to command, upon the late glorious result of their arduous and honourable enterprize. It confirms him in the opinion he had so justly entertained of their discipline, firmness, and gallantry, and it affords a memorable proof to the enemies of the British Government, that British soldiers, when united by those valuable qualities, must not only conquer, but be irresistible. It was the conviction of their supereminence, that determined him in a measure where nothing but bravery could succeed ; and it was the assurance of their intrepidity that urged him to an assault, where multitudes of men were prepared for resistance. The event has proved that his confidence was by no means misplaced. The enemy has been routed from a regular fortified position, and seventeen thousand armed men have been conquered and dispersed. The person of the Sultan has been safely secured, and the circumstances attending his seizure, reflect so much credit upon the troops in general, that the Commander of the Forces cannot sufficiently express his admiration and applause. In the heat of the storm, his person was respected, his family was placed in security and protection, and no part of the property was either pillaged or molested.

" This remarkable instance of steadiness and discipline, shall be brought to the notice of higher authority, and it will be the duty of Colonel Gillespie, to obtain for this force the approbation they have so justly earned.

" To Lieutenant-Colonel Watson, who commanded the leading column, the Commander of the Forces cannot convey the high sense he entertains of his distinguished bravery, and of the quickness and alacrity with which he conceived and executed the attack.

" The animated style in which Captain Johnston and Lieutenant Hunter crossed the Ditch, and, at the head of the 14th Grenadiers, escaladed the Ramparts, under the fire of the East Bastion, could only be equalled by the order and zeal of their gallant followers.

" The prompt and decisive movement of Lieutenant-Colonel M'Leod, to force his passage to the Prince's Gate, and support the leading column, was equally daring and meritorious. The long detour of Lieutenant-Colonel Dewar, and his battalion, towards the Southern Gate, and his well-timed entrance through that passage, con. tributed materially to the success of the day ; and indeed, the whole of the officers and soldiers employed upon this spirited assault, have distinguished themselves so equally well, that it will be difficult for the Commander of the Forces to discover what part was more conspicuous than another. It is right, however, to specify Captain Leys, and part of the Light Infantry Battalion, who crossed the Ditch at a fordable part, and climbed to an embrazure on each other's shoulders *.

---

* These Sepoys, after crossing the Ditch, rapidly passed along the Berm, and let down the Draw-bridge, at the Prince's Gate, for the admission of Lieut.-Col. M'Leod's column.

" It is also just to mention the conduct of Major Forbes, who attacked the right of the Sultan's Square, and detached Lieutenant Douglas, with a small party of His Majesty's 78th Regiment, to cover the guns that were directed with so much spirit and effect by Lieutenant Cameron, of the Bengal Artillery. It would also be wrong to omit mentioning the spirited conduct of Major Dalton and his battalion, who scoured the ramparts to the left, and admitted Lieutenant-Colonel Dewar at the South Gate, after preserving the life of the Prince Royal *. He therefore requests that those Officers will accept his best thanks for their valuable services, and commucate them to the troops under their several commands. It appears that Lieutenant Douglas had the honour of capturing the person of the Sultan, with his small detachment of the 78th Light Company. Major Butler, and the Foot Artillery, Captain Byers, and the Royal Artillery, Captain Rudyerd, and the Horse Artillery, and Lieutenant Dudley, and the Hussars, were all conspicuous for the same gallantry and zeal ; and the Commander of the Forces communicates his thanks to Captain Byers, for his active exertions in joining Lieutenant-Colonel M'Leod's detachment, with the Ordnance Stores ; and the same approbation is also due to Captain Colebrooke, of the Royal Artillery, whose activity has more than once been noticed. Captain Byers, and Lieutenant Black, rendered effectual assistance to Lieutenant-Colonel M'Leod, in blowing open the Prince's Gate, with one of the Horse Artillery guns. This valuable corps is always conspicuous when its services are required.

" It now remains for the Commander of the Forces to particularize instances of personal intrepidity, and amongst these may be classed the conduct of Lieutenant Hill, of His Majesty's 14th Regiment, who, with a Havildar, of the 4th Volunteer Battalion, reconnoitered the Fort, before the advance of the troops, ascertained the depth of the water in the ditch, and furnished a most correct report for the guidance of Lieutenant-Colonel Watson. The behaviour of this officer will be brought to the

---

* As a countermarch could not be effected, it now became the turn of the Bengal Light Infantry Battalion, under Major Dalton, to lead the column, in sweeping the rampart round to the left, and which was done most gallantly.

notice of His Excellency the Commander in Chief in India, where just claims to dis tinction are never disregarded.

" It is also reported to the Commander of the Forces, that the conduct of Private John O'Brien, of the Horse Artillery, was particularly conspicuous, in having per. formed an important point of duty, under circumstances of the greatest personal hazard, and he therefore merits public approbation.

" The conduct of Lieutenant Hale, and his party, has already been mentioned in terms of just applause; but the Commander of the Forces cannot refrain from again testifying his sense of the activity and exertion that have been manifested by Captain Dawes, and the officers and men of His Majesty's 22d Dragoons, during the progress of the service.

" The central attack was conducted by Major Grant, of the 4th Volunteer Bat. talion, whose well-established gallantry is acknowledged and recorded. It is therefore requested that this officer will receive his warmest thanks for his active exertions, and communicate the same to the officers and men placed under his immediate com- mand.

" The Commander of the Forces performs a pleasing task in recognizing the valuable services of Major Butler, commanding the Artillery, who has uniformly dis- played his wonted zeal and indefatigable exertion. The Commander of the Forces is therefore happy in the opportunity of bearing public testimony of the professional superiority and valuable acquirements of this excellent officer.

" Major Butler, Deputy Adjutant General; Major Thorn, Deputy Quarter- Master-General; Captain Hanson, Military Secretary; Captains Parsons and Taylor, who were acting as Aides-de-Camp, and all the Staff, with the troops, continue to deserve the approbation and praise already bestowed upon former occasions; he there. fore requests that these Officers will accept of his warmest acknowledgements for their assiduity, activity, and attention. Lieutenant-Colonel M'Kenzie, of the Engineers, and Major Thorn, Deputy Quarter-Master General, whose gallantry and conduct have been always conspicuous, were exceedingly serviceable in arranging the plan of attack. The former of these officers having been detained upon the Island, upon professional duties, the Commander of the Forces was particularly fortunate in the opportunity of benefitting by his valuable talents and exertions.

" Lieutenants Harris and Baker, of the Bengal army, have manifested great anxiety to forward the benefit of the service.

" Majors Johnson and Campbell, Captains Jones, Bethune, and the Officers of the Honourable the Lieutenant Governor's Staff, attended the Commander of the Forces during the action, and he is much indebted to those, as well as to many others, for their active assistance and exertion.

" It would be injustice to omit the name of Captain Teesdale, of the Royal Navy, who accompanied the Commander of the Forces, and acted as an Aide-de-Camp, in which situation he displayed all the energy and zeal so common to those of his honourable profession, and the Commander of the Forces regrets that he was wounded so early in the service.

" The conduct of Lieutenant M'Lean, of his Majesty's 14th Rifle Company, of Lieutenant Robinson, of His Majesty's 78th, and of Lieutenant Paul, of the Bengal Native Infantry, has also been reported zealous and meritorious. They were wounded in the assault; and although the Commander of the Forces cannot help deploring the loss, however small, that we have sustained during the progress of the service, he cannot avoid reverting to the ardour and rapidity of the attack, which ensured to the gallant troops a most complete victory, and lessened those bitter feelings of regret, which the loss of a brother soldier must always produce.

" Russa Khan, Havildar, of the 4th Volunteer Battalion, and Marwam Sing, Sepoy, in the Light Infantry Battalion, are promoted to the rank of Jamidars; and Roop Maran Sing, of the Light Infantry Battalion, is promoted to the rank of Havildar, for their distinguished and conspicuous gallantry. These appointments are to be considered as having taken place during the action, and they will also be sub- ject to the confirmation of Government.

" The exertions and assistance that were afforded by Mr. Crawford, Resident, Mr.

Robinson, Mr. Deans, and Mr. Hardy, shall be brought to the attention of the Honourable the Lieutenant Governor.

(Signed) " RICHARD BUTLER,

" Deputy Adjt. Gen."

General Orders by His Excellency the Commander in Chief in India.

" Head Quarters, Cawnpore, Sept. 30th, 1812.

" His Excellency, the Commander in Chief in India, having, while at a distance from the seat of Government, received from Major-General Gillespie, Commander of the Forces on the Island of Java, the official reports of the success of the Expedition to Palimbang, and of the glorious result of the assault on the strong fortifications of Djoejocarta, on the 20th June, 1812, offers his cordial congratulations to Major General Gillespie, and all the Officers and Troops who had the honour of serving under his personal Command on both those important occasions, but more particularly on the ever memorable assault of Djoejocarta.

" Although the feeble use which the enemy made of his extensive means of defence and annoyance at Palimbang, deprived the Expedition against its barbarous Prince, of that character of brilliancy which peculiarly belongs to active operations in the field, the Commander in Chief considers the troops employed in that difficult service as highly deserving of his approbation and thanks, for their exact discipline, patient endurance of fatigue and privation, and forwardness on every occasion which seemed likely to require their active exertions.

" The personal intrepidity and presence of mind displayed by Major General Gillespie on this occasion, by which the lives and property of a numerous population were rescued from impending destruction, and placed under the safe-guard of British humanity and good faith, reflect additional lustre on the high reputation which that Officer had already acquired in his distinguished career of public service.

" Nor are the wise and prudent arrangements, by which Major General Gillespie accomplished in a short time all the important objects which Government proposed by the Expedition to Palimbang, less deserving of the Commander in Chief's public approbation and applause.

" Whether the Commander in Chief views the well-timed promptitude and decision with which the resolution to assault the Crattan of Djoejocarta was adopted ; the judgement with which the attack was planned ; the order, rapidity, and gallantry with which it was executed by the brave troops, who, emulating the example of their leader, and relying on his established character and talents, and their own valour and discipline, disregarded numbers superior beyond all proportion in ordinary warfare, and surmounted every obstacle to complete success ; his Excellency must ever consider the storming of the Crattan of Djoejocarta, by the troops under Major-General Gillespie, as ranking amongst the foremost of those great achievements which adorn the military annals of our country, and have increased its power and reputation in Asia.

" The Commander in Chief in India, desires to offer the tribute of his warmest thanks and applause to Major-General Gillespie, commanding the forces on Java, for the energy, skill, and valour evinced by him, in the conduct of the arduous service in question, the successful termination of which has superadded to all the splendor of heroism, the substantial advantage of establishing the British supremacy over Java, and the tranquillity of the Island, on the solid foundations of justice and power.

" His Excellency also desires to express his warmest thanks and highest approbation to the undermentioned Officers, who are particularly mentioned in the Major-General's Dispatches, and to all the Non-commissioned Officers and Privates of the several corps, European and Native, employed under them.

" To Lieutenant-Colonel Watson, of his Majesty's fourteenth Foot, for the gallantry and judgement displayed throughout the principal attack, which he led ; to

Lieutenant-Colonel M'Leod, of his Majesty's 59th Foot, for the prompt and decisive movement which he made to support the leading column; to Lieutenant-Colonel Dewar, of the third, Major P. Grant of the fourth Bengal Volunteer Battalion; Major Dalton, of the Bengal Light Infantry Battalion; Major Forbes, of his Majesty's 78th, for their distinguished conduct at the head of their respective parties; to Major Butler, commanding the Artillery, for the professional ability and zeal displayed by him during the progress of the service; to Captain Rudyard, of the Madras Horse Artillery, and Captain Dawse, of his Majesty's 22d Dragoons, for the distinguished bravery evinced by them, and the detachments of those corps under their respective Commands; to Major Butler, Deputy Adjutant General, and Major Thorn, Deputy Quarter Master General; Captain Hanson, Military Secretary; Lieutenants Parsons and Taylor, Aides-de Camp, for the able and zealous assistance rendered by them on this and every other occasion of service on Java; to Lieutenant Colonel M'Kenzie, of the Madras Engineers, who being detained on the Island by professional duties, afforded all the aid of his valuable talents in the formation of the plan of attack, and to Majors Johnson and Campbell, and Captain Jones, of the Bengal Establishment, as well as the Staff of the Honourable the Lieutenant Governor, who attended the Commander of the Forces during the action, and of whose assistance and exertion he reports in such favourable terms.

" It is difficult to particularize individual merit, where the good conduct of all was so conspicuous; but the undaunted resolution and bravery, under circumstances of particular difficulty and danger, which Major General Gillespie reports to have been displayed by Lieutenant Hale, of his Majesty's 22d Dragoons, on the evening of the 18th June, and by Lieutenant Hill, of his Majesty's fourteenth Foot, who, with a Havildar, of the fourth Bengal Volunteer Battalion, ascertained the depth of the ditch previous to the assault, demand to be honourably recorded.

" The Commander in Chief cannot conclude without expressing the satisfaction he derived from the honourable and ample testimony borne by Major-General Gillespie, in his reports to His Excellency, to the distinguished zeal and gallantry of the detachment of Bengal Volunteer Battalions, employed at the assault of Djoejocarta, during which they eminently sustained the long established character of the Bengal Sepoys, for courage and discipline.

(Signed)   " C. STUART,

" Acting Adjutant General."

General Orders by the Right Honourable the Governor General in Council.

" Fort William, August 14th, 1812.

" Official accounts of the successful assault of the fortified Palace of the Sultan of Djoejocarta, on the island of Java, on the 20th June, having been received at this Presidency, the Right Honourable the Governor General in Council, deems it proper to direct, that the annexed documents, containing the details of that most brilliant achievement, be published for general information.

" In discharging the satisfactory duty of expressing his admiration of the professional talent, personal zeal and intrepidity displayed by Colonel Gillespie, and the heroism which animated all the Officers and men of the Detachment, headed by that distinguished Officer on this occasion; his Lordship in Council has only to signify his unqualified concurrence in the applause bestowed on them by the Honourable the Lieutenant Governor of Java, in his General Order of the 28th of June, and in the high commendations which the Detachments in general, and the several officers, particularly noticed in the General Orders of their gallant Commander, have had the honor to receive.

" In the promptitude of decision, ardor and ability of execution, which inspired the conduct of their leader, and in the persevering courage, zeal, and energy which pervaded all ranks of the troops under his direction, in the successful accomplishment of this arduous enterprize, his Lordship in Council recognizes those eminent qualities the display of which had already conferred immortal honour on the brave officers and men, who, under the guidance of their illustrious Commander in Chief, effected the conquest of Java; and contemplating the formidable difficulties opposed to them by the strength of the enemy's works, and the vast superiority of his force, his Lordship in Council, cannot but consider the storming of the Palace of Djoejocarta among the number of those extraordinary efforts of gallantry, which will ever hold a distinguished place in the annals of the British arms.

" His Lordship in Council deeply laments the severe wound which Colonel Gillespie received in the moment of victory, but has the satisfaction to observe, that it was not of a nature to excite apprehension.

" The Governor General in Council has great pleasure in confirming the highly-merited Promotions which are specified in Colonel Gillespie's General Order of the 21st of June.

" By order of the Right Honourable the Governor General in Council,

(Signed)   " N. B. EDMONSTONE,

" Chief Secretary to Government."

STATISTIC AND HISTORICAL SKETCH

OF

J A V A;

Being the result of Observations made in a Tour through the Country;

WITH AN ACCOUNT OF ITS DEPENEDNCIES.

———————

IT does not enter into the design or limits of the present work, to give State of the Island. a copious description of the Island of Java and its Resources; nor to treat circumstantially of the different Tribes inhabiting that country; which are subjects that would, if fully delineated, as their importance deserve, extend far beyond the limits here prescribed; and require more ample opportunities of examination than in the present instance were enjoyed.

Java, and the Eastern Islands, open a wide field for speculations, Political, Commercial, and Agricultural. By a radical reform in the internal administration, and the blessings of peace, this celebrated colony may hope to revive from its drooping state, to the possession of a consequence similar to that prosperity, which, for two centuries, imparted power to ancient Holland, and placed that country in the rank of one of the most flourishing Nations in Europe.

But the depth of misery into which the revolutionary war had sunk the Dutch at home, materially affected their colonies abroad. Subject to the paramount authority of France, the separation of Holland from the British interests, exposed her trade to numerous losses, which rendered all intercourse precarious and unsafe, while multiplied disappointments and failures in commercial speculations proved fatal to the spirit of enterprize. The mismanagement in the affairs of their East India Company, occasioned by the depredations and the want of morality and public spirit in its servants, added considerably to the mischief. No new settlers of respectability from Europe arrived to replace those whom the sickly climate carried off, so that Batavia, which was formerly styled the " Queen of the East," being thus deprived of a great part of its inhabitants, having also the accustomed influx of wealth cut off, and labouring at the same time under the yoke of French domination, sunk into a state of languor and wretchedness.

The great depreciation of the old Batavia Paper Currency, accelerated this general decline, and the means which were adopted to remedy that evil, failed in producing the desired effect. Specie became extremely scarce, and the want of an accredited circulating medium caused an entire stagnation in trade. The rate at which the Paper was fixed by a Proclamation issued under the authority of Lord Minto, viz. $6\frac{1}{2}$ Paper Rix Dollars for one Spanish Dollar, was very soon doubled, and in the Chinese market, and Exchange shops, the value of Silver rose over that of Bills to the height of one Spanish Dollar for fourteen or fifteen Rix Dollars of Paper. This loss, while it affected the Public Treasury in its receipts under the circumstances above-mentioned, at the same time fell very heavily on the people, who had to make their purchases, and even, perhaps, to procure the necessaries of life, by giving at the lowest price, bills which had been received at their original value. The seller again received no more than the value of his goods, being obliged again to exchange the bills to procure specie, in order to carry on his dealings with the merchant vessels that supplied him with goods; while both sustained a considerable loss in the decrease of sale, because of the privation which the greater part of the people were obliged to impose on themselves. The evil was therefore increasing daily, and to remedy it, the old paper currency was called in, by means of the sales of public lands, the payments being made into the treasury, partly in paper, at $6\frac{1}{2}$ Rix dollars for one Spanish dollar, and partly in specie. The circulation of the old paper currency was stopped, but that of specie did not increase. The general loss of credit was in consequence destructive of speculative pursuits, and those who were possessed of money kept it locked up; which, being so much dead capital, occasioned a complete scarcity of the circulating medium. The consequences were, an interruption of labour, and want of employ; suspension of useful and profitable establishments; a scanty market occasioned by reduced consumption, and a necessary loss to the public revenue. But the successes of the British arms in these regions have opened new sources of prosperity.

The tin from Banca, or Duke of York's Island, supplies the want of Spanish Dollars in the China trade; and establishments on Borneo are also in progress. An armament which sailed in June, 1813, from

Samarang, under the orders of Colonel Watson, against Sambas, achieved its capture, and drove into the interior Anam, the nominal Sultan of that place; but who was in reality nothing better than a formidable Pirate Chieftain, who had successfully resisted the British flag, when an attack was made towards the close of the preceding year by the late lamented Captain Bowen, of the Phœnix Frigate.

Pontiana obtained a British Garrison in compliance with the pressing solicitations of its Sultan. Ambassadors from the King of Siam arrived at Batavia with offers to renew the former relations of reciprocal Commerce with Juthea, the capital of that Empire, where the Dutch had formerly a Comptoir. The long interrupted intercourse with Japan was also about to be re-established by this conquest; two large ships having sailed from Batavia in June 1813, with a valuable cargo for the seat of that Empire.

Thus, a successful renewal of its commercial relations, with the establishment of a new system of landed tenure, must improve the internal revenue, and fix it on a certain basis, unexposed as it had been to the vicissitudes of trade, under that ruinous system of monopoly and forced contingents of the old Government. It is computed, that by this change the land revenue will be augmented more than ten times its former assessments. At the same time, the proposed abolition of all feudal services and forced deliveries, will emancipate the great mass of the population of Java, from that state of vassalage and bondage under which they were so long oppressed, and by the introduction of a free cultivation, and a free disposal of the fruits of labour, that fine country, so much favoured by nature, will, under a wise administration, soon emerge from its gloomy and depressed condition, into a state of wealth and prosperity.

The Island of Java lies between the fifth and ninth parallels of South Latitude, and from the 105th to the 115th degree of East Longitude, being in length six hundred and forty two miles, while the breadth, which varies much, is at the greatest, one hundred and twenty-eight miles.

Face of the Country.

The island is divided nearly in its whole length, by a range of mountains, running almost East and West, the centre of the range, which is however often broken, being the most elevated. Descending to the north coast, it is in its whole extent, low and swampy, intersected by a great number of rivers, and fine bays, with many towns and villages being interspersed along the coast. Some shoal flats are stretched along in several parts, and a few patches lie detached from the shore, but in most parts this coast may be approached to 8, 7, or 6 fathoms of muddy bottom, whereas the south coast, of which, as it has not hitherto been explored, very little is known, rises into high and rugged hills, against which the surf dashes violently, so that, with the exception of a few Bays, this coast is almost inaccessible.

In several hills of the great range of mountains, are the craters of volcanoes, which formerly raged with fury, and poured forth torrents of lava; but, at present, none are known to be in activity, though many emit smoke after heavy rain. In the neighbourhood are numerous mineral springs, possessing different degrees of efficacy and temperature.

To an enterprizing and commercial people, the number of navigable rivers, with the canals that might be cut from them, on the north coast of Java, would supply an endless source of wealth by the benefit of inland communication. Almost all the towns of any note on the coast are situated on large rivers, by which the whole produce of the surrounding country is easily transported in boats or on rafts.

Military Roads.

The great military road from Bantam to the east end of the Island, measuring above seven hundred miles, will ever remain as a monument of the enterprize of General Daendels; though it is to be lamented that this great work was accomplished by a prodigious sacrifice of human lives. About twelve thousand natives are said to have perished in constructing it, chiefly owing to the unhealthiness of the forests and marshes, through which it runs. From Bantam to Batavia, the road is generally flat; and, except through a jungle of about twenty miles in extent, it is made without difficulty. From Batavia to the foot of the Blue Mountains, the road runs nearly level; the ascent then gradually increases, and becomes so extremely difficult, to the summit, that the aid of buffaloes is required to draw up a carriage. Though in this mountainous region of about one hundred and twenty miles, there is very little rock to cut through, still it is evident that the labour by which the work was accomplished must have been excessive. From hence the road runs, with a few exceptions here and there, very level; and, for many miles along the beach, to the east end of the Island, it is conducted through several forests, and over numerous marshes and rice fields. The ordinary country roads in the interior are numerous, but few of them are passable for carriages, except the native Pedatties, or carts, which are drawn by buffaloes; and, during the western monsoon, it is scarcely poss'ble to quit the high roads.

The climate of Java is various. Along the sea coast it is hot and Climate. sultry; but, on proceeding inland, the air becomes keen and pleasant. In some parts, particularly amongst the hills, on the great road, at Salitiga, and many of the inland towns, it is often so cold as to make even a fire desirable. At Weltervreeden, the thermometer is generally at 86 degrees, in the dry season, or the south-east monsoon, which extends from April to October; and from 83 to 90 degrees in the west monsoon, from November to March. In the mountains about Tjipanas, lying only sixty-two miles from Batavia, the thermometer is generally at 65 degrees, and sometimes less, but seldom exceeding 70 degrees of Fahrenheit.

The monsoons are by no means regular. Heavy rain seldom sets in till December, and the heaviest is in the months of February and March. There is a constant succession of land and sea-breezes every day, but varying a few hours in the setting in. From ten in the morning till four or five in the evening, the sea-breeze blows; and then a calm succeeds till seven or eight, when the land-breeze sets in, and continues, at intervals, till day-break. Where the first blows close to the sea, and over a swampy or muddy beach, it is not esteemed wholesome; but the latter, particularly near the hills, is cool and refreshing. The most pleasant and healthy season is from May to October.

Perhaps in no part of the globe is vegetation so richly luxuriant, Produce. or the wants of man so easily supplied, and with less trouble of

2 E

cultivation, as in Java. In the low lands are extensive rice fields, exhibiting the variegated hues of emerald and gold ; one spot, newly sown, being verdant, while close to it is another ripe for reaping, the whole interspersed with topes of cocoa-nut trees. A variety of esculent fruits and vegetables, which may be gathered throughout the year, grow around each cottage, and in every village. On the mountains are lofty trees, fit to be converted into masts, while forests of teak supply the place of oak for building ships, adapted to all purposes. The Kappok and the Jambos grow to a very great height ; and so does that which is called by the Chinese and Malays the Kanarie, which is one of the highest of the forest trees. The Kijatil tree supplies the best planks and timber for all kinds of architecture. The Makandon is a large tree, as also is the Mangam, which is a species of the Palm. To this last are ascribed many virtues. It is consecrated to kings and princes, being placed round their tombs.

The Sagamunda, or Sago tree, is another species of the palm. From it is extracted a sap, which, being mixed with one called Houbat, and other ingredients, constitutes a beverage named Sagouar, which is very commonly used, especially in the Molucca isles, where the colonists have often nothing else to drink. This liquor is intoxicating when drank to excess. The Sago here mentioned is also boiled and made into soup ; and in many places it is the ordinary food of the lower class of people.

The Rossamala, or Turennapi, resembles the beautiful Jati wood, of which such elegant cabinet work is made.

The Kubab Sini, which grows only in the kingdom of Bantam, yields a balsamic oil, or jelly, resembling the much-esteemed Kayoo Pootee oil. It partakes of the smell and taste of camphor, and is taken inwardly, in violent coughs, or disordered stomachs, and also in various other cases.

The odoriferous Benzoin tree is also found on Java. It is a kind of laurel, growing to a great height; and the leaf is not unlike that of the citron, or lemon tree. It produces a gum, which is obtained by an incision under the crown, and is at first very thin and fluent, like water, and transparent, if taken away in time: but when suffered to settle, it turns to an orange colour, and loses its clearness. This gum forms a lucrative branch of commerce. Plantations of cocoa-nut trees surround every cottage; and the peasant considers it a duty most sacred to bestow his principal care and attention on the preservation of these trees, which he transmits with care down to his children, not only in a flourishing state, but augmented by new plantations, thus constituting a regular inheritance from father to son. The Bamboo also is generally planted round the cottager's little garden, in which grows the Dorian and Plantain, with a few culinary plants. Such are the simple articles with which the Indian villager satisfies almost all his wants; while numerous kinds of fruit-trees, dispersed over the fields, produce a superabundance. Of these, the Mangosteen is, perhaps, the most delicate and finest tasted fruit in the East; but it is singular that its growth should be confined to particular spots. In Java, it grows principally about Batavia, and the western parts of the Island, there being comparatively but few in the eastern parts. The Mango and Tamarind, Jamlo, or Jambo, Jaaka, or Jack fruit, are very plentiful. The latter, as well as the Dorian and the Annona, or, as the Malays call this last, Sarborossa, are very favourite fruits with the natives. The Ramboutan is also another of a very pleasant taste; besides which, Pomegranates, Custard apples, Papaya, Billimbing, Guava, Boa-bidarra, Peaches, Oranges of various kinds, with a great variety of other fruits, are produced throughout the Island. The Pamplemousse are here of a very exquisite flavour; as also is the Annanas, or Pine-apple, both being superior to those of Hindostan. Grapes thrive so well, that the colonists might not only produce wine for their own consumption, but for exportation. This was once tried, and the vineyards promised every success; but the jealousy of the Dutch settlers at the Cape, who considered this as likely to break in upon the wine trade, which they had so long carried on, influenced the Government at home to issue an order, prohibiting the culture of vines in Java.

The Areca, called Pinang by the Malays, and Betel plantations, are very numerous. The various kinds of plants, and great abundance of herbs found in Java, would afford ample scope for the researches of the botanist; as flowers exhale their perfumes at all seasons of the year. The Fula Majori, of which whole fields are to be seen, is most extensively cultivated, and the water distilled from it, which is superior to rose water, is used in washing the face and eyes, being supposed to have the virtue of strengthening them. The Boenga dada or Eglantine tree was originally imported from Persia. The leaves and knobs resemble those of our rose trees, but the flowers are smaller. The smell is also like that of our rose, and the water which is distilled from it is in great repute. Among the Heathen nations of India, in consequence of their belief in the metempsychosis, we find the culture of a great variety of herbs and plants particularly attended to ; as their religious abstinence from animal food lays them under the necessity of discovering other articles of sustenance, which they find in abundance among the variety of vegetable tribes, and these of course constitute their principal dependance in the article of living.

This conformity in the Javanese to the practice of the continental Indians, indicates a common origin, besides which, there are many Hindu peculiarities observed among these people, and the ancient traces of Hindu worship found in the island, sufficiently prove that the present race of inhabitants are the descendants of the sons of Brahma.

In addition to the numerous esculents which are cultivated here, the people are in possession of many medicinal plants. The Tanda Rousa is used as such. The Indian Alkanna or Henna, has many virtues ascribed to it by the Malays, particularly the women, who carry their faith in its efficacy to a degree of superstitious veneration. A sap extracted from the juicy leaves of the Magas or Kiati tree, is held in high estimation, as an effectual cure of wounds made by crisses and spears that have been dipped in a poison composed of the blood of the Gekko, and other ingredients. The leaves of the Torre tree are esteemed by the natives to be a powerful remedy for the bite of snakes, as also is the wild Nardus, which grows in great plenty. This last is used by the Javanese in their cookery.

Amongst the great variety of culinary vegetables in most request, the Kurkum is a favourite plant of the Malays, who employ the roots in cooking their fish and flesh, which thereby acquire the colour and taste of saffron. The Pattatas, which is much cultivated, is a root eaten either raw like sallad, or roasted, in which last state it tastes like a chesnut, and is reckoned very wholesome. Focki Focki, when boiled in wine with pepper, tastes somewhat like our artichoke. The Nomeradi, which is a kind of spinach, is in general use; the Assafœtida is also found here; and the Cardamon is much cultivated; all other garden plants, such as endives, cauliflowers, beans, cabbages, pumpions, melons, patacas or water melons, yams, potatoes, &c. are produced in great abundance throughout the island. Maize, or Indian corn, is a favourite article of food with the natives, who eat it roasted.

Tobacco grows very well in Java, though formerly much was imported from Ternate. But the staple produce of the Island is Rice, which is cultivated nearly the whole length of the sea coast, many miles in breadth, and in all low grounds, ravines, &c. wherever water is to be had; but the greater part is grown to the Eastward, whence it is brought to Batavia, and exported in great quantities. Upland Rice and Cotton are grown in-land, and on the hilly parts. Indigo of a very superior quality, yet said to be 25 per cent. cheaper than that of Bengal, is also produced here, and might even be raised in any quantity. With this all the native dresses are dyed, as the Javanese almost universally wear blue or black cloths. Catjang is also much cultivated; and the Chinese, after expressing great quantities of oil from it, with the residue feed their hogs. It is much used throughout the Island, and on board country ships, forming a considerable branch of the export trade. The Coffee Plantations are extremely luxuriant, and cultivated principally on the high grounds. From the profit accruing to the Revenue, they were much extended by the late Government; and in the different Regencies there was a regulation that a certain number of trees should be planted every year; but of late, from the interruption of the trade with America, and the Continent, the regulation has not only been abolished, but the plantations to the Eastward were ordered to be entirely destroyed, and converted to other uses. Pepper is chiefly cultivated in the country of Bantam, whence a certain quantity was obliged to be furnished by the stipulations of the former Government. Great quantities of Sugar are made, chiefly in Jacatra, as well for the consumption of the Island, as for exportation. Wheat and Barley are only grown in small quantities, in the hilly tracts, chiefly in the middle parts of the Island, but enough might no doubt be raised for the consumption of Java and its dependencies, by extending the cultivation. Oats and Bengal Grain thrive likewise in those parts of the Island, and would prove very abundant, were the culture extended.

The natural fertility of the soil renders much labour and tillage unnecessary. In the ordinary cultivation of the Rice and Paddy Fields, the husbandman makes use of Buffaloes. These powerful and often furiously enraged animals, are securely conducted by little children; they seem indeed to forget their own strength in the weakness of the child, and are most willingly obedient to it. Cattle of every description are plentiful all over Java, but the Cows in general are of an inferior kind, and give very little milk. Sheep, Goats, and Pigs are very numerous. Game, however, does not abound here so much as in other countries; though Hares and Rabbits are pretty

Animals.

common ; and Deer and Antelopes are also plentiful. The Malay method of hunting the last is singularly curious. In the Mountain Regencies, Horses are trained for that particular purpose. When the Antelope is started, a Hunter immediately pursues it at full speed : the rider lies forward close to the horse's neck, and without minding the bridle, for the animal having been trained, seldom loses sight of the object, which he follows over every thing like a greyhound. On coming up with the game, the hunter is enabled to throw a noose over its horns, or round the neck and head, by which it is secured till the remainder of the party arrive. Should the rider happen to be thrown, the horse seldom gives up the chace. Instances are even mentioned of his continuing the pursuit alone, and on coming up with the Antelope, of his pawing it down to the ground, and by mouthing and kneeling on the prey, holding it there till the arrival of the hunting party. The Horses, which are very numerous throughout the Island, are small but active, and show a good deal of the blood and make of the Arabian. The Bima breed is esteemed by much the best, and great numbers of them are annually imported. The general size of the Horses in the Island, is about thirteen hands. Wild Hogs and Monkies are found in all the Jungles. The Forests, especially to the Eastward of the Island, are inhabited by various kinds of Wild Beasts. The Royal Tiger is here as powerful and as large as in Bengal. A species of Black Tiger, which is often found, is very ferocious, but of a smaller kind, and in size and shape rather resembles the Leopard. The Rhinoceros is sometimes met with, but principally in the Western parts of the Island, lying in the high grass jungle, remote from observation. Snakes are found here, as in all other hot countries, in great numbers, and of various kinds. Some of these are from twenty-five to thirty feet in length. The Petola Snake, which is one of the largest, has been known to swallow whole sheep, hogs, and other animals ; but it is not venomous, and when gorged, it twists its body round a tree, where it hangs quite motionless, till the food is digested ; in which state it is sometimes killed. The numerous marshes on the sea coast, where the principal towns are situated, are infested with Reptiles and Insects. Lizards of all kind, from the variable Cameleon to the Guana tribe, frequent the bushes, trees, and roofs of the houses. Of these, the Gek-ko is held by the Javanese in the greatest abhorrence, from an idea of its being venomous; it makes a loud barking at times, resembling the sound whence its name is derived. Scorpions abound in these marshes, and the Mosquitoes are particularly tormenting.

Of the great diversity among the feathered tribes found in Java, we may remark the Cassowary, by the Indians called Emeu, which is a very large and powerful bird. White Eagles have been seen here, and every kind of Bird of prey are continually on the wing. Of the Parrot species the Lowrys are very beautiful, and often sold at a high price. Birds of Paradise, from Gillolo, Papua, and New Guinea, sometimes visit this Island. The Java Sparrow is of a peculiar kind, and very handsome. Pigeons, domestic and wild, with the most beautiful plumage, abound here ; Pheasants ; Jungle, and Pea-fowl, are also numerous, together with Quail, Snipes, &c. Wild Ducks and Geese, however, are not common, though Poultry is extremely plentiful.

The Aquatic tribe is equally diversified, and the extensive fisheries along this great line of coast, are highly productive. At some places the fishing-stakes run out six or eight miles into the sea. Of the great abundance daily brought to market, we may notice the Kaacop, which grows to a large size, and is in great repute. The King Fish, which is the best flavoured of any, sometimes measures five feet, and is very wholesome. The Jacob Evertzen is a very fine fish, and often weighs four hundred pounds. Sole, Carp, and many other kinds of fish found in Europe, are very plentiful here. The Clip Fish and Springer are very good when boiled. The Eels are a favorite food with the Chinese. Oysters, and every kind of Shell Fish are in great abundance. At the mouths of the rivers, numbers of Aligators or Caymans, are continually lurking for their prey. The Water Guana, a smaller kind of the Crocodile species, infests rivers and ponds, where they prove very destructive. In the several Bays numerous Sharks swim about the ships; and many Animals unknown in Natural History, abound in these seas.

Manufactures, Exports, and Imports. Java has but few Manufactures. The principal is that of Cotton, which is produced in sufficient quantity to furnish the coarse cloths, handkerchiefs, and other articles of dress worn by the natives. The greater part are fabricated in Java Proper, or the country east of Cheribon, whence they are brought in great quantities to Batavia, and there sold at very reasonable rates. At Solo is a considerable manufacture of Leather and Sadlery. Boots and shoes are made in the Samarang district, and of these great quantities are exported. All kinds of utensils of iron, brass, and tin, are also manufactured here, but these sell at high prices.

The principal articles of exportation are Rice, Sugar, Coffee, Pepper, Indigo, Teak Timbers and Planks, Spices, which are brought from the Moluccas, Tin from Banca, Cotton, Yarn, Salt, Edible Birds' Nests, which are procured in abundance, particularly among the rocks in the hilly range stretching through the Bantam Country, and in the dominions of the Emperor and Sultan.

The imports are European articles of every description, Chintzes, Silks, Hats, which are a favourite dress with the Chinese and Native Chieftains, Tea, Japan Goods, and China Ware, Opium from Bengal, Tin from Banca, Wines, Beer, &c.

INTERNAL ADMINISTRATION.

REVENUE DEPARTMENT.

UNDER the Dutch Government, every branch of the revenue was Old System. farmed out, and sold by public auction once a year; as also the collection of dues on Opium, Arrack, Salt, and of Bird's Nests throughout the whole island.

Coffee and Pepper used to be the first articles of revenue, as they were obliged to be delivered to the Company at a stated price, generally one-fourth of what they were afterwards sold for ; and the forced collections of these and such articles of produce as might contribute to the commercial monopoly of the local Government of Batavia, seems to have been its great object. It is said that General Daendels attempted to exchange the collection of taxes in kind for a specific sum, which the Regent was bound to pay, and left to collect from the poor inhabitants by any arbitrary exactions he chose ; but it had scarcely begun to be acted upon when he was recalled. The residents living in the principal towns of each district received the revenue from the native Regents only, and the mode of collection remaining in the hands of the latter, left the cultivators no security beyond the claims of established usage. Thus, although custom prescribed a certain portion only of the crop to be delivered, there was no positive means of preventing a greater levy ; and while the power and influence of authority could be successfully exerted to stifle complaints, it may be concluded, that the peasant despairing of any relief, had to endure the weight of severe oppression and injustice.

The internal duties comprized those levied in the markets or tolls imposed at stated places on the transport of goods.

The market duties were exacted for every article of manufacture or of agricultural produce, which was exposed to sale, and was not confined to one or two of the chief places in each district, but extended at the pleasure of the farmer, to every petty village that could afford the most distant prospect of gain,

New System.   It is sufficiently apparent from what has been said, that the former system cherished those seeds of corruption which tended to its own dissolution. An amended system became therefore indispensable, and its establishment, which the fall of Djoejocarta was the means of introducing, and rendered secure and easy, promises the most beneficial effects. It is founded on the following basis :

1st. The entire abolition of all forced delivery of produce at inadequate rates, and of all feudal services, with the establishment of a perfect freedom in cultivation and trade.

2dly, The assumption on the part of Government, of the immediate superintendance of the lands, with the collection of the revenues and rents thereof, without the intervention of the Regents, whose office is in future to be confined to public duties.

3d. The renting out of the lands so assumed in large or small estates, according to local circumstances, on leases for a moderate term.

Under the new regulations, the allotments of land fall under the collector's superintendance, who is instructed to continue in possession all such persons as he shall find to be actually holding and cultivating lands, and to receive them as renters from Government in the new settlement. Though such cultivators shall not be able to adduce proofs of any real property in the land, yet long occupancy, improving culture and general good conduct while in possession, are deemed to be just

Landed Tenure.

claims, and to constitute a right in equity and sound policy, of being considered preferable to any others, who have no such pretensions; it is to be understood, however, that no positive right of any nature is to be infringed by this settlement.

The following is the general standard for fixing the Government share, from each species of land.

FOR SAWAH LANDS.

First sort, one-half of the estimated produce.
Second ditto, two-fifths ditto.
Third ditto, one-third ditto.

For Tagal lands, under which description are comprehended all lands not subject to irrigation:

First sort, two-fifths of the estimated produce.
Second ditto, one-third ditto.
Third ditto, one-fourth ditto.

According to these rates, the land rental, exclusive of Batavia or the kingdom of Jackatra and the Preanger lands, but only including the provinces east of Cheribon, amounts for the year 1814, to 3,883,651 rupees; and after deducting the amount of assessment of lands provisionally assigned to native chiefs, there remains a nett land rental of 36,63,611 rupees; add to this, the amount of farms and fixed taxes provisionally continued, and the territorial revenue of the eastern provinces alone, is 42,06,341 rupees.   In addition to this, the salt, opium, and customs, including town duties in those provinces, will give a total of 53,68,085 rupees.

Such of the inhabitants, who not being cultivators, contribute nothing to the land rent, are to be classed as householders, and have a tenement tax levied on them, or small rent for the ground on which their houses stand.   These will be assessed according to the classes, at three rupees, two, or one per annum.

Collectors have been appointed to the various districts, whose office consists in the sole and entire superintendance of the Land Revenue.

Mode of Collection.

They possess no magisterial authority whatever; but must make regularly application to the Resident, as Judge and Magistrate, whenever it becomes necessary to call for his aid in either capacity.

The Collectors will forward to the Resident, who is the sole Treasurer of the District, the several sums of money he may receive in his collections.

A native assistant, taken from among the Bopatis (nobility), Patehs, or Tumangungs, who have been, but are not now, in the actual service of Government, in consequence of the new arrangements in the landed tenure, and such number of writers, opasses, and other servants, as may be necessary, are to form the Collector's establishment.

The simple mode of village administration, which formerly extended throughout the Island, is ordered to be maintained in all the Provinces, as being best suited to the genius of the people, and promising to be most conducive to the interest of the state.

A writer, priest, and other subordinate officers and servants, complete its regular establishment. The head inhabitant, therefore, who has various denominations, according to the custom of the several Provinces, such as Potingi, Bakal, Kuwu, Mandor, or otherwise, will have the management of the Revenue concerns in his village entrusted to him, agreeably to the regulations that have been framed for his guidance. His personal influence, and intimate acquaintance with the situation and concerns of the several inhabitants in it, render him better qualified than any other to discharge this duty; and in consideration of which, a certain portion of land is to be allowed him, free of rent.

The heads of villages are considered in every way subordinate to the Officer of Division, who is selected from among the Bopatis, or the nobility, and who is empowered to take regular cognizance of all transactions respecting Revenue collections, and to inspect, whenever he pleases, the several village accounts.

The Officers of Divisions furnish to the Collector all such papers as may be required, and are diligently to execute the orders they may receive from him, or his native assistant.

The option-of-kind payment in Paddy and Rice, is still left to the renter, on many accounts, principally owing to the scarcity of specie in the Island. But every facility and encouragement is enjoined to be afforded to this description of renter, to induce him to pay the Government dues in money.

The other great branches of the Revenue of Java, are the Teak Forests, which are very productive. Those in the central districts, which were ceded in consequence of the fall of Djoejocarta, afford employment to 200,000 persons, who inhabit these forests, thus rendering that a fertile source of this Revenue, though of the Forest administration, as well as of the Coffee culture, which is equally considerable, nothing precisely is known.

Another very profitable branch is the monopoly of Tin from Banca, which is sold to the China ships.

The Salt Farms, with the exception of a few, have been abolished, and this measure has proved a death-blow to that pernicious influence which the Chinese had been allowed to acquire.

The amount of annual revenue under the present circumstances of the department, is estimated at five lacks of rupees per annum ; while the price fixed for the internal sale of salt, renders it considerably cheaper to the consumer, than it could formerly be retailed at, after passing through the hands of various farmers; while an uniform moderate export price, which before varied at every place of manufacture, is now calculated to promote the exportation.

The Arrack Farm, which formerly embraced the monopoly of the retail trade throughout the Island, has been abolished, and the exclusive manufacture on account of Government is discontinued. Licences are now granted for the manufacture, and for the retail trade.

A duty is likewise levied on Carriages, Horses, Slaves, Houses, and Chinese Queues, which are taxed according to their length.

The Revenues of the Custom are collected at the seaport towns, by means of officers, specially appointed for that purpose. *Port Regulations.*

Vessels from Europe, and Foreigners, among whom are included Arabs and Chinese, not trading from eastern ports, must enter at the port of Batavia.

2 G

The general import duty is fixed at ten per cent. It is proper to observe, that the duty is now only intended to be levied on articles which are actually consumed on the Island; and that the produce of the Eastern Islands not so consumed, is allowed to enter clear of duty; while the establishment of a drawback equal to the amount of import duty on all articles whatever, leaves the transit trader entirely free.

The produce of the Island exported to a foreign market, bears at present a general export duty of three per cent.

The Anchorage Duties on vessels not belonging to the Island, are fixed at the rate of ten dollars for every hundred tons burthen, the payment of which, at any port, exonerates a vessel from further payment for six months. Vessels belonging to the Island are not subject to anchorage fees, but pay an annual duty, at the rate of half a dollar a ton on registry.

The Residents at the different Courts of Bantam, Solo, and Djocjo, collect all the revenues that are given up by those Governments, such as Opium, Birds' Nests, Farms of Salt, Arrack, &c.

JUDICIAL DEPARTMENT.

Formerly there were separate Courts for investigating the conduct of the immediate European Servants of the Dutch Company, and of Europeans not included in that service; but it being resolved that justice, under the British Government, should be administered equal and alike to all classes and denominations, the judicial power of the College of Schepens was abolished, and transferred to the jurisdiction of the Courts of Justice. These Courts, composed of a President and three Members have, since the conquest, been established in each of the three principal towns, Batavia, Samarang, and Sourabaya : the jurisdiction of which extended over the European inhabitants, proceeding in civil cases, by the mode before established ; but conforming in criminal ones, as much as possible, to the laws of Great Britain ; in all cases confronting the prisoner with the evidence, and a jury being called to judge of the fact on the evidence so adduced. Every court is also open and accessible to the public, which was not the case under the old government. All tortures, and every kind of mutilation by way of punishment, have also been abolished.

To relieve the principal Courts from numerous inconsiderable causes, inferior ones, in the nature of Courts of Requests, have been established in these three towns, for the recovery of small debts.

At Batavia is also a Bench of Magistrates, who have the general superintendance of the Police of the town and the environs. A particular Magistrate is likewise appointed for the districts of Batavia, Samarang, and Sourabaya, in the former of which are dispersed several Scouts, or Sheriffs, with Peons, &c. wherever there is any considerable European population.

At Batavia, Mr. Muntinghe, the second Member of Council, is Chief Justice, and Mr. Cransen, the third Member of Council, Chief of the Police.

In the interior, the tranquillity of the country and the duties of police have been provided for, by preserving the original constitution of the villages, and continuing the superintendance and responsibility in the hands of those whose rank enables them to exert a due influ-ence and to command respect.

For the administration of justice, the duties of the Resident, as Judge and Magistrate, have been considerably extended.

In civil cases, the mode of proceeding, and the establishment of petty Courts, have been founded on the practice of the country; while the Criminal Jurisdiction of the provincial Courts has been extended to all cases in which the punishment for the crime alledged, does not amount to death.

In these Courts, which, instead of being termed Landsraad, as here-tofore, are now styled the Resident's Courts, the Panghoolo, or Chief Priest, and the Superior Jaxa, or Native Fiscal, attend to expound the law upon oath. The Bopatis or Regents, with their Patehs, are present, to aid and assist the Resident with their opinion in the course of the investigation, but they have no vote in the decision.

The Resident's Court is held at least twice in every week, in the Passerban, or Residency's public court room, for the purpose of hear-ing and trying all causes, not capital, whether civil or criminal, that occur in the Residency.

Any accused person will be admitted to bail, provided the offence be of a bailable nature; otherwise the Resident shall sign a warrant to the gaoler, to receive and hold him in custody until he shall be discharged by law.

If the crime imputed to him be murder, treason, gang robbery, or any other for which the sentence may amount to death, the Resident must commit him to prison to take his trial before the Courts of Circuit.

One member of each of the Courts of Justice has been appointed a Judge of Circuit, who will be present in each of the Residencies at least once in every three months, and as much oftener as possible.

The Koran, with the Commentaries upon it, and the ancient customs of the Island, form the general law of Java.

In the mode of proceeding, a native Jury, consisting of an intelligent foreman and four others, decide upon the fact.

The right of challenge shall belong, as in the English courts, to both the prosecutor and the prisoner. The persons composing this jury ought to be, as near as possible, on an equality of condition with the prisoner. But no one under the rank of a head of a village shall be competent to act as juryman; since persons in the very lower order cannot be supposed to possess either independence or knowledge sufficient to qualify them to execute justly the duties of the situation.

The sentence of the Resident shall be final, and be immediately carried into execution, in cases where the punishment awarded does not amount to imprisonment, or transportation for life. In the latter case, the approval of the Lieutenant Governor must be obtained; and in all cases originating in the Resident's court, an appeal shall be permitted to the Lieutenant Governor, provided notice of such intention is given on the day of trial, and conforming to certain conditions. These appeals also are limited to the space of one month from the day of trial.

It not having been heretofore usual to employ Vakeels, or native lawyers, persons of that description are not to be admitted into the Courts, but the respective parties shall plead in their own behalf; by this means litigation will be considerably reduced and discouraged.

And as it is most essential to afford easy access to justice, the Resident shall cause a box to be placed at the door of the Court, into which the petitions may be dropped; of this box he shall himself keep the key. and afford the desired redress to the injured persons. By these means. the complainant will not be dependant for a fair hearing, on the officers or servants of Government, who might, from interested, partial, or resentful motives, find means of preventing access to the Resident.

Divisions and Subdivisions.
A Regency is divided into districts, according to population, the extent of land, or other circumstances; and each district is consigned to the care of a Bopati, or native chief.

These districts again are subdivided into divisions, and a fixed station of Police assigned to each, with a competent officer, and such number of inferior Mantris, Peons, &c. as shall be deemed necessary for the execution of the various duties allotted to this office, and the due maintenance of tranquillity in the district.

The officers of divisions shall once a week, or oftener, attend at the station of Police, with their Mantris, for the purpose of enquiring into and deciding on petty offences, as inconsiderable assaults or affrays committed within their divisions; trespass, nuisance, encroachment on boundaries, and other such minor grievances of usual occurrence in villages. These, if proved, they are authorised to punish by fine, not exceeding ten rupees; one half of which shall be given to the party aggrieved, the other to be carried to the account of Government.

They are also empowered to hear and determine on all such petty civil cases as may be referred to them, provided the amount at issue exceed not the sum of twenty rupees.

Whether civil or military, they shall not, in any case, be authorized to arrest or imprison, but must summons the party to appear by the next day of sitting, when the cause shall be heard and decided on without delay. An appeal may be made, in civil cases, from the Court of the Officer of Division to that of the Bopati, at the chief town of the district.

Ten per cent. on the amount of the sentence in civil cases, is, according to the custom of the country, to be taken from the loser of the suit, to be carried to the account of Government.

The Bopati's Court is held twice a week, or oftener if necessary, at the chief town of each district; in which himself, or, in his absence, the Pateh, shall preside, assisted by the Jaxa, Panghooloo, and other appointed law officers. His authority is, however, entirely confined to civil matters, where the amount at issue is not less than twenty, nor exceeding fifty rupees. All cognizance of criminal cases, beyond that already allotted to the Officers of Divisions, being vested solely in the Court where the Resident himself presides.

An appeal, in causes originating in this Court, shall lie to that of the Resident, provided proper notice of the same is given on the day of trial, and the appeal itself be made within a week after.

The heads of villages have the care of the police in their respective villages entrusted to their charge; and for the due preservation of peace, the prevention of offences, and the discovery and arrest of offenders; they are required to be particularly careful that a sufficient night watch be regularly maintained. For this purpose they are authorized to require each of the male inhabitants to take his turn in the performance of his duty; and at any time to require the aid of all in the pursuit and apprehension of offenders, or to execute generally any of the other duties that may occur.

They are responsible for the amount of all property belonging to travellers, which may be lost within their villages, if the same shall have been placed under their charge; and they are required to take charge of all travellers' property which may be brought to them for that purpose.

The heads of villages are enjoined to look on themselves, and to act with regard to the persons under their controul, as fathers of families; to maintain, to the extent of their power, a spirit of harmony and tranquillity in the villages entrusted to them; to curb every approach to feud and litigation; and with the aid of their officers, to interpose their authority in settling, with justice and impartiality, all such petty quarrels as may arise among the inhabitants.

POPULATION AND STATE OF SOCIETY.

The entire population of the island of Java is estimated at five millions; of which, the European Colonists form comparatively a small number; the natives may be classed under the general denominations Malays. of Javanese and Malays. The latter are again subdivided into distinct classes, according to their respective nations; and in large cities, such as Batavia, they have separate campongs allotted them, under a chief of their own, who is answerable for their good conduct to the bench of Magistrates or chief of the police, in the same manner as the China captain is placed over the Chinese. All the slaves brought from Celebes,

Flores, and the other Eastern islands, are classed with the Malays. The free Malays inhabiting the coast are principally traders and navigators, as well as builders of small prows, in which business they are very expert. They are evidently of the same race with the inhabitants of the whole Eastern Archipelago, who had their origin in the colonies which poured forth from the Malayan peninsula, and extended themselves over Sumatra, Java, and the other islands. History makes mention of many bloody wars in the twelfth century, between the Malays and the Javanese King of Modjapahit, who was not only Sovereign of Java, but having possessions in Sumatra and other isles, was one of the most powerful Princes of the East. Having constrained the King of Singa-poera, Siri Iskander Shah, to retire further to the north, in the year 1253, the latter built a new capital, which he called Malacca, whence sprang the numerous colonies, which, in the reign of Sultan Mahomet Shah, who, by his marriage with a Princess, united the kingdom of Arracan to his other possessions, extended themselves and the Malay name far and wide ; being easily excited to desperate enterprizes and emigrations by their characteristic love of plunder, war, and navigation. Their language, which is the softest in Asia, little accords with their character, which certainly has not to boast of many amiable traits. They are generally indolent, but at the same time restless, vindictive. and treacherous, nor can any dependance be placed upon them. Their courage, however, cannot be called in question, and they have evinced, on numerous occasions, an utter contempt of death ; but assassination is their prevailing vice, and they would, at any time, much rather stab an enemy in the dark, than encounter him face to face. They are pas-sionately fond of gambling and cock-fighting, which last diversion

2 H

they formerly carried to such an excess, that among the poorer classes and slaves, after losing their last stake, with such articles of their master's property as they could lay their hands on, their next step frequently would be to intoxicate themselves with opium, and then run a muck, stabbing with a criss all that came in their way, till they were themselves taken or killed.

The gambling houses were, under the former Government, regularly farmed out, and produced a considerable revenue ; but since the abolition of these receptacles of depravity, by order of Lord Minto, humanity has not been so much shocked by those horrid scenes produced by the frenzy of disappointment, which were formerly so frequent, and not an instance of running a muck has occurred at Batavia since the conquest.

It may here be remarked, on the subject of the abolition of torture, introduced in criminal cases, that the opinion of the Dutch was at first against such a measure. They thought that the appalling spectacle of excruciating torments was rendered necessary, from a general idea of the natural obduracy of the Malay character. To frighten the imagination, therefore, humanity was outraged with every cruel invention ; and, instead of preventing crimes, by putting down the nurseries of vice, the gambling houses, which were the source of every evil, continued open, to feed that avarice which derived emolument from the taxes levied on them. The persons who thus encouraged a destructive passion, after indulging the deluded victims in their folly, sat as judges upon those, who, in consequence of the ruin in which they had involved themselves, had become frantic, and committed murder more out of madness than malevolence. These judges, however, having profited by the taxation of the cause, which was the impelling principle to the misery that followed, could coolly consign the unhappy criminals to a protracted death, by quartering and impaling them alive, without feeling the least emotion for the sufferings they had in fact occasioned, or any desire to put an end to the evil which led to a continuance of such atrocities. Yet it is still very difficult to root out strong prejudices and favorite practices suddenly, and the natives continue their propensity to sports of this kind ; but as they cannot indulge it in fighting cocks, they amuse themselves with the combats of other animals, as quails, and even grasshoppers.

The Malays are generally of a brown or light copper colour; the nose much flattened, and the head covered with a profusion of black hair. In their persons, the men are often very muscular, and well made. The Malay language is spoken on all the sea coasts, and is so very distinct and soft as to be called the Italian of the East. It is written in the Arabic character, and has a number of Arabic and Persian words intermixed.

But the great mass of the population consists of Javanese, who inhabit all the interior parts of the Island, and are the general cultivators of the soil. They are an exceedingly indolent race; and nothing short of positive compulsion, the want of the necessaries of life, or the prosecution of some of their favourite amusements, can rouse them from that state of apathy which is almost natural to them. Nor is this, perhaps, much to be wondered at, when the nature of their Government, which is a pure despotism, is considered. No hereditary rights, or privileges, are enjoyed by any class of people, except in some parts of the country, where grants of lands in perpetuity have been bestowed by the sovereign ; and these are strictly heritable. Some of these

Javanese.

grants have been made for religious uses, others as provisions for relatives, or rewards to the higher order of nobility. But the actual proprietary right in the soil was originally vested solely in the sovereign.
The first clearers of the soil became entitled to no more real property
in the land which had been in a manner created by their labour, than to
a claim on the state for peaceable possession, so long as they and their
heirs should punctually pay to the sovereign a due share of the produce,
and this last portion alone was that which the Government could alienate. The intermediate classes between the sovereign and the actual
cultivators, were considered as no more than the executive officers of
Government, who received the revenues of villages, or districts, only
as the gift of their lord, and depended on his will alone for their tenure.

State of Society.
The Javanese institutions, whether civil or military, recognize a
gradation of petty officers, whose titles, rank, and income, bear some
proportion to the importance and responsibility of their charge.

Adipatti is the highest title of Javanese nobility. Tumagong is the
next inferior rank, and which is borne by most of the Regents. Petty
districts are entrusted to officers styled Ingabis, or Mantris, who do
not belong to the class properly denominated the nobility, or Bopati.
The officer of superior rank, whoever he may be, is uniformly understood to possess the privilege of appointing the next immediately
under him. This prerogative is equally exercised by private persons
as by the officers of Government. The Tumagong, or other chief,
who is himself nominated by the Prince, appoints the Demang, or
Mantri-désa, and the Demang, the Bakal, who is vested with authority
over the cultivators, to whom he allots land, or deprives them of it, as
he thinks proper. He may, therefore, be considered, with respect to

the cultivators, or actual occupants, as the actual land-holder, so long as he continues in office.

The tenure of the Bakal is hardly less secure than that of the cultivator; but, from the advantages acquired by actual possession, and the capital thus accumulated, the former, generally speaking, becomes the fittest and ablest person to pay to the superior the full rent of the lands; it is, therefore, the advantage of the latter not to remove him; and thus the interest of the lord gives to his situation a certain degree of stability.

The Demang is accountable to his superior for the entire rent, receiving one-fifth of the rents of all the Bakals under him, besides enjoying a proportion of perquisites. By this plan of settlement, the interests of the body of the people are entirely at the disposal of a numerous set of chiefs, who exercised over them a gradation of arbitrary oppression, and exposed them to a variety of injuries. In fact, the people seem to exist merely for the benefit of their chiefs Without freedom, and a certainty of enjoying the fruits of their labour, the hand of industry is palsied. It has been calculated that, in some of the eastern provinces, a husbandman possessed of sufficient land to maintain two buffaloes, derives from the fruits of his tillage and labour, only one fourteenth part for himself and his family; so greedy are the Chiefs with their numerous dependants, and lazy superintendants, all of whom the cottager is obliged to feed. Notwithstanding these arbitrary exactions, the natural fertility of the soil is so great, as to make ample amends, and in general the people live very well; their food, consisting of coffee, rice, salt fish, poultry, vegetables of all sorts, and curry stuff and chilies; salt pickles of several kinds, sugar, fruit, especially the dorian. Of this last the natives are remarkably fond: and it is said to be possessed of very stimulating qualities.

On all the frequented roads, small sheds or shops are erected at convenient distances, where the above articles are supplied in great plenty, and very cheap to all travellers.

Both Malays and Javanese live in bamboo huts, divided into different apartments, sometimes plaistered with mud, and usually raised two or three feet from the ground. All the villages are surrounded by topes of cocoa-nut and other favourite fruit-trees, encircled round by a thick bamboo hedge. The head inhabitant of a Javanese village, whose office is elective, is invested by his fellow inhabitants with the general superintendance of the affairs relating to that village, whether in attending to the police, settling the minor disputes that occur within its limits, or of collecting its revenues, or more often its services. This limited form of village administration has been continued under the new regulations of the British Government, but with some restraints on the power and influence of the Regents over the lower classes of inhabitants.

The Javanese, who are better featured than the Malays, are of a light brown colour, muscular and well made. The women also have a more pleasing cast of countenance than the Malay females; and in some of the hilly tracts they are really beautiful. They generally wear a long black gown, with a cloth wrapped round to serve as a petticoat; and the men a black cotton frock, with either a cloth tied round the waist or a short pair of drawers. The higher classes are very partial to chintzes, silks, and velvets, which they are fond of ornamenting with embroidery, and in which they generally appear on all festivals and public occasions.

The professed religion of both the Malays and Javanese is Mohammedanism, but mixed with many superstitions. They seem indeed to be so very careless of its rites, that it would be difficult from common observation to ascertain the nature of their faith and worship. Few of them who are not of a religious turn, obey the laws of their Prophet in abstaining from wine, for which both high and low have a great relish, and drink it often in public.

The language both oral and written of the Javanese is quite distinct. Hence it appears that the Aborigines of the country were of a different race from their neighbours the Malays, and the many remains of the Hindoo temples and inscriptions, that have been discovered in the interior of Java, in the Emperor's Dominions, and about the ancient City of Modjapahit, seem to place it beyond a doubt that a race of Hindoos had been originally settled in the Island.

The European Colonists, Chinese, &c. principally inhabit the seaport towns along the coast.

BATAVIA AND ITS ENVIRONS.

The population at Batavia is divided into the following classes. Next to the Dutch Burghers come the Portuguese or half-casts, and other Indian Christians; next to them are the Papangars, or Mardykears, who are emancipated Slaves; the Moors and Arabs. The other classes are distinguished into the Javanese, the Baliers, Bougginese, or Buggese, Maccassars, Amboynese, Boutonneers, or Madurese, Malays, Sumbawaurese, and the Parnakan Chinese; these last are the most numerous and most useful of all the foreign adventurers settled in Java.

Classes of Inhabitants.

Enfranchised Slaves.

The Mardykers, also called Topassers, are Indians of different nations, who have obtained their freedom, and reside in the town and its vicinity. Most of them are in the country, or coasting trade, others who dwell inland, are cultivators of the soil, and bring great supplies to market. They live in good houses, have schools for the instruction of their youth in reading and writing, and the study of their religious tenets, and are altogether superior to other Indians in their domestic and social ways of life.

Arabs.

The Moors and Arabs who formerly possessed the uncontrouled commerce in these parts, till the Portuguese gained the ascendancy, have still detached Colonies in several of the principal Islands. Those who reside at Batavia and Palimbang, navigate these seas, not only in prows, but frequently freight large ships. They are a very fine, active and intelligent race of men.

Javanese.

The Javanese at Batavia, occupy two Campongs, each under a Chief of their own nation, on the right and left of the Great River. They are principally husbandmen, and cultivate the rice fields in the neighbourhood; but some of them are employed in fishing.

Baliers.

The Baliers are very numerous at Batavia, and are divided into several Campongs, under their respective overseers. They are naturally indolent, and hate working; but as they cannot indulge so much in their slothful habits at Batavia as in their own country, they are obliged to exert themselves in useful labour. The Baly Slaves are much esteemed at Batavia, being considered more trusty than others, particularly the females, who are handsome, and in the houses of the opulent, are entrusted with the superintendance of the other slaves, to whom they are superior in every good quality. The Chinese of note generally choose their wives from the Baly females. The men too, are possessed of more bravery than their neighbours, and the Dutch were accustomed to enlist many of them for soldiers.

The Buggese, a short but stout race of people, are partly from Cele- Buggese. bes, from Borneo, and other neighbouring Isles. They are a quarrel-some and revengeful race of people, distinguished also by their trea-chery and impatience of controul. But though they are furiously passionate, yet as slaves, when well treated, they have exhibited instances of great fidelity and attachment to their masters.

The same may be said of the Macassars, though in fact they are the same description of people, and come under the general term of Bug-gese. But their valour having been oftener tried, particularly in their sanguinary conflicts with the Dutch, in their early establishment at Macassar, they have ever been distinguished by that name, from the other inhabitants of Celebes; and throughout the East, the Macassars are held in the same estimation as the Swiss were formerly in Europe. The Dutch formerly used to enlist many of them for soldiers.

The Amboynese occupy a Campong on the left of the Jacatra road. Amboynese. Some of them profess the Mahommedan Religion, but many of them are Christians. They are taller and less stubborn than the Buggese, and as soldiers, acting collectively, and therefore necessarily subject to military discipline, they are preferable to all others. The Dutch cavalry and horse artillery, were composed of Amboynese, intermixed with Europeans.

Madurese.

The Madurese, from the Island of Madura, are generally an orderly and well-behaved people. They are also characteristically brave, and large bodies of them used to be taken into the Dutch service.

Malays.

The Malays in Batavia live in a separate Campong, under a Chief of their own nation. The appellation of Malay here, is confined to those who came originally from the Peninsula. They are very numerous, being chiefly fishermen and boatmen, and few of them are merchants or mechanics. They all profess the Mahommedan Religion.

Chinese.

The number of Chinese inhabitants at Batavia alone, exceeds a hundred thousand. There are also many dispersed throughout the island, in the interior as well as along the coast. They are the most industrious and useful race in the Eastern world, and in general very peaceable subjects. No fresh disturbances have taken place since their rebellion in 1742, and the bloody catastrophe which marked its suppression. Their sole object is making money, in the pursuit of which the Chinese are indefatigable, and their industry embraces every department. Without them indeed the Island of Java would be an unprofitable Colony, as in their hands are all the Manufactories, Distilleries, and Potteries. They are also the principal Traders, Smiths, Carpenters, Stone-masons, Shoemakers, Shopkeepers, Butchers, Fish-mongers, Green-grocers, and in fact, the whole retail trade of Java is in their hands. No work of any kind is done, nor any mechanical business executed, without calling in the assistance of one of the Chinese, who contract for all buildings and supplies. Under the former government they farmed all the revenues and collected the several taxes. But in this last capacity the Chinese practised so many extortions on the poorer Malays and Javanese, as naturally engendered a rooted hatred against them. It is not therefore to be wondered at, that the latter should seize every opportunity that offered, of attacking the Chinese farmer, and plundering him in turn; as was the case during the recent disturbances in the Mataram Empire. Nor did the rich Chinese experience favour or pity, when any cause of alledged delinquency was brought against him before a Magistrate, or into Court. His wealth, whether obtained fairly, or accumulated by peculation, was generally drained from him in some way or other, before he could procure his discharge, and be at liberty to renew his career, perhaps in the same line of knavery, though with more circumspection. Immense sums were formerly mulcted from the opulent Chinese, when bribery, under the pretext of pecuniary fines, was regarded as the lawful perquisite of individuals in power. Very large fortunes were amassed by these means; and the practice was considered as justified by the known depravity of the Chinese, whom the Dutch affect to hold in abhorrence on account of their dishonesty.

The Chinese Company at Batavia, comprizes the whole of the South Western suburbs, and is very extensive. Every house is a shop, and the streets being constantly crowded, exhibit a constant scene of noise and bustle. Their Captain, Oey Hingho, has several Lieutenants under him, who watch over the Police of that numerous population. As no woman is allowed to be exported from China, adventurers from that country intermarry with the Javanese and Malays, or purchase slaves for their concubines and wives, who, as well as their progeny, become completely Chinese.

Their Marriages are conducted with great ceremony, and considerable expense ; and though they have colonized in the Island for centuries back, they still retain in every respect the manners and customs of their nation, which may be greatly owing to the constant intercourse kept up with the mother country, to which the greater part return on becoming possessed of an independence, and from whence new adventurers arrive with every junk. Not less than five thousand of them came to Batavia soon after the intelligence of the capture of Java by the English had reached China.

The Chinese in Java are very fair. They dress in long silk gauze gowns, and loose pantaloons, generally white, black, or blue, with cotton stockings, and high-raised shoes, or boots ; a small black cap is fitted to their heads, which are shaven, except on the back part, where is a small tuft, having attached to it an enormous long tail, for which they pay a tax ; so that, by this capitation impost, the number of Chinese in the Island can be pretty correctly ascertained, on which account, perhaps, the continuance of it is politically expedient.

In their intercourse with Europeans, they are polite and well bred, and very quick of comprehension ; but they are great cheats ; for craft is their profession. A good Chinese workman will earn a rupee, or more, per day ; but they are seldom employed as labourers, and never as domestic servants. They live well, but grossly ; and their tables are three times a day loaded with rice, fish, curry, pork, fowls, ducks, and vegetables ; a dram of arrack being taken at each meal.

The higher ranks indulge in every luxury, and spare no expense in the pursuit of pleasure, and every worldly gratification. Edible birds' nests, to which a fancied invigorating quality has been long ascribed, and all other dainties, however dear they may be, are always found on the table of the Chinese voluptuary; and it must be confessed that, whatever be the crimes of these people, they have at least, in an eminent degree, the virtue of hospitality general among them.

Their festivals are very grand, particularly that in celebration of the New Year, and which lasts the first twenty days in February. On this occasion, the streets in the Chinese Campong are thronged with carriages and crowds of people, men, women, and children of, all countries, colour, classes, and denominations; masters and servants, mistresses and slaves, forming a motley group, parade the illuminated streets till late at night. For eight or ten days all business is at a stand, and every house is the scene of festivity. At these times, the rich and higher classes of the Chinese spread sumptuous tables, replenished with viands, and furnished with every luxury. Many of the European visitors partake of these splendid entertainments, while the master of the mansion strives, by his attention and good humour, to shew how much he is delighted with the honour done him in the company of his respected guests. Plays are exhibited on stages erected in various parts of the Campong; but these pieces, which are called here Wyangs, resemble our mountebank exhibitions. The performers, who are females, trained up to the profession, like the dancing girls of Egypt and the East, are dressed in the Chinese and Tartar habits, and some of them are very beautiful. The subjects of these exhibitions are generally taken from the history of that extraordinary nation, and usually such as give the representations of battles between the Chinese and Tartars. The dialogue is all spoken, or sung, in the Chinese language, amidst a clangor of Gongs, and other musical instruments.

Their Burials are the next great pompous exhibitions of the Chinese. These are solemnized agreeably to the rank of the deceased : that of the Oey Hingho, their Captain, being the most pompous. An immense multitude of Chinese attend on the day of interment, carrying images of men and women, representing the deceased members of the same family, with wax tapers and censers; while a numerous procession of priests, accompanied with musical instruments, precede the corpse, which is carried in a huge coffin, slung on bars, supported on the shoulders of sixteen bearers, in pairs, followed by the relations of the deceased, uttering most piercing lamentations. The cemetery of the Chinese extends over a prodigious deal of ground, on the southeast side of Batavia. Unlike the Dutch practice of placing five or six corpses in the same grave, the Chinese allot a separate sepulchre for each, over which is raised a high circular mound of earth, like a crescent, cased with stone, and ornamented according to the wealth and importance of the deceased. To these receptacles of the dust of their ancestors, the Chinese pay, as a sacred duty, an annual visit; which mournful ceremony takes place in the month of April. Stages are then erected in various parts for the priests, who deliver from them their orations in praise of the dead there deposited; and the neighbourhood of ancient Jacatra, over which their principal cemetery extends, exhibits an affecting spectacle, of multitudes of people, prostrate before the numerous tombs, which are decorated with flowers, spreading also viands and fruits as an offering, and bowing their heads in sorrow to the ground.

Laudable as this respect for their deceased friends doubtless is, it does not seem to have any effect on the moral principles of the survivors; nor can it be traced to any vital religious sentiment, uniting, as it were, the dead and the living in one bond of amity, and in the prospect of a reunion in another state. In fact, though these people have temples erected in various parts of the Island of Java, and one at Anjole, close to Batavia, the structures seem to be formed more out of compliance with custom than for any serious purpose, since religious rites are hardly ever observed in them, nor is any thing like worship practised by the people who build them. An image, with tapers burning before it, representing either a good or evil genius, or both together sometimes, is placed in every Chinese dwelling. This idol is frequently consulted by dropping two or more sticks before it, and in a variety of other ways, which the Chinese interprets according to certain rules, and thus determines the regulation of his trading concerns by lots, not very dissimilar to the divinations of the ancients, and the practice of drawing arrows still observed by the modern Arabians.

The Burgher Class comprehends what is called the Dutch Population at Batavia, but they can hardly be termed Europeans, so completely are they intermixed with the Portuguese and Malay Colonists. The same may be observed of the other great towns along the coast, and of the Dutch Settlements in general throughout the East. With very few exceptions, that which is emphatically called the Mother Land, or Mother Country, is only known to them by name; and this

Dutch Inhabitants.

is particularly the case with the Batavian women, few of whom are
Europeans by birth. Their features, and the contour of their faces,
may, indeed, indicate that origin, but their complexion, character, and
mode of life, approach nearest to those of the natives. Though fair,
they have none of that rosy tint which distinguishes the sex in Europe ;
but a pale, sickly langour overspreads their countenances. Their dress
at home, and on ordinary occasions, differs little from that of their
slaves ; but when abroad, they wear a petticoat or bodice, and a loose
flowing gown over all, called a Cabaya ; their black hair being plas-
tered back and ornamented with diamond pins, combs, and some strong
scented flowers.

After the arrival of the English, the younger ladies, and those who
mix much in society with them, adopted the fashionable habiliments
of our fair countrywomen, and in their manner as well as dress they
are improving wonderfully. The English language is also now much
taught among the youth of both sexes. It is, however, not a little
remarkable, that in such a country and population, no permanent
seminary should have been established for the instruction of youth ; so
that parents desirous of giving a liberal education to their children,
have been obliged to send them abroad for that purpose, which was of
course attended with great trouble, expense, and danger. An attempt
was made in 1745, by M. Van Imhoff, to settle a school at Batavia,
for the instruction of youth in general knowledge, but notwithstanding
the obvious utility of the measure, and the goodness of the plan, the
institution met with slender support, and in 1756 came to an end,
since which, strange to say, nothing has been done for its revival.
Public teachers of any note are not to be found in Batavia, and there-

fore, the culture of the youthful mind of either sex is, at the present day, most shamefully neglected.

The state of society, and the intercourse between the two sexes, are very different from what may be found in Europe. In a large Dutch party, it is common for the men to assemble in one room, where they smoke and drink, whilst the lady of the house entertains her female friends in another with betel, spices, and coffee. The gentlemen also assemble at a meeting called the Society, where they smoke, drink, and play at cards or billiards, every evening, from seven till nine o'clock, when they return home to a hot supper.

An elegant building for the use of that Society was recently erected, at the corner of Ryswick, over the entrance of which is inscribed, in large letters, " DE HARMONIE."

The higher circles, however, have to boast of ladies as well as gentlemen of rather superior acquirements, who are for the most part Europeans, either by birth or education. These meet frequently in convivial parties, entertaining themselves with sprightly dances and elegant suppers. But there are no places of public amusement at Batavia ; nor a single theatre of any kind, and what is still more extraordinary in such a populous capital, there is not a single assembly-room.

The Dutch have been unjustly accused of adding unnecessarily to Slaves. the evil of slavery ; but the fact is, that the imported slaves, and those who have been made free, with their progeny, are the only domestic servants that can be procured. The Javanese are naturally too indolent for employment, and they have besides an unconquerable aversion to

2 K

servitude in families, in which dislike the Chinese participate with still stronger feelings of repugnance.

In the selection of female slaves for the respective duties of the house, great attention is paid to their personal appearance and musical accomplishments, as well as to those qualifications, which might seem to be their principal recommendation. Here the slaves are valued for their beauty, their skill in playing on the harp, and their melodious voices. This peculiarity of Asiatic luxury is carried to such a height, that in some of the houses of the more opulent Europeans, as well as of the wealthy natives, some dozens of these enchanting female slaves may be found, as if the owners thought of realizing the promise of the Mahommedan paradise in this world.

The condition of the slaves in Java is far from being uncomfortable; they are well fed and clothed, and by no means hard worked or severely treated, except perhaps where they are made to experience the resentment of female jealousy; which passion is not confined to the European ladies, as many instances are mentioned of some favoured slaves having taken revenge on their masters for their inconstancy, by different kinds and degrees of poison.

Since the Conquest of Java, the act of the British Legislature for the Abolition of the Slave Trade, has been published and enforced in these seas; in consequence of which, several vessels conveying slaves have been seized by our cruizers, and this has not a little conduced to enhance the value of those at present in the Island.

The City and Environs.

The idea of unhealthiness has become so completely associated with the name of Batavia, as to produce an unfavourable impression against the whole of Java. But while the truth of the first must be admitted to the fullest extent, the injustice of the latter imputation may be proved by many incontrovertible facts. The causes of the unhealthiness of Batavia are so generally known, as to render any minute disquisition on the subject wholly unnecessary.

A town so near the equator, surrounded on all sides by a nearly stagnant ditch ; every street intersected with canals, mostly bordered by trees, into which every thing offensive is thrown to find its way into the common rivers, that have scarcely any current; with a country which is for miles round a complete sheet of tope and rice fields ; ought not to excite any astonishment, when it is found that fevers are prevalent; and that an invitation to the festive board, is often followed in a few days by another, to assist at the mournful ceremony of paying the last funeral obsequies to the remains of one of the departed guests. Death's shafts fly thickest at the breaking up of the Monsoons, which is the most sickly period of the year. Then

> " Gaily carousing,
> " Calling for all the joys beneath the moon,
> " Next night, Death bids them sup
> " With their progenitors—He drops his mask,
> " Frowns out at full,—they start, despair, expire!"

But in no country is the intelligence of the decease of a near friend or relation received with less surprise or concern ; which indeed is naturally accounted for by the rapid succession of scenes of mortality at that sickly period, when every day presents to the view a long line of funeral processions. But the melancholy train is generally beheld with indifference, on account of its frequency; and even the sable mourners commonly smoke their segars or pipes as they move along, with all the unconcern imaginable, though they are paid to mimick sorrow!

Some good has been recently done by reducing the breadth of the canals, and thereby producing a greater depth of water, with more current to carry off the filth.

The town has certainly a fine appearance, and contains many substantial houses, which, in their internal or external appearance or construction, may lay claim to elegance, but in their economy, few come up to what we understand by comfort. The streets are broad, with canals in the middle, on each side of which is a gravelled road for the use of carriages, &c. and on the side next to the houses is a pavement six feet in width, for foot passengers. Rows of trees run along the sides of the canal, and the edge of each foot-path, consisting principally of the Inophyllum and Calaba, the Canary Nut-tree, and the Guettarda Speciosa, with its odoriferous flowers. The canals, which have numerous bridges over them, are generally of the same breadth as the carriage roads. The city, however, is now much deserted, and all the wealthy inhabitants live in the environs, principally on two roads leading to Weltervreeden; the one East, called the Jacatra road, the other West, through Molenvliet and Ryswick. These two elegant roads are planted with shady trees, and exhibit all along a number of very handsome houses, with beautiful gardens or plantations round them, thus forming a very agreeable excursion of about six miles, which therefore attracts much genteel company every evening, who ride or drive hither for their relaxation and amusement. Numerous country houses adorn the environs of Batavia; extending to the eastward as far as Chillingchng, and to the westward as far as Tangerang, which is the boundary of the kingdom of Bantam; whilst southwards from Batavia, they are scattered over a distance of forty or fifty miles inland.

The fortifications of the capital were all destroyed, and mostly pulled down before our arrival. General Daendels directed the demolition of the ramparts, with a view of rendering the city more healthy, by a freer circulation of air; and with the serviceable materials he built the new cantonment of Weltervreeden. The great church of Batavia, built in 1760, west of the Town House, was also pulled down, in consequence of its foundation having given way. The new Lutheran church, near the Castle, is the only one where the Protestant part of the community enjoy the benefit of divine service. The Portuguese church, which stands at the corner of the Jacatra road, is resorted to by most of the native Christians. The Castle at Batavia is very spacious, and contains a number of buildings and extensive warehouses; in the construction of which, prodigious labour and expense must have been incurred. Such, however, was the unhealthiness of the place to the troops, that they were withdrawn, and the spot converted into a depot for naval and military stores, magazines of spices, and other valuable articles, which were destroyed at our landing, by the order of General Janssens.

The hospital between Newport and Diestport, and mostly all other public buildings in the town, and at the wharf, being no longer used for Government purposes, have been sold, and are now warehouses for individuals.

The works erected on the island of Onrust, for building or repairing ships of all sizes, were once the astonishment of every beholder, surpassing in variety, quickness, and facility of operation, any thing of the kind in almost every part of the world. But these works were all destroyed by the naval armament under Sir Edward Pellew; and the want of such an establishment is now much felt in these seas. There are, indeed, still several places for laying down smaller vessels; and every town and fort along the north coast of Java has conveniences of that kind. But it would be very difficult to find the means of building or even repairing any vessels of a very large size. At Onrust, ships were hove down by cranes, erected upon the wharfs, when they required repairs. This little Island had a strong fortress, a handsome church, and spacious warehouses; being, therefore, the great Marine depot, it was crowded with inhabitants, and, in former times, was celebrated even in the poetical works of the Dutch, as one of the wonders of human art and enterprize in the eastern world.

On Kuiper, or Cooper's Island, about half a mile south of Onrust, were numerous warehouses, containing the goods intended to be sent to Europe, and two cranes for loading and clearing ships. At Purmerend, about a mile S. E. of Onrust, was an hospital for infectious and incurable disorders.

Edam, twenty-four miles N. E. from Onrust, had a flag-staff for directing ships from the north and east; and there was another at Middleburg, twelve miles N. W. from Onrust, for ships approaching from the westward. But all these places are now desolate and uninhabited. These, and numerous other little islands, which defend the entrance of the Bay of Batavia from the violence of the sea in stormy weather, render it not only the finest but also one of the safest harbours in the world. It has been observed as a remarkable circumstance, that not a single ship belonging to the Dutch company has been lost in this Bay ever since they founded here, two centuries ago, the emporium of their extended trade, and on its marshy shores erected the proud seat of all their eastern dominions. The Observatory of Batavia is in latitude 6 degrees 9 minutes S., and longitude 106 degrees 51¼ minutes E., by the actual astronomical observations of Johann Mauritz Mohr; and this may be considered as very correct, being the result of many observations of Jupiter's Satellites, taken during his residence at this place.

The principal rivers are the great Jacatra or Batavia river, which Rivers. has its rise in the Blue Mountains, and encircles the town by several branches and canals connected with it.   Ankee river rises in the Salack mountains, as also does the Tangerang, which is a very considerable river. The Slokan is an artificial cut, which unites the smaller streamlets in the mountains above Buitenzorg, and serves to water the rice fields in the plains south-east of Batavia. Besides these, numerous other streams and rivulets intersect the district of Batavia in all directions; and two large canals to the east and west, navigable for large boats, or prows, of considerable burden, connect the communication between the town and the two large villages of Tangerang and Tjilinching, whence large supplies are drawn for the use of the capital and its environs. On the banks of the rivers Ankee and Anjole, which terminate the suburbs to the west and the east, strong redoubts and forts were formerly erected, but they are now all in ruins, as well as the water castle at the entrance, and the numerous other batteries in the old line of defence round Batavia.

Roads.   The roads in the environs, which are very numerous, are shaded with trees, and, for the most part, quite straight, passing over the canals on bamboo bridges, and over the larger rivers and streams on bridges with stone arches, or strong timber props, resting on a stone foundation. Besides the several lesser roads, intersecting one another in a variety of directions, with beautiful villas interspersed in the shady topes; a new one, commenced by General Daendels, and which has since been carried on by the British Government, runs due east through rice fields and tope, for many miles from Batavia, through the country of Crawang, at which place it will join the great Military Road, which crosses the mountains from Buitenzorg to the eastern extremity of the Island. Two miles and a half south of Batavia, is Weltervreeden, and the two elegant roads, or rather streets of sumptuous houses, leading to it, that of Jacatra and Molenvliet, have been already mentioned. On the Jacatra road, besides a number of other elegant buildings, that of Goonong Sarie, the town residence of the late Dutch Governor, is situated. It is no longer public property, having been lately sold with other buildings; but it continues to be used as the Grand Assembly Room on great occasions, being hired by Government at a stated rent. The buildings and grounds belonging to it are spacious. To the east, the eye is gratified by fertile plains, with luxuriant rice fields, exhibiting all that is cheering and pleasant for the comfort of human life; while, on the opposite side, a dismal contrast presents itself, in the vast cemetry, filled with Chinese sepulchres, stretching to a great and melancholy extent. A Free

Mason's Lodge, which is pretty generally frequented, stands within the precincts of ancient Jacatra. Near this, a cross road runs past the Chinese burying-ground into the Molenvliet road, where the Council hold their meetings, in a large building, which also contains the Treasury, and all other public offices, but has nothing favourable to recommend it, either for pleasantness of situation or salubrity of air. In the vestibule are portraits of all the Dutch Governors, to which that of Lord Minto has been lately added. Here is also the Printing-office, being the only press in this large and populous country. Molenvliet House is situated about midway between Batavia and Weltervreeden. At Ryswyck are good barracks, and pleasant officers' quarters for both infantry and cavalry. Turning to the left, the road conducts to Weltervreeden, and is divided in the middle by the principal canal, which conveys the great body of water from the Jacatra river by Molenvliet to Batavia. Continuing straight from Ryswyck, the road leads on the east, past the Champ de Mars; and on the west side, by the overstocked Dutch burying-ground. Of this antique garden of death, which is surrounded by a wall, with palisades, it may be truly said, that its soil is almost become hard with human bones.

The road then continues to the fertile fields of elevated Tanabang, about four miles from Batavia; here a market is held twice a week, to which an immense concourse of people resort from all parts of the surrounding country, and hence the inhabitants of Batavia procure most of their supplies.

Weekly bazars are held at almost every principal place throughout each district, to which the produce of the vicinage is brought in great

quantities, and sold or bartered for other articles under certain regulations. There is something very curious in the manner of conducting
the fish market at Batavia, all fishermen being obliged to bring their
fish thither between the hours of eleven and twelve o'clock every day,
when crowds of people attend, and the neighbouring streets are
thronged with carriages; for, at Batavia, few people are inclined to
walk, and in the streets, as well as in the numerous roads and alleys in
the environs, a constant press of coaches is seen from morning till night.

The fish is sold by public auction to the retailers, and the amount,
after deducting the Vendee Office duties, is paid to the fishermen, who
return directly to renew their labours for similar earnings on the next
day. The retailers, principally Chinese, then spread their purchased
stock out on their several benches in the market, and for this licence
another duty must be paid.

The visitors from the town and country walk leisurely round, and
make such purchases as suit their inclinations and circumstances; and
the concourse of people of all descriptions, male and female, in their
various attire, who compose this fantastic show, is highly amusing.
Here also are supplied with fish the lesser retail shops, which are dispersed about the town and country for many miles round.

WELTERVREEDEN, is a pleasant and very healthy cantonment, and
the Head Quarters of the army. It was chosen as a military station by
the Dutch Government, and is far preferable to any other place in the
neighbourhood of the capital. General Daendels intended to have removed to this place all the public offices, both civil and military; thus,
making this desirable spot the seat of Government, for which purpose,

a very large building, with numerous appendages, had been begun by him, and it was partly roofed in before our arrival, as were also several ranges of excellent barracks, some of which have been finished, and are occupied by our troops. Were the whole of them completed agreeable to the original plan, and the commendable design carried into execution, of draining the Champ de Mars, and uniting it with the Cantonment by a bridge over the river, in front of the new government house, Weltervreeden would be rendered a beautiful and a most excellent military station. The officers' quarters are in general very good, as is also the general hospital, separated from the Cantonment by the river. A large old building, formerly used as a government house, where the council sometimes met, is now converted into a Commissariat Depot. Hence a fine avenue leads through the new cantonment to the China bazar. Near to this has been erected a new Catholic chapel. Half a mile farther, a cross road leads to Tanabang; and here the action of the 10th of August took place, in which the British advance, under Colonel Gillespie, routed the Elite of the French army, who were strongly posted, and drove them within the works of Cornelis. At about 6 pals *, commences the front line of the lately-fortified camp of Cornelis, of which there are now few traces, the works having been all razed, and the natural fertility of the soil and quick vegetation so general in Java, has spread a wide jungle over this field of glory, where British valour wrested the last and most valuable colony out of the usurping hands of French Despotism.

* A Dutch measurement—17 pals are equal to 16 English miles.

FROM BATAVIA TO THE WESTWARD.

Kingdom of
Bantam.

Proceeding westward from Batavia, the road passes through the suburbs, and after leaving Ankee, and a number of old Dutch villas interspersed on both sides for near fifteen miles, but which are now mostly deserted, it arrives at the large Campong or village of Tangerang. This is a considerable place, and before the neighbouring part of the Bantam country was ceded to the Dutch, it was a large military frontier station ; but the fort, barracks, &c. are now nearly in ruins. The foundation of a new one was laid by General Daendels, to command the passage of the river and the high road to Batavia, on the supposition probably, that Bantam would be the landing-place of an English Expedition.

A large weekly bazar is held here, to which the produce of the adjacent country is brought, and thence carried to Batavia, by means of a canal which communicates with the river Tjidanee, by a fine sluice, and then runs parallel to the road the whole way to Batavia. Near this sluice and bridge is a beautiful villa, the late residence of General Lutzow. The country is well cultivated, interspersed with several seats or Dutch farms, producing rice, and the greatest part of the grass for the consumption of the horses in town. As this article is in great demand, and uncommonly quick in its growth, it is of course much cultivated and very profitable.

The river Tjidanee which is broad, and in the rainy season very rapid, is crossed here. It was formerly the boundary between the kingdom of Bantam and that of Jacatra, and from the name of the frontier post, has obtained the name of Tangerang river.

From Tangerang, for the distance of sixteen miles, the country is high and open, cultivated principally with rice and cocoa-nut topes ; but the villages are not numerous. The road then enters a thick jungle and forest, infested by tigers, but having hardly any traces of cultivation, and few human inhabitants, excepting the small villages of Tjikandee and Oonderandy, both on the banks of large rivers, till within seven miles of Ceram, when a country rich in rice fields, and studded with villages, surrounded with fruit-trees, on a sudden opens to the view, and continues to the latter place, which is the present abode of the Resident at the Court of Bantam, from whence it is distant nearly eight miles.

Ceram is a tolerably large village, and is defended by a block-house, 56 miles West from Batavia, which serves also as a barrack for the troops stationed in this district. The country for several miles round appears to be in a high state of cultivation. The road runs from Ceram through rice fields and thick topes to

BANTAM—which once rich and flourishing city, has nothing now but 61 miles West from Batavia, ruins to exhibit, as the sad memorial of departed greatness. The fortifications, both European and Native ; Fort Spielwyck, as well as the Sultan's Fort, are levelled with the ground, and what few European habitations have not been pulled down, are falling fast into decay, and totally deserted. Situated on a low swampy beach, surrounded by jungle, and intersected with stagnant streams, it ought not to excite wonder that the climate should prove so deleterious to European constitutions, and cause the abandonment of the place. Of a recent embassy, consisting of nearly fifty persons, which was sent from Batavia in 1804, on the ceremony of the Installation of a new Sultan, not above eight or ten survived. Even the natives are not proof against the Marsh Fever; and the present Sultan was, at this time of our visit, suffering severely from its effects. He is a young man, and were any one to indulge the expectation of finding here a Court answerable to the dignified title of a Sultan, he would at his arrival be sadly disappointed, and neither fancy himself in a Palace, nor in the presence of a Sovereign.

Bantam Bay is about two leagues and a half S. E. from St. Nicholas Point, which is in lat. 5 deg. 52 min. S. long. 106 deg. 2 min. E., or fifty miles West from Batavia by the chronometer. The Bay is extensive, and contains several Islands, of which Pulo Panjang, a long flat spot, covered with trees, in the West part of the entrance, is the largest. A fine river, navigable for large prows, flows through the city, and joins the bay close to Fort Spielwyk. Formerly Bantam was a free port, and open to the commerce of all nations. The trade, however, was monopolized by the Dutch, in the reign of Sultan Agon, in the year 1683, and they erected Fort Spielwyk to shut out all other merchants. This naturally excited great discontent, and increased the hatred of the people, who were always the bitter enemies of the Dutch; but the struggles of the natives only served to rivet the chains of their vassalage, and in 1742 they fell completely under the yoke of their foreign oppressors. They murmured indeed, and were still refractory, but the Dutch Fort, commanding the whole town, kept them effectually in bonds. Of the commerce carried on here, the Pepper trade is the most considerable, and to this the country of the Lampoons, on the opposite coast of Sumatra, which was formerly tributary to Bantam, contributed largely.

The attention of our Government was called to this kingdom by its troubled state, and the restless ambition of Pangarang Achmet, who, after being long in arms against the Dutch, and presuming on the services rendered at various times to our ships when cruizing off this part of the coast, now took upon him the dominion of the country, to the exclusion of the lawful heir. Our interference, therefore, having become necessary to put an end to the usurpation, the turbulent Achmet was made prisoner, and sent to Prince of Wales's Island; while the person whose rights had been so unjustly seized was put in possession of his territories, and placed on the Musnud without any disturbance.

Since that period, the Sultan, from apathy, and labouring under disease, as already mentioned, has wholly resigned the government of Bantam, and voluntarily retired on a pension allowed him by the British Government, which has taken into its own hands the administration of the kingdom. Subsequent to the arrangement with the Sultan, for taking the immediate management of the country into the hands of Government, a land rental was introduced; and the territorial revenues of the residency under the present arrangements, amount to the sum of 100,000 rupees.

Continuing from Ceram, the road passes through Tjiligon to Marack Bay, a distance of eighteen miles. The country, which has many declivities, is tolerably well cultivated with rice, cotton, and catjan. Approaching the sea, the hills narrowly inclose the site of Fort Marak, and its Bay, which is formed by this promontory, and an

74 miles west from Batavia.

elevated island N.W., on which batteries were to have been erected to strengthen the defences on the main land. But its extreme unhealthiness swept off thousands of the labourers and most of the soldiers stationed here likewise fell a sacrifice to the projects of General Daendels. To this mortality it is to be attributed that the fortifications, now a heap of ruins, were left unfinished by the late Dutch Government, and that the intention of making this Bay to the west what Sourabaya is to the east, was obliged to be abandoned. Nearly a hundred pieces of cannon were, at the time of our visit, lying buried in the high grass, many of them as overturned by a boat's crew from his Majesty's ship Minden, who gallantly stormed the batteries, though defended by two hundred men, a short time before the arrival of the expedition. The anchorage is not very good, and consists mostly of coral bottom. Here, as in many other places in Java, it was evinced that, however ignorant and passive a people may be, oppression will drive them to resistance. The system of feudal service was most oppressive. Independently of demands for the public service, which from the facility of making the requisition, were more unlimited than would otherwise have happened, every public officer deemed it fair to require the service of as many men as he found convenient. The native chiefs followed the same system, and thus there could be no actual check on the part of Government.

Such was the severity of the labour required from the Bantamese in the erection of works, making roads, &c. that these people being obliged to leave their own lands untilled, numbers of them sought refuge in the woods and in the western extremity of the island, which to this day remains entirely unknown to us, waging from thence a destructive and successful warfare. These emigrations and incessant troubles occasioned by the hard treatment to which the inhabitants were subjected, are the cause that the once-flourishing kingdom of Bantam is now reduced nearly to a desert. It is not to be wondered at, therefore, that the authors of so much misery should be detested by them; and to this day their distrust of the Europeans is very great, and this spirit is artfully kept up by the priests. As the ignorance of the lower classes of the Javanese, and their implicit obedience to the orders of their chiefs, render them liable to be influenced on any occasion by their priests, it has been in contemplation to endeavour to ascertain the situation of those who possess any influence in the districts under our Government, and to secure their attachment, by granting them a certain allowance from Government, to be continued during good behaviour. Still all the endeavours of the British resident to conciliate the confidence of the mass of the people, have been hitherto unavailing. Nor can it be expected that the state of almost constant warfare they were in with the Dutch, should incline the Bantamese very favourably towards Europeans in general; but the more equitable administration, of which the British Government has laid the foundation, will, it is to be hoped, in a short period, produce more conciliatory habits, and restore that distracted country to tranquillity and confidence.

Anjier, in latitude 6 degrees, $3\frac{1}{2}$ minutes South, about two leagues to the Eastward of the Fourth point, is situated in a bay formed by that point and the point of Marak bay. It has a good block-house with cannon, and excellent quarters for a proportionate garrison, encircled by a mud parapet and wet ditch. It is at present far from healthy, 78 miles West of Batavia.

which may be owing to the surrounding jungle, and its stagnant ditch, as well as a small river, which deposits the filth thrown into it, on one of the sides of the fort. The removal of those causes would make it an eligible military, as well as naval depot, it being our Westernmost post on the island, and conveniently situated for watering as well as supplying refreshments to all ships sailing through the Straits of Sunda. A fine streamlet of excellent water, which flows from the mountains, might with little expense be conveyed by an aqueduct into boats lying at anchor. This place is now generally the rendezvous of the homeward and outward bound China fleet, as it is considered one of the healthiest parts of the coast, and affords very good anchorage. The village here is large and populous, and well stocked with poultry, &c.; buffaloes are also easily procured, and plenty of turtle. Fruits and vegetables would also abound were encouragement given for their cultivation. Towards the interior, the country rises gradually and is very beautiful. Nothing indeed seems wanting but an adequate population to make this extensive district one of the finest and most productive in Java.

From Anjier to Tjiringhin, a distance of 25 miles, the road runs near to the beach over a partly-woody country, across many small rivers and inlets from the sea, and passing through several large fishing villages. At intervals near the hills, which in many parts run close to the beach, much rice culture is seen. The shore, with the exception of a few fine bays, is rocky, chiefly coral, and much indented.

103 miles west from Batavia.

Tjeringhin, is a considerable fishing village, and was formerly a military post with a block-house, which was burnt by our ships of war. It is situated at the mouth of a river, which is navigable a long way up, for small prows affording a ready conveyance for the rich products of a country South East of this, the finest and best cultivated district of any in Java. For about twenty miles farther west, the road continues along the sea-coast to Tjibonger, the favourite haunt of insurgents, who, from their numbers, frequently render detachments from the military necessary to disperse them, as happened not long since. A formidable stand was made here by the refractory Bantamese against Marshal Daendels, a few years ago in a small fort; the parapet of which being composed of tiers of cocoa nut trees, was from their elasticity impenetrable to balls; and when a storm was ordered, the besieged quietly walked off in the night, and found a secure refuge in the neighbouring woods and the Western extremity of the island, where no European had ever penetrated, and of which consequently nothing is known.

Leaving the sea-coast, the road takes a South East direction from Tjiringhin inland, and the country rises considerably towards the hills with occasional declivities. This is an extremely beautiful and well-cultivated tract, with a numerous population scattered in small villages at short intervals; and luxuriantly surrounded by topes of cocoa nut and other fruit trees.

Near Kuddo Helud, about ten miles, the road runs along the foot of the high mountain Poelassarie, which was once a volcano, and still emits smoke. Proceeding further, the country rises still higher, after which a fine and nearly champaign country, interspersed with numerous villages, with some irregular declivities between the hills of Poelassarie and Carang, which furnish a thousand rills for the culture of the fertile ridges of the sloping grounds, presents a beautiful appearance. Here, on turning round, and looking back to view the extensive prospect which the height we had gained enabled us to contemplate, the eye was gratified by one of the noblest sights that can charm the admirer of picturesque beauty. The day was now declining, and before us lay stretched the verdant and romantic country over which we had just passed, sloping gradually towards the sea; while, as it were, in the back-ground of this delightful picture, the rays of the sun, just setting in the ocean, gilded the tops of the distant isles in the Straits of Sunda; and the gently-diminishing splendour, spreading a fiery veil over the distant horizon, terminated the prospect.

The same fertility and beautiful scenery continues fifteen miles further, to Pondok Gelang, distant from Tjiringhin twenty-five miles to the south-east. This is a fine elevated post, and still exhibits a ruinous parapet and ditch, by which it is surrounded; and which would form an eligible military station for the troops serving in the Bantam country, being situated in the midst of a populous, rich, and healthy district, commanding a ready communication with Ceram, Tjiringhin, Bantam, Batavia, and Buitenzorg. Continuing from hence, we passed through an equally productive country, and over a range of small hills, for about ten miles, when a thick jungle, where the tiger and rhinoceros divide the command, commences, covering a low range of hills. Little cultivation and no villages are to be seen from the road, which the inhabitants seem purposely to avoid; but several of them are interspersed at different distances in the jungle, which appears nearly impenetrable. The villagers communicate with one another by means of very intricate path-ways, only known to themselves, which makes this tract a secure refuge for the turbulent and discontented, and a very difficult one for the passage of troops.

In the heart of this jungle, a refractory chieftain, inhabiting a village very near some thatched roofs, where darkness had obliged us to take up our abode for the night, menaced our destruction in the night, which, from our small number, being only three Europeans and some black servants, without any guard, he might have easily accomplished. But being perhaps fearful that such a step would lead to a premature discovery of the more sanguinary plot which he was then contriving, he left us undisturbed to continue our course through the wilderness early the next morning. This chief, with fifty of his gang, were afterwards seized and transported; it being discovered that he had at his command ten thousand men ready at a signal to rush on the neighbouring districts, with the view of plundering and murdering the inhabitants. After proceeding about thirty miles through this dreary jungle, the road becomes more and more difficult, passing over numerous ravines, and the two considerable rivers of Oondarandy and Tjicandee, which are navigable thus far for small prows. The road then generally declines, till within a few miles of Tjisingha, where it enters a more open and better cultivated country.

Tjisingha, which is about thirty-five miles from Pondok Gelang, is a very fine Dutch farm, belonging to Mr. Reintz. It is agreeably situated on the river Tjidorean, which, in the rains is very rapid, and scarcely passable. A road leads from hence through Tangerang to Batavia. After crossing the above river, and still continuing in a south-east direction, our road passed over a low chain of hills, covered mostly with jungle, and divided by a number of rivulets, with steep banks; so that this tract is rendered impracticable to carriages, and difficult even to horses.

At a distance of about ten miles the road turns due East to Sading, another Dutch farm belonging to Mr. Moatman, which is situated on a fine river, and nearly surrounded by hills, some of which produce the edible bird-nests. Continuing on to Tjiampion, about seven miles further, we had to cross the rivers Tjikanakee and Tjiantan, and passed through a country high and more open with better cultivation. Here is another Dutch farm, the property of Mr. Rymsdyck, with a large bazar; and several hills belonging to it containing also the edible bird-nests. It is astonishing what an immense revenue is produced by a single rock, the caverns of which are frequented by the little grey swallows; for the nests in some of them clear from twenty to forty thousand Spanish dollars annually, on a moderate computation.

The Dutch farmers who possess rocks of this kind on their estates, are therefore very careful of them, and watch them closely to prevent the Chinese or others from privately stealing the nests; they are also very particular in preventing the discharge of fire arms near the spots, for fear of frightening away the birds. These little swallows abound chiefly among the hilly tracts, invited thither by the insects which hover over the stagnated pools. Their nests are constructed in regular rows, adhering to the sides of the cavern, and to each other. The whiter and more transparent the viscous matter is that cements the fine filaments of which the nests are composed, the more valuable are they reckoned, and they always fetch a very extraordinary price. A couple of eggs only are laid in each nest, which are hatched in about a fortnight, and the proper time for taking them is after the young ones are fledged. The business of taking these nests is generally repeated about three times a year, and is attended with much danger ; many serious accidents having often happened. The superstition of the people usually employed in the work, leads them to make many vows and sacrifices with the view of propitiating the demons, who are supposed to dwell in the caverns and dark recesses of the mountains.

After passing the river Tjidanee, near Tjiampion, the road passes through a country high and well cultivated ; and joins at a few miles distance the great Western road, which runs from Tangerang to Buitenzorg. The distance from Tjiringhin, where we left the coast to Buitenzorg, by the route described, is one hundred and four miles.

FROM BATAVIA TO THE EASTWARD.

Proceeding from Batavia, on the new Eastern road towards Buitenzorg, every advantage is presented for quick and convenient travelling. This excellent road, which is kept in the best repair, with regular post stages at every five or six miles, greatly to the public convenience, extended till very lately as far as Kalatigus, a distance of nearly seven hundred miles East of Batavia. But the relays of post-horses, stationed between Buitenzorg and Samarang, have recently been done away with, and consequently the facility of passing through the Regencies does not now exist.

After passing through Weltervreeden and Cornelis, and by several elegant country-seats, farms, and villages, enveloped in topes of cocoa-nut and fruit-trees, the road breaks through the mass of tope which encircles Batavia, and enters on a more open and more elevated country. In this neighbourhood, between Campong, Macassar, and

Route to Samarang.

Tanjang Oost, the difference of climate is very sensible, though the distance is not more than twelve miles from Batavia. Several of our officers have temporary villas here, which being situated near Welter-vreeden, they can easily pass backwards and forwards daily, and thus their health derives essential benefit from the change of air and exercise.

About seven miles farther, at Tjimangis, which is another Dutch farm, temporary barracks have been erected on a high, and agreeable situation, for the occasional accommodation of the military details during the dry season, to practice field manœuvres. The temporary removal of the European troops from Weltervreeden to this place, after the breaking up of the Monsoons, when fevers are so prevalent in the low lands, would be attended with the most beneficial effects in preserving the health of the soldiers. Such a measure would also prove advantageous with regard to the military exercises, and particularly the artillery practice, which could be carried on here at such times, not less for the good of the service, than for the welfare of individuals. A fine hospital for convalescents, with every convenience, delightfully situated on the borders of a beautiful lake is belonging to it, and the country around is extremely pleasant. Being situated half-way between the coasts and the hills, the climate partakes of the advantages of the land and sea breezes, with occasionally cool refreshing showers, without being deluged by the rains from the mountains, as is the case at Buitenzorg *.

* Possessed of these advantages, it is to be regretted that this post should have so long remained unoccupied; and that any trivial economy should suffer these buildings to go to decay, which might be so profitably employed for the general good.

Leaving Tjimangies, the road passes by Tjibinong, which is another of Mr. Rymsdyk's farms, and by Tjiloar, distant thirty-one miles from Batavia. This last is a very pretty place, and was for some time the country residence of Major General Gillespie. It was built by the late Mr. Tantzie, who had another very pleasant villa and farm at Soucarajah, three miles from hence. Tjiloar had a large-sized brig, full rigged, and mounting guns, sailing on an elevated tank or lake made by Mr. Tantzie, and being seen a long way off, the traveller is very agreeably surprized on first beholding this vessel under sail, apparently moving through the surrounding rice fields.

The house at Soucarajah, which is situated in the midst of a large tank on stone pillars, is a very beautiful place. On the North side is the entrance, over a long passage on pillars, with a drawbridge; and on the South side a beautiful avenue is presented, laved by a crystal stream, which, covering the whole breadth of the avenue like a mirror, glides gently down on the banks of the tank, and flows into the lake close to the house.

Half-way between Tjiloar and Buitenzorg, the road leads over the great river. A bamboo raft is used for crossing the carriages and horses over, without the necessity of quitting the carriage or taking out the horses; the float being fastened to the sides of the river by a strong cord or bamboo-twist; one man, by pulling towards the one or the other end, easily moves it across, and the carriage and horses pass on without delay or trouble. Most of the large rivers in Java are crossed in this manner; but others which are more rapid and broad, or much swoln by the rains in the monsoon, are crossed on a bamboo raft fixed on light boats like a flying-bridge, either by hauling or rowing,

2 N

carrying over carriages, horses, artillery, and other articles safely and expeditiously.

36 miles
South from
Batavia.

Buitenzorg, which signifies in Dutch, rural care, is the country-seat of the Head of the Java Government. Being situated at the foot of the Blue Mountains, the climate is very healthy and cool; but to debilitated constitutions, the rain which falls almost every evening, renders this place far from salutary. The principal building has a handsome appearance and is very spacious: the village also is large, with a good bazar, besides several other houses, barracks, stables, &c. The country round is naturally very strong, intersected by ravines and two considerable rivers; in the space between which last, the French had erected numerous batteries to defend every possible approach to the place; but these are now going to decay. The road runs from hence South East, through a hilly but finely cultivated country, and passes several very agreeable country residencies and farms. At Pondokgedee is one beautifully situated, belonging to Mr. Engelhardt, formerly Governor of Samarang, and opposite to it is another farm of Mr. Rymsdyk. Close to this, on the top of a high hill, is a new farm of the late Mr. Tantzie, which overlooks the entire plain of the kingdom of Jacatra, and in clear weather the shipping in the bay of Batavia may be distinguished from thence.

The whole country, after quitting the topes of Batavia, is open, and rises gradually towards the mountains with alternate hill and dale, the lower parts being cultivated with rice, and the higher with pulse, katjan, and cotton. Much however is allotted to pasture for cows, and a great part is overrun with jungle, owing to a scarcity of population. For this deficiency many reasons might be assigned. One of the principal is the constant compulsion to labour on all public buildings, roads, canals, &c. particularly during the Government of General Daendels, when so many of these works were undertaken. Another cause of the scanty population undoubtedly is, the small proportion of Sawah, or rice land, which the inhabitants greatly prefer to all other cultivation. When it is considered also that the whole of those lands from Batavia to Tjicerora, as far as the interior of the mountains, and for many miles in all other directions, belong to a few Dutch gentlemen, no wonder can be made at the scarcity of population, and the existence of so many uncultivated districts. The high demand for bird-nests, and the wealth thence accruing to the few individuals who possess the immense tracts where they are found, cannot fail also to draw the attention of the landed proprietors from the improvement of their estates, and to repress that spirit of useful industry which properly exerted and encouraged, would be beneficial to the natives, and advantageous to the colony in produce and population.

The distress which the poor in Batavia often experience in times of dearth, when contrary winds delay the arrival of vessels with supplies of rice from the eastern districts, thereby raising that article from five, six, to seven hundred per cent. above the standard price, affects not the rich landlords, who might prevent, or at least lessen these evils, by grants to encourage the culture of waste lands, or by adopting such improvements as would in a short time abundantly supply the whole population in Batavia, and the neighbourhood. That the soil is in general capable of such improvement, has been evinced in the farms of the late Mr. Tantzie; by whose active exertions large tracts of

barren heath were converted, in a few years, into the most flourishing rice fields. In the hilly tracts, the soil is extremely fertile, and
esteemed superior to what is to be found in other parts.

50 miles S.
from Batavia.

Near Tjiceroa, the last of Mr. Rymsdyk's farms, the steep ascent of
the road commences, and the use of buffaloes becomes indispensible.
Two or more of these powerful animals are put before the horses, and
together draw the carriage up without any danger; though, in some
parts, the precipices on the sides of the road are really frightful.

55 miles S.
from Batavia.

Having reached the summit of this pass, a beautiful view breaks at
once on the sight; in which, the stupendous scenery extending over
the lesser mountains is awfully contrasted by the dreadful abysses
immediately beneath; while, in a clear day, the ocean on the one
side, and the north coast on the opposite, may be easily discerned.
At the highest point of the east side of the road, a plain wooden
pillar commemorates the successful efforts of General Daendels in
making this great road, over an extensive mountainous country, the
labour expended on which must have been prodigious.

62 miles S.E.
from Batavia.

The road, taking a more easterly direction, continues over very steep
hills, to Tjipanas, where is a small government-house and a large
garden, which supplies abundance of fine vegetables. At this place
is a hot mineral bath, which was formerly much frequented; and has
its origin most probably in a volcanic hill at a little distance, from
whence smoke is still emitted. The climate here is very salubrious,

and has proved highly beneficial to invalids. At night, however, the cold is sensibly felt, and the evening sky is generally overcast with clouds and rain ; but the mornings are very delightful, and are always clear and serene.

Here commence the fine coffee plantations, which extend considerably through these hilly regions, and are exceedingly valuable. The rich produce of these regencies, so called from having had the administration entrusted to native chiefs bearing that title, was formerly collected into the Government storehouses and magazines for exportation, on the public account. On the late sale of crown lands, these extensive districts, which in Europe would be considered as constituting large principalities, were converted into private estates, the property of a few individual adventurers, who purchased them at a very inferior price to that of their actual value. But nothing precise is known of their real worth to Government, under the present circumstances, though their increased value, since the period of the destruction of the other coffee plantations, in the eastern parts of the Island, is evident.

The first principal town in these highlands through which the road leads, is Tanjore, which is the seat of the Regent of the district, and till lately also that of an European resident. The country round is very delightful. Passing through Byabang, a large village, pleasantly situated on the banks of a river, the next principal town is, *73 miles from Batavia.*

BANDONG, possessing the same residencies as the former, but neither so agreeable in its position, nor healthy, being in the midst of a swampy *120 miles from Batavia.*

soil. The country, however, soon reassumes a smiling face, when arrived at

144 miles
from Batavia.
SAMADONG, another large town, with its several residencies, the beauty of the cultivated fields spreading the most luxuriant fertility over hill and dale, mountain and valley, succeeding each other in a charming variety, afford a picturesque and highly-gratifying scene.

The inhabitants here are fairer in their complexions, and possess softer features, than in the other parts of the island; the women also are gracefully shaped, and some of them are very beautiful.

168 miles
from Batavia.
At Karang Sambong, the road leaves the mountains, after having traversed one hundred and twenty miles of perhaps as fine a country as any in the world, or rather one that is capable of being made so. Except in the towns where the Regents reside, and a few villages scattered here and there, a want of population is generally discernible. The soil is uncommonly fertile, as exhibited in the cultivated parts, and in the coffee plantations, which flourish most luxuriantly. Wheat, barley, rice, and all kinds of pulse and vegetables, are produced in perfection; and as the climate is most salubrious, if these districts were divided into farms of about fifty to one hundred acres, and superintended by European farmers, the benefits would be incalculable. This country is, indeed, particularly advantageous for new settlers, if a liberal encouragement was offered to adventurers of good character and ability.

Karang Sambong, is a considerable inland town, situated on a fine river, which is navigable for large prows, and runs through Indramayo into the sea. The Dutch had a large factory at this place, from whence a shorter inland communication to Batavia is now establishing, by means of the new road, and by the way of Crawang, which is also a considerable town, situated on a river of the same name ; the ancient boundary between the kingdoms of Jacatra and Cheribon.

The road now descends into a more populous and champaign country, cultivated chiefly with rice ; and here it regains the coast at Cheribon, distant about thirty-five leagues to the eastward of Batavia, but mea- 178 miles suring one hundred and ninety-eight miles by the post-road. This from Batavia. was a considerable military station in the former government, and the European town, which contains many good houses, was well peopled till within a few years of our arrival, when a pestilential disease swept off the greater part of the inhabitants, since which it has been nearly deserted. It is remarkable, that this contagion did not extend on the west side of the town more than two miles ; as the family of the Resident dwelling at that distance entirely escaped. This malady has been ascribed to a morass, extending many miles to the eastward of the town, and over which the wind blows at particular periods of the year ; while others attribute it to a cold drying wind, issuing for a considerable time through an opening of the mountains from the southward.

The great hill of Cheribon was formerly a volcano, and still emits smoak in some seasons.

This town lies at the bottom of the deep bay formed to the southeast of Point Indramayo, to the westward of which there is good anchorage in the easterly monsoon. The bay is well sheltered from the north-west monsoon by a shoal bank, which stretches from the north point of the bay to the eastward.

The commerce of Cheribon consists of rice, sugar, coffee, pepper, cotton yarn, edible bird-nests, &c. ; but the splendour of its former Sovereigns is sunk with their power. No less than four Sultans reside at this place, to whose ancestors the whole of the territory once belonged; but by different stipulations and treaties, the greater part came into the possession of the Dutch, who suffered the former lords to retain the empty title of Sultan, with very small districts for their maintenance, out of which they were even obliged to pay a certain proportion of the produce to their new masters. They are all, of course, miserably poor; though one, who is a very old man, is looked up to as the head, and is called by way of distinction, the Sultan.

Since the conquest an arrangement was concluded with the Sultans, by which they were relieved from future contingents and forced services. They consented that the internal administration of the country should be exercised by our Government, in consideration of their being secured in the possession of certain tracts of land, with a continuation of the annual pension in money, which they had previously enjoyed. Accordingly the capitation tax was abolished, and a land rent introduced, calculated according to the produce of the soil, in lieu of all arbitrary contingents formerly delivered to Government. The abolition of feudal services was proclaimed to the inhabitants, and Government engaged to pay at an equitable rate for all articles of produce, or the labours of the people, when they might be required for the public service.

According to this arrangement, the territorial revenue of Cheribon, including the duties on salt, opium, and town customs, are stated for the year 1814, at 255,306 rupees, without reckoning the assessment of lands provisionally assigned to Native Chiefs, and which amount to 34.270 rupees.

At a little distance from the town is a venerable mosque and mauso-
leum, erected to the memory of Sheik Melana, who is said to have
introduced Islamism into the Island of Java, but at what period is not
ascertained, though in all probability it was soon after the ninth century, between which, and the fourteenth, the Arabs are supposed to
have had the uncontrouled commerce in these parts. This building
is held highly sacred by the Mussulmans, and its precincts can only be
entered by the Sultan's family, which ceremony takes place once
a year, attended with much pomp and ceremony. It is now much
decayed, and in a few years more will be entirely crumbled into
dust.

Leaving Cheribon, the road proceeds due east, in many parts close
to the water's edge, and after passing the neighbouring marshes, it
continues through several native towns, to Losaric, Bribos, &c. and a
delightfully fertile country to Taggal. The long line of coast from 244 miles
from Batavia.
above Cheribon to Samarang, and thence to the Straits of Baly, was
much exposed to the inroads of pirates, who, having often shewn
themselves off the principal towns near the sea, rendered the erection
of forts indispensible, for the protection of the inhabitants, and to serve
as secure depots for the produce of these fertile shores. Appropriate
garrisons, with suitable supplies of military stores for their defence,
are kept up in each ; which measures became more especially necessary, as the Java gun-boats were not much better calculated under the
Dutch Government to protect the coast, than they are at present. The
vessels are fine, but badly manned, and worse commanded, being without a single European to navigate them ; and therefore the most pru-

2 o

dent course the crews can adopt is, to run away, which they always do when they meet a piratical prow, to avoid being taken. These pirates are determined fellows, who will rather die than yield, of which an instance occurred not long since off Indramayo, when one of our cruisers fell in with half-a-dozen of these armed prows, the crews of which obstinately refused quarter, and when floating on the water, after their vessels were sunk, they still resisted with their crisses, and would not suffer themselves to be taken on board to save their lives.

The country about Taggal is extremely fertile, and the whole of this part of Java, and further to the east, is the rice granary, not only for the supply of Batavia, but for exportation to the Eastern Isles. The net land rental, under the new arrangement and territorial revenue of Taggal, for the year 1814, is stated at 245,653 rupees.

Taggal, which is prettily situated on a broad river, has a church and a small fort, exhibiting with the town a very neat appearance. The resident's house is a commodious and very handsome building.

At this, and most other places to the eastward, a mounted police guard, (Djyant Secars,) is maintained by the several De Patties for the service of the interior. These men, who are under the orders of the resident in each district respectfully, are mounted on Java horses, with suitable accoutrements, armed with sword and pistols, and uniformly clothed in blue, with caps or helmets. In large towns they are under the charge of European officers, to superintend their exercises, &c. Proceeding through Pamalang, and several considerable native towns, the road conducts us to Paccalongang, another small European town and fort, like Taggal.

Paccalongang is also the seat of a Landdrost, or Resident, and has *282 miles from Batavia.* a numerous population of natives and Chinese, but there are not many Dutch families. Near this place is a forest, many miles in extent, which is so dreadfully unhealthy that four thousand people are said to have perished in cutting the great road through it. With the exception of this particular place, nothing can surpass the fertility of the country, or the number and population of the villages. Agreeably to the same statement before alluded to, the territorial revenue of Paccalongang amounts to 346,176 rupees. The road, for the whole way to Samarang, runs generally level, close to the beach, crossing numerous rivulets and inlets from the sea, over bamboo bridges.

SAMARANG is the principal central station of the Island, and is a *343 miles from Batavia* large town, with a considerable European population. It is defended by a stone parapet and rampart, with bastions, and a wet ditch; but only calculated for defence against a native power. The line of fortification along the coast had been destroyed before our arrival. Between the town and sea-coast is an impassable morass, which prevents any approach to the town but by two fine roads, east and west; both of which are raised and communicate with each other, by one running parallel to the coast, and close to the water. Ships are obliged to lie at the distance of five or six miles from the shore; the anchorage being six fathoms, and a muddy bottom, in lat. 6 degrees 53 minutes S., long. 110 degrees 34 minutes E.; or a ship may anchor in 5 or $4\frac{1}{2}$ fathoms nearer the shore. The Bay is bounded, on the east side, by the high land of Japara. The river, which is navigable for prows and coasting vessels up to the town, runs between the west side of the city and the Chinese campong. In blowing weather, the bar, at the mouth of the river, is deemed very dangerous.

The town has a neat appearance, with a number of good houses. It has also a fine large church, a new town-house, and a variety of other public buildings, both elegant and commodious, within and without the city. Here was formerly a public school, where numbers of Dutch and half-cast children were educated for the military profession.

Samarang was always the seat of a separate Governor, having the denomination of Governor of Java Proper, and exercising very extensive powers under the sanction and controul of the Governor General and Supreme Council of Batavia. All political and commercial regulations with the neighbouring Courts of Solo and Djoejocarta, were under the immediate authority of the Governor of Samarang, whose influence extending over so great a territory, made this an exceeding lucrative office. But the establishment has given way to the less expensive institutions of a Civil Commissioner, and Residents for the transaction of business.

The climate of Samarang, though not very salubrious, is far preferable to that of Batavia. The European inhabitants appear much more healthy, and instead of the gloomy indolence of the Batavians, we find here a pleasing sociability of disposition and hilarity of behaviour. The environs have numerous villas, which, from their commanding situation, overlook the stately topes and the neat garden houses that peep through the shady groves among the verdant fields; while the beautifully-variegated hills and dales towards the interior, greatly enliven the scenery. The Chinese and native population here is very considerable. Crowded villages overspread the neighbourhood, and the general bustle in the town and vicinity was not a little increased at the time of our visit, by the great concourse of strangers, and numerous bodies of horse attending the Crown Prince of Solo, who had arrived in consequence of the proffered terms for a pacific treaty between the Emperor and the British Government, after the capture of Djoejocarta, and the discovery of the treacherous alliance that had been made between the Soosoohoonan and the late court of the Sultan.

Under the new system of land rental, the territorial revenue of Samarang for the year 1814, amounts to 508,830 rupees, exclusive of the land assessments provisionally assigned to native chiefs. The salt revenue is stated at 200,000, opium at 24,080, and the town duties at 200,000 rupees, which gives a total of 1,032,910 rupees, without reckoning the profitable collections made on the edible bird-nests, which are given up by the native courts, and a variety of other customs.

FROM SAMARANG TO THE SOUTH COAST.

Proceeding from Samarang to the South, the road soon begins to ascend, and passes through Oonarang, a small European town and fort. Near this place, General Janssens made his last stand for the island of Java, with troops which he had collected from the native chiefs, formidable in numbers, but unable to encounter in the field a few well-disciplined soldiers. The country is pleasing and very healthy, and in its neighbourhood an eligible station for troops has been chosen, where barracks are now erecting for a battalion of Europeans. Until

11 miles S. from Samarang.

28 miles S.
from Sama-
rang.
lately the head-quarters of the troops in the Samarang district had been at Salatiga, which is another small town and fort most delightfully situated, and in a populous and extremely well-cultivated country, yielding provisions, vegetables and supplies of all kinds, cheap and in great abundance. Continuing to the village of Silimbi, the road crosses the river Damak, over which is a fine bridge ; and stretching through the middle and most elevated part of Java, it arrives at

44 miles S.
from Sama-
rang.
Boyolallie, another small town and fort situated in a delightful and most fertile country. Fifteen miles west of this is the famous burning mountain called Meer Appi, which formerly sent forth burning lava as far as this place, where the print of a human foot and hand, probably of some unfortunate fugitive, whose faltering step was arrested by the torrent, is seen to this day in the broad and now flinty tract. The ascent up this mountain is extremely steep and fatiguing ; but when the traveller reaches the summit, he forgets his toil in the contemplation of a sublime prospect.

By the light of the moon we had been enabled to gain a considerable height before the dawn of the morning, and the sun on his rising appeared through the gray mist which enveloped the objects below us, like an immense fiery balloon.

When we arrived at the summit of the mountain, the crater presented to our astonished sight a tremendous abyss, the depth of which cannot be perceived for the smoke, which is continually issuing from below. This frightful gulph we contemplated by leaning, at great hazard to our safety, over a vitreous and sulphuric substance which overhangs the precipice, but the danger was sufficiently evident from the numerous fissures that presented themselves all around us. Vast pieces of the superincumbent mass had been recently detached from the edge of the crater, and precipitated into the depth below.

The mountain seems split to its foundation, and the central gulph, formed by explosion, gives it the appearance of three separate mountains. The crater still bursts forth after heavy rains, and the bed, through which the lava made its way, exhibits a rough surface, like the undulating waves of a stormy sea. On turning from this height to view the vast expanse below, the habitations of men and all other objects are lost in one undistinguishing mass ; and even the solitary mounts of Cheribon, Taggal, &c. appear like insular rocks rising from the bosom of the ocean, enveloped in clouds.

The gardens of the town of Selo, situated at the foot of this mountain, produce most kinds of European fruits and vegetables ; while a small Dutch farm affords good lodging, and comfortable refreshment after a fatiguing excursion. Here, during the night, and till the sun has risen considerably above the horizon, the cold is so intense, that a blazing fire is very desirable, though the place is but seven degrees from the equator. The whole of this part of Java is delightfully fertile, and even the summits of the highest mountains are in a state of cultivation. Wheat and barley thrive remarkably well here ; and the population appears to be very great all over the country.

The road continuing on to Carta Soura, divides at that place in the direction of the two Native Courts. This was formerly a principal link in the chain of forts from Samarang, by which the Dutch were enabled

56 miles S. from Samarang.

to keep open a communication with either of these courts, and to con-troul both, by supporting the one against the other according to convenience. Any union of the natives against the Dutch, was care-fully guarded against by the Residents at the two Courts, and pre-vented by the subtle artifice of fomenting jealousies and aggravating existing dissensions.

The forts in this chain of posts, which extend within half-gun shot of the Crattan, or residence of each of these two principal Courts, are nearly similar; being well built, of a square form, with four bastions, mounting from six to eight guns in each, and surrounded by a wet ditch, with draw-bridges. They have in each commodious barracks, both for officers and soldiers, with arsenals and powder magazines; but, of the latter, few in the Island are bomb-proof. The forts are mostly covered with shingles, for which this reason is assigned, that the powder is less liable to spoil under them than under vaulted roofs, which are supposed to retain too great a dampness in this country; but this opinion appears to be erroneous, as the powder in the magazine of Fort Klattan, the only one that is bomb-proof, loses nothing of its quality. There is, however, great danger in the ordinary practice of covering these magazines with shingles, for the want of secure roofs was strikingly instanced in the late bombardment of Djoejocarta; when the spreading conflagration round our fort threw such a quantity of burning embers on the roof of the powder magazine, as threatened the most dreadful consequences, and an explosion was only prevented by the great quantity of water which was poured upon the building. Some of those forts which are the farthest from the two Crattans, have only demi-bastions, and are placed in such situations as to be com-manded by the surrounding heights. They form, nevertheless, safe depots, and are sufficiently secure from a coup-de-main. The one at Carta Souro was taken, and razed to the ground by the Chinese and the Emperor's troops, in 1741; and the neighbouring plain, extending to the borders of a large lake near this, was afterwards, in Van Imhoff's time, the scene of dreadful slaughter, when 20,000 Chinese are said to have perished. It was lately the favourite retreat of robbers, who, concealing themselves here, took advantage of the momentary troubles at Djoejocarta, in committing dreadful outrages, and they generally sealed the crime of plunder with the blood of their victim.

Proceeding south-east, the road conducts to Solo, or Soura-Carta; 61 miles the capital and residence of the Soosoohoonan, or Emperor. This is a from Sama-rang. very large and populous town, intersected with broad and shaded avenues, or streets, running at right angles. The Crattan, where the Emperor resides with his Court, is very spacious, and comprizes several palaces in its area. The other chiefs and nobility live in villas, sur-rounded by high walls, interspersed through the town and neighbour-hood. The European town and fort are very neat. The latter, which is not above eight hundred yards from the Crattan, contains a British garrison; and close to it is the Resident's house, which is a large and very handsome building.

The Emperor, or Soosoohoonan, is said to be of Arabian descent, and the same may be said of all the native Princes, from their affinity to each other; such as the three principal courts of Soura-

2 P

Carta, Djoejocarta, and Bantam; though now they are completely Javanese.

The Emperor, who is about fifty years of age, is courteous in his manners; and in his visits to the British resident, he is generally accompanied by his favourite wife. There is little pomp observable in his Court, and his troops, though numerous, are mostly of a motley description; but one regiment in his service of mounted carabineers, makes a tolerable appearance.

A fine river which flows near this town, and, passing through the dominions of the Sultan and Emperor, falls into the harbour of Gressie, affords, in the rainy season, a ready conveyance for the various productions of a large tract of country, in exchange for commodities which are sent up in boats from the coast.

68 miles from Samarang.

87 miles from Samarang.

Returning to Carta-Souro, the south-west road conducts past Pakkies to Klattan, another of our forts, in which is a small garrison; and, continuing by Prambanon, which was laid in ashes by the Sultan's banditti, during the attack at Djoejocarta, it leads over several difficult passes for carriages, to the capital of the Sultan of Mataram. The name of Djoejocarta will ever bring to mind the heroism of British soldiers, displayed in the attack and capture of a strong line of fortifications, under very disadvantageous circumstances. Already had multitudes of armed men cut off the communication with Samarang, and both the Emperor's and Sultan's troops, in countless numbers, were prepared to fall on our rear; but the energy of General Gillespie frustrated at one blow these designs, by the successful assault on Djoejocarta. Our most implacable foe was thus hurled from his throne, and the hostile confederacy was dissolved. The loss of several valuable provinces, and the destruction of the defences of the Crattan, on the north side, facing our fort, with the removal of the best part of the ordnance, completely reduced the power of the Sultan of Mataram, and prevent him from again committing any acts of aggression. Among other acquisitions, the rich Province of Codoe has been ceded to the British, the annual territorial revenue of which amounts to nearly 600,000 rupees; besides some other districts, containing the most valuable forests of teak in the Emperor and Sultan's dominions; and, to ensure a continuance of tranquillity, a third power has been set up, in the person of Prince Nunga de Suma, brother of the Ex-Sultan, who had thrown himself on our protection at the commencement of hostilities, and has obtained considerable estates out of the Emperor's and Sultan's cessions. Thus the once powerful empire of Mataram, formerly possessed entire by the Soosoohoonan, is now divided among three Princes; and the long meditated attempt of the native chiefs to overturn the European Government in Java, has ended in the full and complete supremacy of the latter over the whole Island; thus promising a general termination of those violent commotions which formerly proved so destructive to all the inhabitants, who have now a fair prospect of enjoying permanent peace and prosperity.

The present Sultan of Djoejocarta, who is about forty years of age, is tall and stout, but without having any thing prepossessing or dignified in his manners. The interior of the Crattan is filled with palaces, the most remarkable of which is an ancient edifice in the midst of a large lake. The only entrance to this building is by a subaqueous passage, of which nothing more is seen above the water, except the tops of some detached turrets with windows, by means of which light is communicated to the vaults below. This extraordinary covert-way is very long and spacious, and, thus concealed, connects the insular Chateau with some pleasant little gardens, fountains, &c. on the opposite land, formerly composing a seraglio, but which had of late been converted into a foundery and arsenal. The water-palace is a singularly antique structure with numerous apartments, which communicate with each other in so intricate a manner as to bewilder a person, and a stranger would stand in need of the friendly help of another Ariadne to extricate him from this curious labyrinth.

The walls, though exceedingly thick, are now cracked in many places, and this extraordinary edifice is falling fast to decay. The lake is of considerable depth, and extends across the whole breadth of the Crattan, which is about three-quarters of a mile, and in the opposite bason it has another curious building not yet finished, resembling a citadel or tower which surmounts the highest trees, and has a prospect of the whole country round. On the Platte-terre are ramparts defended with small bastions, bordering the lake. As no access appears above ground, it is probable that another subaqueous passage communicates here with the insular castle; an extensive bamboo scaffolding, on which the labourers carried their materials, raised in a shelving manner across the broad lake, conducted us nearly to the top of the tower, which in appearance recalled to mind what fancy had often figured of the Tower Babel.

The whole of the interior area of the Crattan is intersected with high walls, enclosing palaces and numerous court-yards. The palace in which the Sultan actually resides, has nothing in it very magnificent. The audience-hall and other places of public resort, are simply spacious Platte-terres, surmounted with a roof ornamented within, and supported by numerous and variously decorated colonnades. In the private apartments, which have nothing extraordinary in their construction and furniture, a guard of Amazons is always in attendance, particularly at night, when every man is excluded from the palace and the immediate neighbourhood. These heroines are armed with spears, and are agile horsewomen. They are trained to a domestic, as well as to a military life, and for the most part are the daughters of petty chieftains, in the service of, or dependant on, the Sultan. Their number, at the time of the late capture, was computed at about three hundred.

The population, contained within the walls of the Crattan, is very considerable; and besides being the constant abode of the Princes and families belonging to the Court, it also forms the temporary residence of the principal Pangerangs and nobles, who are vassals of the Court, and obliged to reside there themselves for two or more months in the year, or to give domestic pledges of their fidelity to the Monarch.

At the grand entrance on the North side, is an extensive square, where exhibitions of wild beasts, fights, and various tournaments, are often practised. The amusement of a buffalo and tiger fight is very general throughout Java : the animals are shut up in a large circular court, enclosed with strong bamboos, and covered in at the top, where men are placed to goad on the combatants. The buffalo is usually the victor, and the tiger is killed almost instantaneously. Another favourite amusement is, to form a circle of three or four ranks of men, armed with pikes, around a tiger, who is turned out of a cage, which is generally obliged to be set on fire, when the animal, after fiercely taking several rounds, makes a spring, and is caught on the pikes, stretched out to receive him, and is soon dispatched.

A very handsome mosque, and numerous villas, belonging to the Sultan and other Native Chiefs, are dispersed through the surrounding country. The house of our Resident is large and commodious ; and the fort, in which is a British garrison, is in good repair, and contains very good quarters for the troops. In the European town, which has some very good houses, reside several Dutch families, who are chiefly pensioners, and prefer living here, like those at Solo, on account of the cheapness of provisions, and the salubrity of the climate.

From Djoejocarta to the south coast is about eighteen miles, and the roads tolerably good as far as Krattock, a large village, near which we crossed the broad and deep river of Allantjiengan, which four miles from hence falls into the South Sea. Having been hospitably entertained here, at the house of a Chinese farmer, or collector of customs, we proceeded to

104 miles from Sama-rang.

SPOLONK, where the great South Sea arrested our progress in this direction ; and at a considerable distance from the beach, our tract led over high sand-hills, thrown up by the waves, on the flat shore in the neighbourhood ; while on most other parts of this great line of coast, stupendous cliffs oppose the roaring surf, and render the shore in many places inaccessible. Unlike the north coast of Java, which affords a facility for landing throughout its whole line, that of the south, from the great violence of the surf always beating on it, and iron-bound by steep cliffs, has very few places where vessels can take shelter, or where any expedition could be prudently disembarked. There are no European settlements along the south coast; but the Bay of Pagitan, south-east of Solo, was intended to have been fortified in the time of General Daendels. This bay is in the form of a horse-shoe, and from its neigh-bourhood to the two capitals, and the principal native courts, it appears well adapted for the accommodation of shipping. In general, the Bays nearly midway between Bally Strait and Java Head, ap-pear to be the safest on this coast, but they are seldom visited.

Of the districts that run along this coast very little is known; but the parts which we visited appeared to be very fertile, and the green hillocks dispersed in this neighbourhood give a pleasing and romantic aspect to the surrounding scenery. The country had lately been much in-fested by banditti, and the frightened cottagers were still keeping themselves and their little property concealed in the cavities of rocks and hills. Only the night before our arrival, the village of Spolonk had been the scene of plunder; but the chiefs of the band being taken the following day by our small escort, the peaceable villagers returned to their habitations.

Near this is shewn a cave, celebrated as the retreat of a Prince of Mataram, who for many years had eluded all his pursuers. Close to the beach are several bungaloes, appropriated to the Sultan, or persons of his family, who sometimes repair hither for the advantage of bathing in the sea. Adjoining is a beautiful grotto, formed by the petrefaction of the trunks, roots, and lower branches of a small grove, through which runs a crystalline stream, which falling from a height, like a sun-beamy shower, into the midst of the variegated substances, exhibits a most brilliant spectacle, and the imagination delights in exercising its powers on the various figures around, which bear a resemblance to numerous objects in animated nature. Near this petrifying spring is a small temple, embosomed among the trees, which gives an air of sanctity to the place, and serves to increase the pleasing melancholy excited by the calm tranquillity and romantic beauty of the charming scene. A few hundred yards west, on the beach, are hot mineral springs, close down to the water's edge. These springs, which are nearly inclosed and covered in, have a strong sulphureous smell, and one of them is 122 degrees of Fahrenheit.

———

CONTINUATION OF THE EASTERN ROUTE.

Continuing from Samarang to the eastward, the road conducts across the river Torabaya, through a flat country, with numerous rice fields, villages, and topes of cocoa-nut trees, to

358 miles E. from Batavia.

DAMACK, which is a large populous town, and was formerly the capital of a kingdom of that name. In the neighbourhood is a considerable tract of marshy land, which continues many miles, and is succeeded by a level plain, spreading to a considerable distance, and exhibiting signs of great fertility. A fine canal, navigable to the distance of twenty miles from Samarang, runs along the left side of the road, and terminates in the river Tanganamis, which is also navigable for small vessels. Beyond it a road leads off on the right to Oonorang by Serondole. The country here is intersected by numerous canals and rivulets, which cross the road, and after passing through

Codoes and Patti, two very considerable towns, and each the seat of a De Patti; the road conducts to Joanna, situated on the east side of the promontory of Japara.

JAPARA, is a place of great antiquity as a commercial mart of the Europeans; and was among the first of the Dutch establishments in the eastern seas. The town and fort are on the west side of the Peninsula, having contiguous to it some islets and rocks, with four or five fathoms of water.

390 miles from Batavia by Kodoos.

The Chinese inhabitants are very numerous at Japara, where they have a temple similar to that at Anjole, near Batavia, and a few other places in the island.

There are many small isles and rocks scattered along the shore of the bay to the eastward. On the south west part of this bay stands

JOANNA, which is a pleasant spot, and far from being unhealthy. The fort and town are a few miles up the country, on a fine river, which is navigable to vessels of considerable burthen, and has a rapid current. The fort is in good repair, and a very excellent tavern close to the river offers the best accommodation to travellers. Several European families also continue to make this place their residence. The territorial revenue under the new system of Japara and Joanna, is stated at 342,902 rupees for the last year.

396 miles from Batavia.

The river is crossed at this place, on a floating raft or bridge, fixed upon boats, and after passing through rather a swampy country at first, the road soon enters on fine culture again, and conducts to

2 Q

REMBANG, situated near the east part of the bay, formed by the Japara promontory. The Dutch used to build here their principal craft and gun-boats for the protection of the coast; and they also maintained a considerable garrison on this station.

The fort is situated close to the sea, which washes its walls. The town, which is large and populous, has a number of very good houses; it appears to be a cheerful and very pleasant residence, being healthy and abundantly supplied, owing to its advantageous situation for trade, as well by land as by water. A considerable quantity of sea salt is manufactured in the neighbourhood, and exported from hence to different parts of the island, and other places. The territorial revenue of Rembang, is stated at 256,092 rupees. The principal district of this residency is set apart for the forest department. A road runs from Rembang to Solo, through a high and open country. Nine miles farther on the road passes through

LASSAM, a considerable trading village, situated at the eastern angle of the bay, on which Rembang and Joanna are seated, and opposite to all of which, vessels anchor in three or four fathoms among the shoals.

Lassam is the residence of the De Patti, and has the advantage of a fine navigable river, which runs through the town. The road from hence lies partly over low hills, skirting the sea; and the country is bold and irregular. Near Sarang, which is eighteen miles from Lassam, are swampy and waste-lands; but in advancing to Toubang, the neighbouring country is soon overspread with extensive jungle.

TOUBANG, the seat of a De Patti, has an ancient mosque, and is a 470 miles from Batavia. large and very populous town. About fourteen miles further on the road crosses a fine river. Extensive forests of teak from hence stretch over these rocky and hilly tracts, to the neighbourhood of Zedayo; on a near approach to which the land becomes level and extensively cultivated.

ZEDAYO, is a town of considerable importance, being situated at the 509 miles from Batavia. entrance of the harbour of Gressie; and the coast may be approached with safety from the eastern point of the bay that forms Lassam Road to the entrance of the strait of Madura. Zedayo is also the seat of a De Patti; and the present chief holding that office is a man of very superior talents, conversing pertinently with us, both on ancient and modern history, and displaying correct notions of universal geography; an extent of knowledge rarely met with in a native of these regions. All the De Patties are remarkable for their hospitality. They live in great splendour, their mansions having the pomp of Asiatic courts; and though not educated in the school of European manners, they are far from being deficient in politeness. A striking instance of liberality, indeed, occurred in our route, for the De Patti of Toubang, who was travelling in an opposite direction, happening to meet us just as our carriage broke down in the midst of a dreary jungle, and far distant from any town or village, immediately alighted, and in the most courteous manner insisted on our acceptance of his own vehicle to proceed on our journey, though in so doing it was probable that he would have to pass all night in the wilderness, before another convey-ance could be procured.

A short distance from Zedayo, the river Sambaya, or Solo river, is crossed by a ferry, and the passage defended by a strong battery. This river, the largest in Java, is navigable, in the rainy season, as far as the residence of the Soosoohoonan, or Emperor of Solo; and it appears, from a recent survey, made by Captain Colebrooke, of the Royal Artillery, that the impediments which obstruct its passage in the dry season, might be removed without much labour or expense, thus facilitating our commercial intercourse with the interior of that fertile and populous country.

From Solo river, the country is almost an entire swamp, and covered with low jungle, intersected with numerous salt-water creeks and canals. At Banur, nine miles from Zedayo, the road crosses the river Maniar, over a bridge; the land then rises to the right, and is well cultivated; while, to the left of the road, salt-pans, which are very productive, extend as far as the town of Gressie. Siloar river, ten miles further, is crossed by a ferry; the battery for the defence of which passage is advantageously situated. The country now gradually brightens, and the road enters on the fertile and pleasing plains that environ Sourabaya; which is a large town, with a numerous population, European, Chinese, Malayan, and Javanese.

540 miles
from Batavia. SOURABAYA, in latitude 7 degrees $14\frac{1}{2}$ minutes S., and in longitude 112 degrees 55 minutes E., is situated on a fine river, which allows vessels of considerable burthen to come up to the town. The river once emptied itself into a marsh close to the town, but of late years a bank, nearly a mile in length, on which is a path-way for tracking boats, confines its course, and greatly adds to the depth and the current. The mouth is defended by Fort Calamaas, a circular battery, mounting

forty guns, placed on a rising spot, on the east side of the river. This battery has a commanding sweep across the strait of Madura, which is narrowest here, being opposite to the S. W. end of the Island of that name. It was intended, under the Dutch Government, to have erected Sourabaya into a port of consequence, for their trade to the eastward of Java; and with this view General Daendels expended large sums in the construction of works for the defence of the harbour. The eastern entrance into the straits of Madura, being impassable for very large ships, the batteries there were only just begun, and are still incomplete; but the north-western entrance is defended by Fort Ludowyk, which is distant from Gressie about six, and from Point Panka five miles, and is situated immediately on the narrow winding channel by which alone large ships can enter. It presents, low on the water, a very formidable battery, of a hundred pieces of the finest ordnance, mounted on traversing carriages, besides some heavy mortars.

The insular fort stands at the extremity of a mud-bank, which projects into the channel about 1400 yards from the Island of Manarie; but the bank is not visible even at low water. The foundation for the fort was formed by sinking rocks, and raised to its present elevation by means of stones and earth brought from the neighbouring land, and kept in by large piles of wood driven round. The approach is defended by rows of strong piles driven into the bottom of the sea, at the distance of sixty or seventy feet from the ramparts, and forming a close palisade all round, which prevents the passage of boats, and effectually guards against a coup-de-main, or escalade.

The barracks, which are built of bamboo, plaistered over and white-washed, may lodge eight hundred men. The ordnance stores however are greatly exposed, having no bomb-proof magazines, and the water required for the garrison is brought from Sourabaya, nearly twenty miles distant, by means of floating tanks, which, being often delayed by contrary winds in the Western monsoon, the garrison is sometimes put to great distress. General Daendels intended to have connected fort Ludowyk with the island of Manarie by a causeway, which was to have been erected on the intermediate ocean, by a similar expense and labour that had been employed in the construction of the fort. The principal depot for the garrison was to have been established on Manarie, and difficult as the undertaking might have been, the marshal felt the importance of this post so much, as affording an effectual security against the attacks of our navy, especially after the destruction of the Dutch shipping in the harbour of Gressie by Sir Edward Pellew in 1806, that he resolved to spare no efforts in rendering this passage impenetrable by an enemy, and thus making the straits of Madura the grand port and naval depot of his nation in the East.

The anchorage for large ships is off the town of Gressie, till within one mile to the North-west of the mouth of the Calimas river, which runs through Sourabaya; but vessels going to that place require pilots to carry them through the straits.

GRESSIE, in latitude 7 degrees 9 minutes South, is not near so considerable a place now that it was formerly. The town has comparatively but few European inhabitants, but the native population and the Chinese settlers are still numerous. The saltpetre-works here are extensive, and the establishment for its manufacture is very complete; but the want of good water, and the general unhealthiness of

Gressie may be considered, in a great measure, one of the causes of its present decline.

In proportion as this place has fallen into decay, the new town of Sourabaya has risen rapidly in population and prosperity; and the improvement which it has experienced within these few years is astonishing. A fine arsenal, and other extensive works calculated for equipments on a very large scale, were formed by General Daendels at this place. Here guns are cast, and carriages of all descriptions constructed. Vessels also, with their various appointments, are built and equipped at Sourabaya, in the neighbourhood of which are considerable forests, from whence plenty of timber is easily procured, which is floated down the river Calimas, that takes its rise, as it is said, from a large inland lake encircled with high mountains. A mint is likewise at work here, on a new silver and copper coinage.

The new Government-house at Sourabaya, begun by Daendels, was designed to be a splendid edifice, and like that of Weltervreeden, was to have contained the various public offices collectively, instead of being scattered as hitherto, all over a sickly town; but the foundation of the front range having sunk, and endangered the building, it has been abandoned, and that part which continues firm has been converted into store-rooms.

The river separates the European part of the town from that of the Chinese and the native quarter. A fine bridge, with draw-chains to raise it up for the passage of vessels, connects the European town with that of the natives.

The houses are very good, and some are elegant, particularly the newly-erected country-seats of private individuals. The house at Simpang, where the British resident resides, is a fine large building, close to the river ; and near to it the general hospital is an attracting object. This structure is about two miles from the town, situated on the banks of the river, and for elegance, extent and commodiousness, has scarcely its equal.

The roads and avenues round Sourabaya are delightful. The ground is rather low, being chiefly cultivated with rice, interspersed with numerous topes of cocoa-nut and other fruit-trees. The country about Sourabaya is considered much healthier than most other parts of the sea-coast; and the district throughout is exceedingly populous, and highly productive. De Noyo cantonment, which is the present quarter of the military in the Eastern division, is about four miles from Sourabaya, and close to the river. The low situation however, and neighbouring jungle, make it very unhealthy, and in the rains it is altogether uninhabitable, as at that season, the river frequently overflows its banks, and totally inundates the cantonment. Higher grounds rising in form of a crescent, eight or ten miles from Sourabaya, appear to offer much better situations for a military quarter than De Noyo, particularly on the side of the river, six miles South of that place.

The land-rental of Sourabaya exceeds that of any of the other districts. Without reckoning the assessment of lands provisionally assigned to Native Chiefs, to the amount of 72,302 rupees, the landed revenue under the new system is stated at 667,178 rupees, salt at 50,000 ; opium 100,000 ; and town customs 50,000, which gives a total for Sourabaya of 867,178 rupees.

Continuing on to the eastward, the road leads through an agreeable country, diversified with rising grounds and vallies, well cultivated and populous, to

PASSAROUANG, a small European town and fort, situated on a fine river, which is navigable for brigs of considerable burden. It is a delightful place, with a very healthy climate, and its native population numerous; but the European inhabitants are few, being chiefly old pensioners and half-cast families. The Resident's house, and several other buildings here, are very handsome. 576 miles from Batavia.

PROBOLINGO, twenty-four miles farther east, is the capital of a province of that name, which was lately the property of a Chinese individual, who purchased it from the former Government, for ten millions of rix dollars, payable by instalments. The lands, which measure about forty miles in length and breadth, were at that time mostly waste; but so rapid were its improvements, and so productive its soil, when private interest was concerned in its advancement, that ten years cleared the purchase; in consequence of which, it has now become one of the richest provinces of Java, and is very populous. 600 miles from Batavia.

The China Major, which was the name given to the proprietor of Probolingo, lived here in great splendour, with every enjoyment that riches could afford, when, in one hour, and while engaged in the exercise of humanity, he was unfortunately cut off in a most tragical manner, having, for the companions of his fate, two very valuable British officers.

The 18th June, 1813, was the fatal day on which this atrocious act was perpetrated. A small party, consisting of Lieutenant-Colonel

2 R

and Mrs. Fraser; Captains M'Pherson and Cameron, and Lieutenants Robertson and Cameron, of the seventy-eighth Regiment, had repaired to Probolingo for the benefit of their health; the climate of that country being esteemed very salubrious. On the afternoon of that day, a report came that a banditti had descended from the mountains, and were close to the town; upon which, the China Major proceeded in his carriage, with Colonel Fraser, accompanied by the other officers of the party, to meet them; imagining that they were merely a set of robbers, who might be easily dispersed. But the chief of the insurgents, seeing them approach, concealed his men among the bushes, till, at a signal, they suddenly rushed out on our officers, who, finding themselves abandoned by their native followers, and in danger of being surrounded, after several ineffectual discharges from their pistols and fowling-pieces, now tried to make their escape back to the town; but, exhausted with fatigue, Colonel Fraser fell down, when attempting to step into the carriage, and Captain M'Pherson also, through the weak state of his health, being easily overtaken, they were seized and bound by the insurgents, and, with the China Major, were all basely murdered. The other officers succeeded in regaining the house; and, after vain efforts on the part of Captain Cameron, to rouse the Chinese and the tenants to defend the China Major's house, which, being enclosed, held out to him the hope of making a stand, and thereby of gaining an opportunity to sally out for the rescue of his unfortunate countrymen, of whose fate he was still ignorant, he found, to his great grief, the place gradually deserted during the night. Despairing, therefore, of doing any thing for his unhappy friends, he turned his attention to the agonized Mrs. Fraser, and, getting into a boat with the sad remaining few of the party, hurried off, and stood out to sea. They had just left the shore when the murderous banditti appeared in sight, rending the air with their horrid shouts.

Thus oppressed with feelings, the bitter pangs of which may be easier felt than described, was the disconsolate Mrs. Fraser exposed to the burning sun all day, in an open boat, and on the wide ocean, till she at last reached Passarouang, with her afflicted companions.

No sooner did the intelligence of this sad catastrophe reach Soura-baya, than Major Forbes, with a party of the 78th Regiment, set out on horses borrowed from the officers and other individuals, on which he mounted his soldiers, to expedite their march, and rapidly pushed forward to stem the rising torrent. On his arrival at Passarouang, the Major was joined by Captain Cameron and his surviving friends; and, on the 21st of June, they fell in with the insurgents, who had already increased to many thousands, supported by guns, and in full march to the above place, which they threatened to destroy. After forcing their advanced position, Major Forbes continued to press forward, and at last came upon the main body, drawn up across the high-road, about midway between the two towns, and commanded by their chieftain, who boldly advanced to the attack with colours flying; which flag being yellow, the standard of the Soosoohoonan, gave rise to a sus-picion that the Emperor of Solo must have been a party concerned in this revolt.

The bold advance of the enemy rendering every precaution necessary on the part of Major Forbes, in his disposition for repelling such a furious multitude, the detachment was drawn up on the sides of the road, in such a manner as to bring a cross-fire on the main body of the

2 R 2

rebels, while, on the road towards the rear, were stationed some Djyang Secars, provincial horsemen, armed with swords and pistols, and a party of irregulars from Passarouang. Thus prepared, Major Forbes waited the attack; and when the rebels were within a few yards, a well-directed fire brought down numbers of them to the ground; but the Chief, furiously irritated, at the head of a more desperate party, rushed on; and, though wounded in four places, he passed through our fire to the rear, where he was secured, and breathed his last. Many others died in the same manner; and about 150 were left dead on the field. The rest fled, and their guns were taken.

The bodies of Colonel Fraser and Captain M'Pherson were found tied up in sacks, that of the latter was much mangled, and pierced quite through with a number of wounds. Besides the one who fell, several other chiefs had been discovered, and steps were taken to extend an enquiry into the cause of this rebellion.

Probolingo was completely ransacked by the insurgents. The chief, who was slain had proclaimed himself the Vicegerent of Mahomet, and published that he was ordained to make conquests in the name of that prophet. Melancholy as this catastrophe was to some most meritorious individuals, their fate may perhaps be considered as having proved the means of saving the inhabitants of Sourabaya, and of the eastern districts of Java, who were, by the measures immediately adopted, and the bravery displayed, rescued from a general massacre.

The Chinese, in consequence of their exactions, had always been objects of hatred on the part of the Javanese, and the disturbance in this province necessarily led to a change in its administration. Since

that occurrence, a new settlement of the land revenue has been introduced, upon such principles as were considered to be best suited to the
circumstances of the country and inhabitants at that particular period.
The deceased renter's family received a compensation, whilst, at the
same time, the cultivators were relieved from the accumulation of nominal arrears and alledged debts, which it had been the policy of the
landholder to keep hanging over them, and was a perpetual source of
oppression and abuses in the administration.

The newly-regulated territorial revenue of these districts, of Passarouang, Probolingo, including Poagar and Banyowangy, are stated
for the year 1814, at 1,246,000 rupees.

After passing through Besoekie, a considerable town, and Pana-
roekan, where is a small fort, the ramparts of which are cased with
bamboos, we arrived at the river Kalatigas, where the carriage road
terminates. The fine military road from Batavia to this place, measuring six hundred and eighty-four English miles, has scarcely its
equal in any part of the world. From hence, we pursued our journey
on horseback, for about fifty miles, through a hilly country, covered
with jungle and wood, chiefly teak; and after passing the night in the
forest, at the small village of Sambrawary, and the next day passing
through another, Bajuramaty, the only two villages in this long tract,
we arrived about noon at Banjowangy.

The scene of wilderness, and the danger of being devoured by tigers,
or assailed by robbers, certainly made this no very safe ride for only two
persons, unattended by servants, except one Malay boy, or guard
of any kind. The mode of travelling, usually pursued through
these wilds, is by Caravans, the better to secure mutual protection.

Having passed this dreary solitude, the deadly silence of which was occasionally interrupted by the loud roar of the tiger, or the cry of some other wild beast; we, on a sudden, emerged from this dark passage, and experienced the most delightful sensations, in being freed from a state of gloomy apprehension, to the enjoyment of the cheerful contrast afforded by the prospect of the beautiful Straits of Baly.

728 miles from Batavia.

BANYOWANGY, situated in the Straits of Baly, and in lat. 8 degrees 7 minutes, is a place of some consequence as a military post: an efficient garrison being requisite here, to prevent the depredations of pirates, who frequent these parts, being sheltered by the creeks on the Baly shore, where they generally lurk for their prey.

The town has a numerous population of natives, and a few Dutch half-cast families. The fort is on the banks of a river, which washes its walls on the side fronting the sea, and from which the river is separated by only a narrow sand-bank, that terminates about half-a-mile lower down, and uniting it there with the ocean. The country is very fine, extremely well cultivated, and the climate healthy. The cattle procured here to supply the ships, are imported from the opposite shores of Baly.

The north entrance of Baly Straits on the west and north-west side, is bounded by Cape Sandanah, the extreme of the high land that forms the N. E., and of Java, in lat. 7 degrees 46 minutes south*. At Banyowangy, where the Strait is narrowest; the entrance from the southward is five or six leagues wide, and the view of the bold

---

* In the Dutch Charts, the given latitude is 7 deg. 52 min. S.

shores of Baly, and of the immense high mountains behind, is very romantic.

Balambouang Bay, farther south, on the Java side, had a small establishment formerly, for the convenience of ships touching there; but from its unhealthiness, it has been abandoned. In these Straits, not far from Goonong Ikan, which is in long. 114 deg. 20 min. east, and 8 deg. 22 min. south latitude, are the Deptford Rocks, which are very dangerous.

The south-east point of Java, is in latitude 8 deg. 41 min. south, and in longitude 114 deg. 25 min. east; Table Point, the southern extremity of Baly Island, is in latitude 8 deg. 50 min. south. This forms the eastern boundary of the south entrance of the Straits.

From Banyowangy, we sailed in his Majesty's sloop Baracouta, over to Samanap, distant about one hundred miles. This is a large and populous town, and the residence of a prince. It is situated on the south-east side of Madura, on a fine bay, which though rather shallow, will admit of large brigs or country prows, lying close up to the town. *Island of Madura.* *82 miles from Bancallang.*

This place carries on an extensive commerce; and the country abounds in rice, and teak timber for building. Here the Dutch used to build then largest ships for the country trade. Few European Dutch settlers are now remaining here, but the half-cast population is still considerable, and the number of native inhabitants is very great. The bay is much frequented by merchant vessels, which adds greatly to its importance.

The fort is much out of repair, and its situation is badly chosen, so that in fact, it is only of use as a depot. The British Resident's house, and a few others belonging to individuals, are fine buildings.

The old prince of Samanap, worn out with age, has surrendered the reins of government to his second son, who appears to be of a mild disposition, and is greatly esteemed by the people. The heinous character of the old Sovereign may be read in his countenance, which is of a most diabolical cast. The Princes live separately, but their courts shew little or no splendour.

47 miles from Bancallan.

Continuing from Samanap through the interior of the island, the next place of importance is Parmacassan, situated nearly in the centre of the island, and the residence of the second son of the Sultan of Madura, who attends to the administration of this part of the Sultan's dominions ; this prince is indeed a fine young man.

On our arrival at Bancallan, the residence of the Sultan of Madura, we passed the night at his court, which, though not splendid, has some degree of stile. The Sultan is a respectable old man, above eighty years of age, of a cheerful temper, and much pleased with the society of European visitors, whom he entertains very hospitably, and sometimes in a sumptuous manner. Both he and his sons, from their long connection with the Dutch, cast off all prejudices when they sit down to partake of the pleasures of the table. His eldest son, who appears to be a well-disposed young man, resides here also, but separately from the father. He held the rank of Colonel in the Dutch service, and the younger brother was an honorary Aid-de-Camp to General Daendels, which mark of distinction flattered their youthful vanity very much, and stimulated them to raise men themselves, or use their influence in enlisting the Madurese into that service.

The town of Bancallan is large and populous. The fort is close to the palace of the Sultan, and the environs are pleasant with good roads, along which are interspersed pleasure-grounds and several country-seats. The road which runs along the beach west of the town, and opposite to fort Ludowyk, is particularly fine.

That from Sanap to Bancallan, alternately passing over hill and dale, is also very good; the scenery is picturesque, and the country throughout fertile and tolerably cultivated. The Madurese bear a higher character than their neighbours, but the population throughout the island appears in general to be very thin.

Kamal, directly opposite to Sourabaya, is distant about ten miles from Bancallan, and the new road between these two places is very beautiful. We crossed the Straits in the Sultan's barge in two hours.

Of the islands belonging to Madura, the most considerable are Gallion and Pondi. The former, which is very populous, and well cultivated, is situated about twelve miles east of Madura, and abounds in cattle; the latter is smaller, and is also well cultivated, and both have a pleasant appearance. *Gallion and Pondi Isles.*

The only remaining island worth noticing, as immediately apper- taining to Java, is Carimon Java, which lies directly north of Sama- rang, in about lat. 5 deg. 50 min. South, and long. 110 deg. 34 min East. It is a high island, with a hill in the centre ; and adjoining to it are several small lands and rocks. The Dutch kept up a small esta- blishment here under a resident, and an officer's guard is still con- tinued, to prevent pirate prows from visiting the place, which abounds with deer; and ships anchoring here may procure both wood and water. *Carimon Java*

THE EASTERN ARCHIPELAGO.

The position and extensive resources of Java, which has been justly denominated the mistress of the Dutch possessions in the East, cannot fail to give a relative importance of corresponding magnitude to its several dependencies. But the various commercial advantages possessed by the countries which constitute the Eastern Archipelago ; and their immense productions, must at all times render these regions an interesting object of inquiry to the statesman, the trader, and the man of science, independent of other considerations. In the present memoir, indeed, it is to be regretted, that much information cannot be given adequate to the extent of the subject, and the numerous points of inquiry which a minute and regular survey would embrace. The numerous islands are here barely exhibited to view, as objects worthy of consideration, from their relation to Java ; and as meriting particular research, from having been hitherto but little explored, and that little still less accurately represented *.

The inhabitants of these isles are supplied from Java with rice, as well as other articles of subsistence, and their safety depends so imme-

---

* In ascertaining the latitude and longitude of the several places here enumerated, the recent and much approved " Indian Directory" of Horsburgh, compared with other documents, appears to come nearest the truth. To the obliging communication of several gentlemen, who having personally visited those islands, the writer is indebted for many particulars. Those of the late armament against the Moluccas were extracted from original documents, imparted by an Officer of the Royal Navy who was employed on that service.

diately on that of the principal settlement, that, if the latter were in possession of an enemy, Amboyna and Banda could not be retained without the expense of an extensive military establishment. And the same may be said of Macassar, Timor, and all the other establishments, with their several dependencies, which the events of the war have consigned to the British nation, and the garrisons of which are supplied and maintained from Java.

The establishments to the westward of Java, on Sumatra, Banca, &c. have been already mentioned, in the account of the Palembang expedition. To the eastward, the colony farthest distant in the chain of islands nearly in the same parallel of latitude as Java, and washed by the great southern ocean, is Timor, an island which is about 240 miles in length, and from sixty to seventy miles in breadth. The Dutch conquered it from the Portuguese, in 1613; who had established themselves in various parts of the island; and who still retain several distinct establishments here, on the north-east side. But the principal settlement on Timor, is Coupang, a considerable town built on the south side of the Bay of that name, and defended by Fort Concordia, where the Dutch have always maintained a large garrison. The Bay is situated at the south-west end of the Island, and is very extensive. Two safe passages lead into the Bay to the anchorage. The Island is mountainous, and the south coast may be safely approached, within a moderate distance, in most places. The Portuguese population is very considerable. The Dutch, not satisfied with having driven the early adventurers of that nation from all the Spice Islands, followed them to this their last place of retreat; and though there was nothing peculiarly inviting in the produce of the Island, yet, on account of its

Timor.

Coupang Town and Fort Concordia.

neighbourhood to the Moluccas, they established themselves in Fort Concordia. The inhabitants now consist of a mixed body, made up of half-casts, with the Chinese and native inhabitants. Coupang is a populous town, conveniently situated for ships, which obtain here all kinds of provisions, both cheap and in abundance; particularly buffaloes and poultry. Since its occupation by the British, this place has been the general resort of our south-sea whalers, and vessels trading to Sydney, in New South Wales, and other places.

The flag-staff of Fort Concordia is in latitude 10 deg. 8½ min. S., longitude 123 deg. 35 min. E.

The Portuguese settlements in Timor are Dilly or Diely, and Batoo Gady, situated on the North side of the island; and abounding in hogs, buffaloes, and vegetables.

In general the natives of Timor are much more hospitable and friendly than the Northern Malays. The first island subject to Timor is Semao, situated at the South-west end, and fronting Coupang bay. It is of considerable extent, and moderately elevated. The channel, which is navigable with deep water, affords secure shelter to ships, during the strength of the Westerly monsoons.

Rotto island, to the South-west of Semao, is considerably larger, being about forty miles in length.

Savu island is the smallest of the three, being no more than twenty miles in length; but it has the advantage of several bays. The chiefs of all these islands, as well as of Kisser and Roma, lying to the Northward of Timor, are under the authority of the resident at Coupang. Kisser has a town and fort, with a small bay on the Western side, in latitude 8 deg. south, and long. 127 deg. 7 min. east. The principal articles of trade are wax, sandal-wood, edible birds'-nests ; and, till lately, a number of slaves might have been purchased at these isles, but, thanks to the British Legislature, this inhuman traffic is now forbidden.

Separated by a passage of about twenty miles to the Westward from Timor, lies Ombay or Mallooa island, which is about fifty miles in length, and inhabited by a fierce and treacherous people, which renders it dangerous for ships to touch there.

Nearly in a straight line, between Ombay and the East of Java, lie a number of islands of considerable extent, forming a chain of about twelve degrees of longitude, and intersected by several straits. That of Flores is formed by the Eastern part of the island of that name, and the islands of Solor and Adenara, or Sabraon, in extent about twelve leagues. The South entrance is in lat. 80 deg. 40 min. south, long. 123 deg. 3 min. east.

FLORES, or MANGERYE, is an extensive island, subject to the Sultan of Beema, who derives a considerable revenue from the quantity of birds'-nests found here. Its length is upwards of 200 miles, and its breadth in some parts from forty to fifty; but nothing is known of the interior. Flores.

Crossing Sapy strait, which has a number of little islands separating it into small channels, that by causing rapid tides, makes it inconvenient for ships, we reach

SUMBAWA, extending nearly 200 miles in the parallel of nine degrees south latitude. Near the North-east end, on a fine bay which stretches seven or eight leagues South into the island, is situated the town of Beema, where the Dutch had formed an establishment, by invitation from the Sultan of that place, who, at some former period, applied to Beema.

their Government at Macassar for aid to resist a threatened attack from his neighbours at Tambora, which is another considerable town in Sumbawa. This request was readily complied with, and a garrison was sent to Beema, which place has continued ever since under the Macassar government.

The sides of the harbour at the entrance are bold and high, and the approach to it is safe ; but the passage through is sometimes attended with inconvenience, from the strong current that generally prevails, and the great depth of water ; as a hundred fathom line, though close in shore, will hardly reach the bottom. When, therefore, ships cannot pass through, they are obliged, for the want of anchorage, to return to sea, and there wait for a more favourable wind. The batteries erected on each side of the entrance, and opposite to one another, are no longer capable of defence; and are, in fact, gone to ruin. The channel, in some places, is only 150 or 200 yards across ; but there is no danger whatever in the passage*; and a ship of the line may sail along either side within thirty yards of the rocky mountains. These give a grand and picturesque appearance to the channel, which terminates in a safe and commodious bason, presenting one of the finest

* The Dutch charts represent this passage as being extremely dangerous, full of shoals and rocks. This, however, is the general character of their charts of these seas, which are so extremely erroneous, stating dangers where none exist, to multiply the apparent difficulties of access, and marking that as safe where a ship would inevitably meet with destruction, as to make it appear less a mistake of ignorance than the effect of design. This perversion of truth, however, is easily accounted for, by the base spirit of self-interest and monopoly, which endeavoured as much as possible to prevent other European nations from holding any intercourse with countries which, for two centuries, they have kept exclusively under their own controul.

harbours in the world, both for capaciousness and security; extending a considerable way inland, and encompassed by lofty mountains. On the east side of this bay stands the town of Beema. The landing here is very unfavourable, owing to a mud-bank, which extends three-quarters of a mile from the town. The Sultan of Beema is named Abdul Ahmed; and the population is computed to be eighty thousand. Mr. Beth, the British Resident here, transacts the usual commercial relations; and the monopoly of the sappan wood, which continues to be the exclusive privilege of the British Government, at one rix dollar per picol. Besides that article, the island furnishes rice, horses, salt-petre, sulphur, wax, birds'-nests, tobacco, &c., though there is but little trade carried on now at this place. The island, however, has means of great improvement, and would be highly productive, if the inhabitants could be roused to exertion, and their labour turned to industry and agriculture. The number of horses annually exported under the appellation of Beema horses, is very considerable. The finest of these are procured from the small island of Gonong Api*, situated at the north-east end of Beema harbour, about three or four miles from Sumbawa Point, and forming the west side of the north entrance of Sapy Straits. It is a large volcanic mountain, which termi-nates in two high peaks, and the soil is astonishingly fertile. Another

---

* According to a superstitious tradition of the natives, the sea-horse is supposed to pay a visit every five years to the mares of this place, who, after copulating with him in his own element, return to their rich pasture, at the foot of the mountain, and bring forth the breed which is so beautiful and valuable. The horses are small, and the prevailing colour of those in the island is a jet black, though few of that description are to be seen among those which are brought from hence.

volcanic mountain on the north coast of Sumbawa, is said to be responsive to that of Goonong Api; an explosion of the latter being
immediately answered by an irruption from the former; for which
reason the inhabitants of Goonong Api are looked upon with a superstitious veneration by those of Sumbawa. The great depth of
water here makes it dangerous for vessels, except prows, to approach
the shore sufficiently near to find anchorage.

Ships may be plentifully supplied with refreshments, as buffaloes,
calves, sheep, fruit, and vegetables, both at Beema, and the town of
Sumbawa. This last place is situated on a large bay, open to the
north and north-west, and a good harbour stretches inland, between
the reefs at the west side of the entrance. Sumbawa is about 100 miles
to the westward of Beema, and is governed by a chief denominated a
Rajah, whose name is Mahomed, but subject to the authority of the
Sultan. The other towns, or districts, are Dompoo, Tambora, Sangur,
and Pekat; all under their respective chiefs. Tambora is the place
mostly resorted to by the dealers in horses. Gold-dust is found on
Sumbawa, particularly in the district of Dompoo; which also supplies
teak-timber, and is the best cultivated district in the Island. Pearls
are fished for in the large Bay, to the westward of Beema Bay, as also
at Pekat. Between the west coast of Sumbawa and the east coast of
Allas Straits. Lombock, is Allas Strait, called Gilleesee by the natives, in extent
about forty-five miles. It is the safest and most convenient strait east
of Java, having soundings, whereby ships are enabled to anchor when
necessary, with moderate tides; and the plantations and villages on
the coast of Lombock, which is low close to the sea, afford supplies
and refreshments.

Lombock Peak, in latitude 8 deg. 21½ min. south, long. 116 deg. 26 min. east, rises in a pyramidical form, to the height of about 8000 feet above the level of the sea.

The inhabitants of Lombock are chiefly emigrants from Bally and Sumbawa. They retain many Hindoo customs, particularly that of burning their dead ; and the widow also, as in India, immolates herself on the funeral pile of her husband.

Appenan, or Amppannan town, in Lombock, is situated on a large Bay of that name, in the Straits of Lombock, nearly opposite to the road of Carang Assem, and is very populous, as also is the level country adjoining the Bay. The several small rivers which discharge themselves into this Bay, make it very convenient for watering ; and supplies of bullocks, hogs, goats, poultry, and vegetables, may be obtained here in abundance. Contiguous to this place is Mataran, the residence of the Rajah of Lombock, who is tributary to the Sultan of Baly.

BALY ISLAND is very mountainous, but capable of great fertility and cultivation. The coast rises gradually towards the interior, about ten miles to the foot of a chain of mountains, which run across the island from west to east, and are terminated on the east end by the Peak of Baly. At the foot of this mountain, which is volcanic, and has a crater, the town of Carang Assem is situated, in the midst of a rich and populous district, which is well cultivated.

Carang Assem, which is the most considerable town, and the largest district in Baly, is the only harbour or place of anchorage for ships. But vessels may receive refreshments upon any part of the north coast, where they may stand on and off during their communications with

2 T

the shore; and there are, indeed, no reefs, rocks, or other local dangers, on any part of this coast. The next place of note is Boleeling. This town is nearly screened from observation by the gardens, topes, and rich cultivation, with which it is everywhere surrounded. It is the residence of the Rajah Amy Boean Gidee Carang, who is said to be a very pleasant and hospitable character. The name of another Rajah is Moeda, whose martial exploits appear to have gained him some celebrity among the people of Baly. These two, and the Rajah of Lombock, are brothers.

It is remarkable that the title of Rajah, which in India is exclusively confined to Hindoos, is in this instance adopted by Mussulmans, or at least by Chiefs professing themselves of that faith. This is a circumstance which serves to prove that the Aborigines of all these islands were Hindoos.

The Island of Baly is divided into eight districts, *Currang Assem*, *Boleeling*, *Taman Baly*, *Koolong Kong*, *Toeyanyer*, *Mongoewie*, *Tabana*, and *Badong*, each under its own chief, and all independent of one another. The district of Badong is that opposite Java. The Dutch had formerly a small establishment at the capital, which has since been evacuated. The refractory spirit of the Chieftains rendered it expedient for the expedition under Major General Nightingale, to touch at Baly, in April 1814; and their appearance happily averted actual hostilities, by effecting the timely submission of the chiefs.

The Island produces rice in great abundance; not only sufficient for home consumption, but exportation to other settlements. Oil, tobacco, and salt, are also produced here, but wood is entirely supplied from Java. There are no forests in Baly; teak is wholly unknown there.

Roads for horses are said to communicate throughout the island, from one district to another ; and the population is stated at 100,000, which, however, seems to be much below the real number.

The inhabitants are able-bodied men, and possessed of more industry and application than the Malays, or Buggese. They appear to be generally wealthy, and articles of European workmanship, woollen cloths, &c. never fail to meet here with a ready sale.

Recruiting for the colonial service of Java and the eastern islands, properly managed, is likely to succeed at this place; and, except the Amboynese, the people of Baly seem to be the best adapted, among the eastern tribes, for making good soldiers, from their ready subjection to discipline.

The religion of these people partakes of the Hindoos. They burn their dead, and the widow is frequently consumed with the body of the husband ; a recent instance of which was witnessed, when the Hecate touched at Boleeling, in a late cruize to the eastward, on occasion of the death of a Rajah, with whose body were burnt his two wives. On the other hand, they eat pork, which proves them not to be of the bigotted Musselman faith; and beef, which makes them unlike the prejudiced Hindoo. One of their deities is named Deewa.

The Chinese population is very considerable in Baly, particularly at Boleeling. Opium, which, before the conquest of Java, used to be brought to Boleeling by English traders, was thence smuggled into Java, at an enormous profit ; but, at present, the monopoly of this article by our Government has excluded private persons from participating in so valuable a traffic.

Proceeding to the northward of Java, one of the largest, and

2 T 2

probably one of the richest islands in the world presents itself to the view ; though little comparatively is known of its internal state or productions, as hitherto all attempts to penetrate beyond the coast have proved ineffectual ; nor has any friendly intercourse been established with the jealous natives.   This vast island is

BORNEO, of which the kingdom of Lava, comprising the interior of the Island, is only known by name ; and the people are called Biajos; but of their civil institutions, language, and religion, nothing satisfactory can be ascertained ; while the coasts are inhabited by tribes of savage Malays, Moors, and Buggese, who unite to a treacherous malignity the most brutal ferocity of manners ; of which many melancholy instances have occurred to unfortunate voyagers on these shores.

The Portuguese, as early as the year 1526, endeavoured to establish themselves in Borneo, but they were, for the most part, murdered under the appearance of friendship, in a time of profound peace.

About three or four thousand converts to Christianity, the labour of the Portuguese missionaries, on the river Culjong Cajamp, were also massacred about the year 1690, by order of the king of Banjirmassin ; since which time christianity has been entirely extinct in the island.   The Mahomedan religion prevails on the coast, and paganism in the interior of the country.

The Dutch, in 1648, succeeded in forcing the king of Banjirmassin to a treaty, by which he surrendered to them the exclusive pepper trade, and in 1709 they erected fort Tatar.   The Dutch also gained possession of the commerce, with Landan and Succadana.   The latter town is situated in 1 deg. 30 min. south latitude, on the principal or southern outlet of a very large river, which is navigable 150 miles up for prows. This place is celebrated for the large diamonds found here, as also the best camphor.

Banjirmassin still continues to be a dependency on Java, and Fort Tatar is garrisoned by colonials, under the orders of the British resident. It is situated about four degrees to the Northward of the East end of Java, on a fine river, and from its commerce and great population, is a place of considerable importance. A great quantity of gold is found in the mountains of the king of Banjirmassin's territories, and in the sand of almost all the large rivers in Borneo. Iron, copper, and tin are also found in this country; pepper grows in abundance, and these articles, with the gum called dragon's-blood, camphor, and sandal-wood, edible birds'-nests, benzoin, cambac-wood, eagle-wood, canes, reeds, wax, with some cloves and nutmegs in the mountains, constitute the principal productions of Borneo. Pearls are found on the northern coast, and gold and diamonds enrich almost every part of this extensive island. These are brought by the natives of the mountains and the interior to the sea-ports, where they are exchanged with various objects of merchandize. The articles which find the readiest sale here are red agates, bracelets of copper, coral of all kinds, porcelain, rice, opium, salt, onions, sugar, linen, &c.; and this profitable trade is carried on principally in Chinese junks.

The king of Banjirmassin usually resides at Cota Tengah, to the westward of the river of Banjirmassin; and a number of large rivers, with considerable towns or sea-ports, are very favourable to the commerce of his kingdom. That of Mandawy, which is very large, runs through a country which furnishes much gold, bezoar-wax, dragon's-blood, canes, and works in reeds. The mouth of the river Sampit is remarkable for its great breadth, and terminating in a spacious bay, forms an extensive and safe harbour.

Pontiana, on the west coast of Borneo, has very recently placed itself under the British protection. It is situated on a fine navigable river, nearly under the equator. The Sultan of that place, fearing the vengeance of Anam, the Chieftain of Sambas, applied for a British garrison, which was granted; and the subsequent capture of Sambas will no doubt strengthen the existing relations, and improve the commercial interests in that quarter.

Sambas river has a wide entrance, and is in lat. 1 deg. 12 minutes north, long. 109 deg. 5 min. east. The town is about forty miles up the river, on the south branch.

The houses here, as in almost all the other sea-port towns in Borneo, are built of timber and bamboos, raised on wooden stakes or piles, on low swampy morasses. The Sultan is a powerful Prince, but at the period of the late capture by the British armament, he retired into the interior of his territories.

The predatory and piratical pursuits of the inhabitants generally, made it very unsafe for the European trader to venture near any part of the extensive coasts which skirt this great island, and particularly the north-west part of Borneo; where armed prows were continually on the watch, both in Sambas and the river Borneo proper, to dart on the unprepared and defenceless merchant vessel, which they not only seized, but with circumstances of horrible barbarity on the unhappy crews. A large Portuguese ship, with a very valuable cargo, which was thus assaulted and carried to Sambas by the pirates, under the orders of the before-mentioned Anam, was the principal cause of the first attack directed against that chieftain, in October 1812, by the late lamented Captain Bowen, of His Majesty's ship Phœnix.

Of a second attack, which was successfully made by Colonel Watson, the following official statement will give at once an interesting representation, while it affords also an accurate description of a place which till this event was hardly known.

To the Honourable the Lieutenant Governor in Council, &c. &c.

" HONOURABLE SIR,

" I Have the honour to inform you, that I arrived off the Sambas River on the 22d ult. with the force under my command, after touching at Pontiana, to procure boats, &c. On my arrival, I found Captain Sayer commanding a squadron of his Majesty's ships, and the following morning we commenced getting the ordnance and stores into the boats, and on the 25th the troops entered the river. Previous to our advance, a letter signed by Captain Sayer and myself, was dispatched to the Sultan, by Lieutenant Bayley, of the Madras Native Infantry, requiring him to surrender the defences of Sambas; also the Pangerang Anam, and his piratical adherents. This letter it appears was received by the Pangerang, the Sultan having previously withdrawn to the interior, but no answer was returned. We then moved up the river, and anchored on the night of the 26th off the branch leading to Sambas. From all the information I could obtain, the access to the batteries was so difficult, that I determined to employ our whole force, divided into different attacks, one of which at least I hoped would be able to penetrate to the batteries. I accordingly sent a detachment of his Majesty's 14th Regiment, with Captain Morris's party, to land from the main river, and penetrate in that direction, which Captain Morris was

confident was practicable. This officer was obliged, however, by severe illness, to relinquish the command of this column to Lieutenant Bolton, the next senior officer. Another party, composed of the Royal Marines from his Majesty's ships, with one hundred Sepoys of the 3d Volunteer Battalion, under the command of Captain Brookes, of the 2d Bengal Volunteer Battalion, had to pass through a cut higher up, leading into the Sambas river, down which they were to come in rear of the town. This party, if not in time for the attack, I hoped might intercept the retreat of the enemy.

Each of those divisions was also accompanied by a party of armed seamen, to assist in carrying the ladders, and in making a way through the jungle.

With the remainder of the force, I proceeded up the Sambas river, and anchored on the night of the 27th instant, out of reach of gun-shot from the batteries. As a little a-head of our anchorage the ground appeared rather firm, from the report of Lieutenant Bayley, whom I sent to reconnoitre the place, I determined on landing there another party, consisting of one hundred of his Majesty's 14th Regiment, eighty Sepoys of the Third Bengal Volunteer battalion, and a detachment of Artillery, with a party of the seamen. This column was commanded by Captain Watson, of his Majesty's 14th Regiment. It was disembarked at 3 A. M.; and after surmounting many obstacles from the nature of the country, came in sight of the batteries at half-past nine o'clock. Captain Watson immediately commenced the attack, and, in little more than half an hour, carried by assault the two principal batteries, and three redoubts in their rear, although resolutely defended. A battery and five redoubts on the opposite side of the river, were then evacuated by the enemy.

" On the commencement of the firing, I pushed up the river, with a party kept as a reserve, in men of war's boats, to second whichever column began the attack. The front battery fired at the boats advancing, although Captain Watson was at that time in its rear, endeavouring to force an entrance. It is difficult to ascertain the loss of the enemy, as many were killed endeavouring to escape in boats and across the boom. From the best information I can obtain, it amounts to about one hundred and fifty men, including a brother of the Sultan's, the eldest son of Pangerang Anom, and twelve others. Pangerang Anom made his escape in a small quick sailing-boat.

" Captain Brookes found the cut through which he had to pass, much smaller than had been represented, and rendered impassable by trees felled across it. A little beyond this cut, he found a boom across the main river, defended by two forts, which opened on a reconnoitering party, and killed the boatswain of the Leda. Being late in the evening, Captain Brookes determined to attack them early on the following morning; when, as he was moving for this purpose, a canoe brought a letter from the Chief; the purport of it was—' That his batteries had fired by mistake; that he was the friend of the Europeans.' At this moment arrived his Majesty's ship Procris, which had been sent up the main river. Captain Norton sent to inform the Chief, that he wished to anchor off the battery, and desired the boom might be opened. This request not being complied with, a party of seamen was sent to cut it. Just as they had succeeded, the batteries commenced firing, which was returned by the Procris. Captain Brookes then landed his party to attack them; but the enemy immediately evacuated their forts, and fled into the jungle. In this affair two Sepoys were killed, and a ship Lascar wounded.

" Lieutenant Bolton's party, it appears, took a wrong direction at first, and from the difficulties they had to encounter, did not arrive in time for the attack.

" I have the honor to transmit a return of our Killed and Wounded during the operations; also of the Ordnance found in the enemy's works.

" Considering the number and difficulty of access to the batteries, which prevented the possibility of exactly timing a combined attack, or of moving a large force in any one direction, our loss is perhaps less than might have been expected.

" It is with much regret I have further to relate the death of Captain Morris, on the 1st instant. This zealous officer, although very ill, persisted in accompanying me. He fell a victim to his unbounded zeal for the service.

" The pleasing part of my duty now remains, to bear testimony to the general good conduct of the whole of the troops, and to the cordial co-operation of Captain Sayer, commanding His Majesty's squadron, who placed under my orders the marines, and also a body of disposable seamen.

" From the Honourable Captain Elliot, with whom Captain Sayer entrusted the immediate arrangement and command of the armed boats of the squadron, I experienced every assistance and readiness in complying with any of my suggestions. My thanks are due to the whole of the officers, seamen, and marines, that landed from His Majesty's Ships to second our operations, particularly to Captain Leslie and the party under his orders, which accompanied Captain Watson's column. To Captain Watson and his division every praise is due ; the result of their attack fully corrobo-rates the report made by him, that nothing could exceed the coolness and intrepidity of the men composing it.

" I am much indebted to Lieutenant Bayley, of the Madras native infantry, for his assistance. This officer landed with Captain Watson's column, which he volunteered to lead ; and after much perseverance, succeeded in cutting a passage through the jungle.

" From Captain Dyson, His Majesty's 14th regiment, major of brigade, and Lieu-tenant Gunn, of the Bengal light infantry volunteer battalion, quarter-master to the troops, I also derived every assistance in the previous arrangements, and during the operations of the service.

" I have the honor to be,

Honourable Sir,

Your Most Obedient Servant,

(Signed)   JAMES WATSON,

Lieutenant Colonel of the 14th Regiment, Commanding the Troops.

Sambas, July 3, 1813.

Return of Killed and Wounded during the Operations against Sambas, including that of Captain Brookes Detachment up the Main River, July 3d, 1813.

Regiments or Corps, and Ships Names.	Killed and Wounded.	Officers.			Non Commissioned Officers, Rank and File.				Seamen on Shore.		Grand Total.			
		Captains.	Lieutenants.	Ensigns.	Sergeants and Havildars.	Drummers.	Rank and File.	Gun Lascars.	Boatswains.	Seamen.	Officers. Killed.	Wounded.	Non-Commissioned Officers, Rank and File, and Seamen. Killed.	Wounded.
His Majesty's 14th Regiment, - -	Killed						3							
Ditto, ditto, - - - -	Wounded	1	1				20							
Third Bengal Volunteer Battalion, -	Killed						3							
Ditto, ditto, - - - -	Wounded		1			1	13							
Bengal Artillery, - - - - - -	Killed							1						
Ditto, ditto, - - - -	Wounded							6						
His Majesty's Ship Leda, - - - -	Killed								1					
His Majesty's Ship Hussar, - - -	Wounded		1							16				
	Total										0	4	7	55

NAMES OF OFFICERS CORRESPONDING.

Captain Watson, His Majesty's 14th Regiment, slightly.

Lieutenant Jennings, ditto   ditto.

——————— Trist, 3d Bengal Volunteer Battalion, wounded severely and dangerously.

——————— Hoghton, His Majesty's Ship Hussar, severely.

(Signed)   J. DYSON,

Major of Brigade.

Return of the Ordnance Stores captured in the different Batteries
at Sambas.

	GUNS.											Total.
	Pounders.											
	32	24	18	12	8	6	4	3	2	1	½	
Brass Ordnance, - - - ·					1		1		2	20	7	31
Iron ditto, - - - - - -	1	6	2	8		2	4	3	10			36
Total	1	6	2	8	1	2	5	3	12	20	7	67

Round Shot, different sizes,   .   .   .   6000

Bar ditto,   ditto, ...   30

Gun-powder Barrels, ...   26

(Signed)   A. CAMERON,

Lieut. Com. Detach. Bengal Artillery.

A true Copy,

(Signed)   J. DYSON, Major of Brigade.

The whole trade of Borneo has long been, and still continues, in the hands of the Chinese, of whom great numbers are settled in the country, and where they carry on a very extensive commerce. At the town of Borneo, which is situated fifteen miles up the country, on a fine navigable river, the Chinese build junks of four hundred tons burthen, which are navigated by themselves, and in which they export pepper, camphor, which is here of the very best quality, spices, with a variety of other valuable productions of the country, and wares of different sorts. These are conveyed to Java, Sumatra, Celebes, Tonquin, Siam, and other parts, from whence the Chinese bring back to Borneo all kinds of Eastern and European goods, together with such articles as can be procured in China from Japan by the way of exchange. The Diamond mines in Borneo are very productive. Some of the stones are exceedingly fine, and weigh from twenty to thirty and forty carats ; but such large ones are seldom offered for sale, being religiously preserved in the families of the principal chiefs, and handed down from father to son, or given as marriage portions. Those sold are generally of the smaller kind, from five to six carats, and the rose and table diamonds seem to be valued in the East nearly as much as brilliants.

PASSIR, on the east coast of Borneo, and situated on a river in the Straits of Macassar, was formerly subordinate to the Dutch, and considerable for its commerce ; carrying on a great trade in gold and other merchandize, particularly spices, which are produced in the mountains.

Of the smaller islands, to the northward of Borneo, that of Balambangan presents every convenience, with fine harbours to invite the establishment of a colony ; though the attempt of the English to settle there, in 1773, was soon abandoned, owing principally to the jealousy and power of the Dutch.

MACASSAR Strait is about 350 miles in length, and generally from 110 to 140 miles wide, except at the north entrance, where it contracts to 50 miles.

Macassar Town, or Fort Rotterdam, is situated near the southwestern extremity of the island of Celebes, in latitude five degrees nine seconds south, longitude about one hundred and nineteen degrees thirty-nine seconds east. The town and fort have a pleasing appearance from the sea, and the road is protected, in a great degree, by the isles and banks to the north and south ; and these afford also the means of a profitable trade in the *Beach de Maar*, collected here for the China market. This article which literally signifies " Insect of the Sea," has the appearance of a large leech when first gathered, and being properly dried and cured, is considered as a great delicacy, particularly by the Chinese. Unlike most other Dutch settlements, which are encompassed by swamps, and divided by numerous canals, the country round Macassar is high, fine, and healthy.

The fort, which is irregular and ancient, is considered by the natives as impregnable. Towards the sea-face is a strong battery, which commands the roads to a great distance ; and the water is so deep, that line-of-battle ships might lie within pistol-shot of the shore. A British garrison of regulars, and some colonial troops, are stationed here.

The town is surrounded by a stone-wall, sufficiently low to admit a defence from the houses, and yet high enough to prevent a sudden surprise from a nightly escalade, or guard against a coup-de-main. The settlement is flourishing ; and Chinese junks from this place, carry on a direct trade with China ; so that the mixed population of Dutch and half-casts, Chinese and natives, is very considerable.

The Island of Celebes is nearly circular with several large Bays, and is above five hundred miles in length. The interior has hitherto been little explored ; and consequently its natural history is as little known as that of Borneo. The climate is temperate, and the country diversified with hills, dales, and mountains, affording a variety of beautiful landscape scenery.

The Dutch, after the expulsion of the Portuguese from the Moluccas, became masters of the entire trade of this extensive Island ; the possession of which, though not very lucrative, they deemed of so much importance as to sacrifice seventy or eighty thousand guilders annually, to defray the surplus expenses of their establishments on Celebes; in order to keep out strangers, and prevent a smuggling trade with the neighbouring spice islands.

The conquest of the country cost much blood and treasure; the ferocious temper of the natives, and the intrepidity of their chiefs, long opposing a powerful resistance to the settlement of foreign intruders. So formidable were these people in former times, that one of the kings of Macassar, Krain Samarloka, is said, in their early history, to have sailed with a fleet of two hundred vessels, in the year 1420, to attack Malacca. In their protracted conflicts with the Dutch, the Macassars murdered many Europeans, and plundered their ships; and it was not till after repeated fights, and various unsuccessful attempts to effect their expulsion, that the kings of Macassar, and lesser chiefs, were at length, in 1699, compelled to make peace with the Dutch; by guaranteeing to them the exclusion of other European traders from the island.

The Buggese, or inhabitants of Celebes, are trained from their childhood to martial exercises; and they are, in consequence, very dexterous in the use of the spear. The criss, which is constantly worn by them, too often proves the fatal instrument of assassination. Numerous instances are related of their inflamed passions bursting forth in sudden and violent starts; and sometimes, without the least provocation, they are known to have attacked persons in the public streets, of whom they had not the slightest knowledge, cutting and stabbing them to death, from no other motive, frequently, than to try the metal of their crisses or choppers. An occurrence of this kind was very recently witnessed. While a Buggese was carrying wood through the town of Macassar, a man whom he had never seen stabbed him in passing, with his criss in the shoulder, without the smallest offence having been given. The person attacked turned instantly with his chopper ; and, after a desperate battle, at noon day, in which no person interfered, the aggressor was at length completely cut in pieces.

Another recent instance, equally shocking and barbarous, is related of a native who had been banished for his crimes, by the Rajah Boni, to another district, where he continued his villany to such an extent, that at length the Chief was obliged to give an order for his execution, according to the customary mode among these people ; which is, by dispatching an armed party to the house of the culprit, about midnight, and, when he has no suspicion of danger, to fall suddenly upon him, and cut him to pieces. Such was the course intended to have been adopted in the present case, but the criminal unluckily had heard of their approach, and was prepared for their reception. He inquired who were his visitors at that hour ; on which he was told—" The servants of the Rajah Boni." " Come in," said he, " I shall be happy to see you." The instant one man raised his head in the apartment, as instantly he was crissed ; a second followed, and shared the same fate ; at length, after several unsuccessful attempts, which were all equally fatal to the servants of the Rajah, a consultation was held by the rest, how this desperate fellow was to be taken ; and whilst they were thus deliberating, he extinguished the light in the apartment above, and threw a log of wood down the ladder, which had instantly a number of crisses planted in it, the men mistaking it at first for his body. Amidst the general confusion that prevailed, he rushed frantically forward, denouncing death to his pursuers ; and he certainly fulfilled his threat with wonderful success, for before he fell under the crisses of his assailants, he had killed upwards of twenty men ; and his wife, refusing to be removed from the body, suffered the same fate.

The general state of agriculture in Celebes is very low, owing to the extreme indolence of the natives in all works of utility and industry. They are, however, keen sportsmen ; and deer, and every other game, abound in the island. Their mode of running down the former, is the same as that which is practised in some parts of Java.

Though Mahommedanism is the professed religion of the native inhabitants of Celebes, they appear to be little scrupulous in the performance of its precepts.

They were formerly idolaters, and the objects of their worship were the Sun and Moon, to which luminaries their adorations were paid under the open firmament of Heaven, as they conceived that nothing on earth was excellent enough to compose a temple worthy of the divinity.

The Buggese are possessed of many good qualities, which, if better cultivated, would give these people a great superiority to their neigh- bours, and produce a good effect in influencing their intercourse with strangers. They may be rendered very faithful by liberal treatment, and in many cases they have evinced a sincere attachment to those by whom they were employed ; but they cannot endure ill usage, nor will they easily forget an injury. They are remarkably courteous in their behaviour to each other, and will very rarely descend to personal

abuse; though it must be confessed, that while they consider it as dis-
honourable to make use of scurrilous language, they have no scruple
in avenging the slightest affront with the murderous criss, which in
fact they seem to regard as the only legitimate arbiter of their real or
pretended wrongs. When roused by a sense of danger, or by the
desire of revenge, these people have been known to perform the most
extraordinary exploits of valour and intrepidity. They will, indeed,
sooner rush on death in a thousand shapes than suffer themselves to be
overcome in their contests at sea with their piratical neighbours. A
Buggese prow was lately overpowered by an armed pirate; and when
the crew saw no chance of escape, they set fire to a barrel of gun-
powder on the very instant that the victors boarded them; and thus
they and their foes were launched into eternity together.

The Dutch entertained a number of Buggese among their colonial
troops; and, both at Cornelis and Djoejocarta, they fought desperately;
but all attempts at recruiting among them have of late proved
unsuccessful.

Macassar receives its principal supplies of rice from Bally. The
beef and mutton here are tolerably good; but the only supply of cattle
that can be relied upon procuring at this island, are buffaloes.

The principal articles of export trade are gold, sapan, and sandal-
wood; camphor, cotton, some kinds of hardware, arms for the
Indians, ginger, long pepper, pearls, &c.; and the chief imports are
tin, copper, iron, cloths of various kinds, &c.

Besides the subordinate residency of Beema, with its tributary isles,
the Government of Macassar exercises a controul over several other

establishments and places in the neighbourhood, under the general authority of the British Government in Java.

BONTHIAN, situated to the south-eastward of Macassar, at the bottom of the bay, is very fertile in rice and paddy, and affords excellent anchorage near the village, in seven or eight fathoms sandy bottom, at the north part of the bay. Here is a fine river of very good water. The inhabitants are accounted the subjects of the Company, and pay to the Resident the tenth of their landed produce ; as do those of Booloe Comba, another small settlement farther to the eastward, and under the inspection or superintendence of the Resident at Bonthian. The Fort of Boolo Comba was gallantly attacked and taken the 12th January, 1810, by a party of one hundred men, landed from the Cornwallis, commanded by Captain Montague, attended by Captain Forbes and Lieutenant Duncan Stewart, of the Madras service. This small party, after capturing the Fort from the Dutch, had to sustain, on the following day, a furious attack, from a numerous body of the confederate natives, headed by their chiefs, in all the terror of Malay warfare. They were, however, repulsed, after great efforts on the part of Captain Montague and his gallant party. One instance of devotedness deserves particular mention on this occasion. A soldier of the Madras European regiment, who received a shot through his leg, fell, calling for assistance when the enemy were close upon him. Lieutenant Stewart, observing his perilous situation, nobly stepped from the line, threw him on his back, and, at the imminent risk of his own life, succeeded in carrying the poor fellow to the rear in safety. A fine river of good water, and navigable on the east side of Boolo Comba Bay, marks the European boundary from the dominions of the Rajah Goa, at first the most powerful Chief on Celebes; but Rajah Boni having become the principal ally of the Dutch, he was, through their means, raised to the supremacy on the island. As late as the year 1780, the Buggese of Goa shewed great firmness in their attack on the Dutch Fort of Rotterdam, at Macassar; but they were beat off with great slaughter.

Warjoo is another rival of Boni, but who was always opposed by the Dutch in support of their ally. All these governments are much spoken of in history, as is that of Manado, or Mandar. Sapin and Seluidrin are inland governments. They are monarchical and elective, partaking greatly of the ancient feudal system of the European nations.

The restless and ambitious disposition of the native chieftains of Celebes, had long been, as already stated, a source of trouble to the former government of this colony. The recent conduct of the Rajah of Boni, equally hostile and insulting, rendering an example necessary, an expedition was fitted out at Java, in April 1814, under Major-General Nightingale; which having arrived at Macassar, on the morning of the 7th of June, prepared to attack the Rajah; as that chieftain had declined to make the reparation demanded of him, and refused to surrender to the British Commander the somdang or regalia of Goa, which he had forcibly seized. The troops commanded by Lieutenant-Colonel M'Leod, were in consequence ordered to assault the town and palace, as soon as the day should dawn. All the barriers were carried successively, in the most gallant stile, though not without some loss; and the whole town and residence of the Rajah were in the possession of our troops in little more than an hour from the commencement of the attack. But the Rajah had effected his escape during the night, attended by a few followers. His residence being the principal depot, with a great quantity of gunpowder, fell into our hands, as well as five pieces of cannon, of small calibre, several stands of colours, and arms of all descriptions. The residence was set fire to, and entirely consumed. The strength of the enemy was about three thousand men ; and their loss, in killed and wounded, was considerable.

These measures terminated in the deposal of the Rajah from the authority which he had held in Celebes ; and, by the subsequent arrangements which have been adopted, the tranquillity of the country has been secured, while a happy reconciliation between the contending houses has enabled the General to re-establish an efficient adminis- tration for the country, on principles equally conciliatory to the people and satisfactory to Government.

Maros, to the northward of Fort Rotterdam, is also subject to Macassar. Five rivers, running close to one another, separate the two places, and the country, which is intersected by a great number of smaller streams and rivulets, is productive in rice and paddy, of which one-tenth is paid to the Resident. Saltpetre is also procured in this neighbourhood, principally near the village of Soudang, situated at the foot of a mountain, bordering on Maros river. Of the insular depen- dencies on Macassar, Salayer Island is the first, and gives its name to the Straits formed betwixt its north end, and the south-east point of Celebes. It is about 30 miles in length, very populous and well-cul- tivated. Salayer cloths manufactured here, and cotton yarns, were among the articles of taxation or tribute drawn from the inhabitants of this island by their former masters, the Dutch.

Booton Island, which is well peopled, is considered as tributary to Macassar. Some Dutch generally reside at the town of Booton, situated a little inside the south entrance of the Strait, in lat. 5 deg. 27 min. south, long. 122 deg. 48 min. east. This island is imperfectly known, as also is the eastern coast of Celebes, which is formed of extensive Peninsulas, and the approach to which should be very cautious, taking the greatest care to guard against treachery from the inhabitants.

Buggese Bay, presents a dangerous and intricate navigation, stretching near 200 miles from the south point of Celebes to the northward, into the middle of the island; and towards the bottom of it, and on the west side of the Bay is situated the town of Boni, on a fine river, where is good anchorage in eight or ten fathoms water.

The next great Bays are those of Tollo and Tomminie, or Goonong Tella river; on the banks of which the Dutch had several small forts for the protection of their trade with the nations of those parts, consisting principally in wax and gold-dust. After the reduction of Amboyna, Captain Tucker, of his Majesty's ship Dover, directed his attention to these subordinate stations, and on the 16th June, 1810, having arrived off this harbour, he established a friendly intercourse with the King of this part of Celebes, who resides at Fort Nassan, about five miles up the river; and the Dutch flag, which had been waving on the batteries that defended the harbour, was exchanged for the British. The village, which is two miles up the river, supplies every kind of refreshment, and horses, buffaloes, bullocks, sheep, goats, and poultry, may be procured here.

Manado, with Fort Amsterdam, is the northernmost of the Dutch settlements on Celebes: whence they procured much gold in exchange for opium and Hindostan piece goods, chiefly blue cloth, fine Bengal stuffs, iron and steel. This place also surrendered to Captain Tucker, on the 24th June, 1810. In the fort were found fifty guns mounted, with plenty of ammunition, stores, and provisions. The garrison consisted of one Captain, three Lieutenants, and one hundred and nine soldiers. The bay and town is situated in lat. about 1 deg. 28 min. north, on the west side of the north-east end of Celebes. This place is fertile in rice, with which it supplies the neighbouring Molucca Islands; and it was consequently placed under the direction of the more important Residency of Ternate.

MOLUCCA ISLES.

TERNATE, the northernmost of a chain of islands adjoining to the west coast of Gillolo, was formerly the seat of sovereignty over all the adjacent Molucca Islands, Ternate, Tidore, Bachian, Motir, and Machian, the great work of the Portuguese who first visited them in 1510. The King of Ternate was one of the most potent monarchs of the East, extending his sovereignty over seventeen or eighteen other islands, and maintaining a considerable naval force. But on the expulsion of the Portuguese from the Molucca Isles by the Dutch, in 1607, the native princes were forced to submit to the humiliating conditions of their new conqueror; by which they were interdicted from all trade and intercourse of any kind with any nation but the Dutch.

Thus they soon shared the fate of the conquered provinces of the East, and dwindled away into a state of political insignificance, poverty, and dependence ; while their new masters secured to themselves the valuable spice trade on their own terms. The King of Ternate, however, is still the most powerful of the Molucca Princes. One of that race, in 1722, embraced the Christian Religion ; but the present Sultans of Ternate and Tidore, both profess Mohammedanism. Next in power is the King of Tidore. The former possessing the northern part of Gillolo, with Mortay Bachian, Motir, &c., and part of Papua, whence he receives a tribute of gold, amber, and birds of paradise ; and the Sultan of Tidore holds the southern part of Gillolo, with Mysole, and some other isles. It is not unfrequent in the Oriental Archipelago, to observe similar instances of small isles having been selected for the seats of Monarchy, to which the large and more extensive islands are subject.

Ternate is of small extent but high, and the Dutch erected three forts on it, named Orange, Holland, and Williamstadt. That of Orange was the principal fort, on the east side, where the chief town is situated, in lat. about 0 deg. 50 min. north, long. 127 deg. 32 min. east, with good anchorage near the shore. Here Captain Edward Tucker, of his Majesty's ship Dover, having taken on board a reinforcement of one hundred men, from the garrison at Amboyna, effected a landing on the morning of the 28th August, 1810, and with a handful of men, achieved the capture of a place which had withstood the repeated attacks made upon it by the English in the former war. The troops, commanded by Captain David Forbes, consisted of the following detail :—

Madras European Regiment Artillery	-					74
Amboynese Corps	-	-	-	-	-	32
Royal Marines	-	-	-	-	-	36
Seamen	-	-	-	-	-	32
Total	-	-	-	-		174

It was intended to have landed under the walls of Fort Kayo Meirah, and to have instantly stormed it, but a strong current not only impeded their progress, but compelled them at day-light to bear up and seek a landing place at Sasa, a village screened by a point of land from fort Kayo Meirah, and out of its line of fire.

This place they reached at seven o'clock, and having made good their landing, a party under Lieutenant Forbes, was immediately moved forward to occupy the heights, and a gun was got up after great exertion, on account of the steepness of the hill, and placed in a commanding position, while with the remainder, Captain Forbes proceeded towards a height which had been represented to him as completely commanding Fort Kayo Meirah, and as having been the spot occupied by our troops in the preceding war.

In the mean time, a summons was sent from the Dover, to the Governor, Colonel Mittman—who returned a spirited answer—and the evening having now closed in, and there being no anchorage, the land-wind and currents rendered it impossible to prevent the ship from drifting out of the harbour.

Captain Forbes having determined to storm Fort Kayo Meirah that night, set out with the greatest part of the troops on shore, at seven o'clock, by the inland road, accompanied by Lieutenants Jefferies,

2 y

Royal Navy, Higginson, Royal Marines, and Forbes and Cursham, of the Madras service.

After advancing a short distance, they found it impossible to proceed further by the road they were then pursuing, the enemy having, in the course of the day, cut down a great number of immense trees, and thrown them in heaps across it; turning therefore to the right, and following the tract of a rivulet, after great labour, and in total darkness, the party reached the beach, and about ten o'clock arrived within a few hundred yards of the fort undiscovered.

Having advanced within a hundred yards of the place, the enemy's out-sentry fired his musquet, which gave the alarm, and a volley immediately followed from a strong detachment, with a brigade of guns.

This party of the enemy were driven in at the point of the bayonet, and though under a most galling fire of grape and musquetry, our brave assailants, led on by Captain Forbes, resolutely crossed the ditch, and placing the ladders on the flank of the bastion, to the right of the bridge, escaladed the walls, and carried the fort instantly. Many of the garrison were killed, and the commanding officer and sixty-eight prisoners were secured. The British loss was one sergeant-major, two privates, killed; and one lieutenant, one sergeant, one seaman, one guide, and twelve privates, wounded.

At day-light, the battery of Kota Barro opened a heavy fire. This, however, was silenced by the Dover in the afternoon of the 29th, as soon as the wind and current enabled her to pour her grape and cannister shot into the place, which quickly drove the enemy from his guns. Observing it to be silenced, the Dover stood on for the next battery, by which she opened another, and the sea-face of Fort Orange, and was hotly engaged with the whole, when the enemy again entered, and recommenced a fire from Kota Barro; thus exposed to a heavy cross-fire, the Dover was compelled to resume her station off the latter post, and with a sweeping fire of grape and cannister, which nothing could withstand, she silenced it a second time. A party, under Lieut. Higginson, were just proceeding on shore, to spike the guns in Kota Barro, when a party of our troops were seen engaged with a detachment of the enemy at a short distance in its rear. This party, under Lieutenant Cursham, had been detached by Captain Forbes, to make a diversion in the rear, while the Dover was engaging Kota Barro in front; and after forcing a body of the enemy, with two field-pieces, that opposed his progress, this party arrived to secure possession of the battery, just as the Dover had silenced it.

Kota Barro being now secured, the Dover recommenced a rapid and well-directed fire against the Strand Batteries, Fort Orange, and the Towa, with very great effect. The enemy, however, returned it with spirit for an hour and three quarters, when many of the inhabitants having been killed, and his losses otherwise great, Colonel Mittman, at 5 P. M. hoisted a flag of truce, and all firing ceased on both sides.

The terms of capitulation being settled, possession was given of Ternate, and all the forts and batteries, on the morning of the 31st of August. These works were defended by ninety-two guns, mostly of heavy calibre; five hundred regular troops, of whom many were Europeans; besides the burghers, and a considerable number of the Rajah's troops, both of Ternate and Tidore.

The Dutch had spared no pains nor expense to render the fortifications of Ternate as formidable as they could, in order to keep off foreign intruders. But not content with the exclusive possession of the spice trade, they further resolved in 1638, to confine the culture of the clove and nutmeg, exclusively to the Islands of Amboyna and Banda ; and accordingly every such plantation in all the other places where they used to flourish in the time of the Portuguese, was destroyed. A small pension in money was granted to the Princes and Chiefs, to induce them to lend a helping hand in this work of general devastation within their respective dominions, and an establishment for the annual renewal of the measure, to prevent the growth of any spice plant in these isles, has ever since been maintained at an expense of four thousand pounds a year, in order to keep up the high prices of these articles in the European markets and throughout the world.

At present, Ternate produces only a little rice, though the trade it formerly carried on with New Guinea, and the Chinese, on Gillolo, &c. was very considerable.

Tidore, and the other islands, were all provided with defences and forts ; but like those at Ternate, they are now falling into decay. It is nearly of the same size as its neighbour, from which it is separated by a safe channel, with good anchorage near the town, on the east side of the island.

Gillolo Island, partly tributary to Ternate, and partly to Tidore, is of considerable extent and well inhabited. Oxen, buffaloes, goats, deer, and wild hogs abound in this island, but sheep are very few. The sago and bread-fruit trees, flourish here in great abundance. Ossa town, situated on the south side of the great Bay of that name, in lat. 0 deg. 45 min. north, long. 128 deg. 22 min. east, affords every convenience for ships touching here, either for water, provisions, timber for spars, or other necessary articles. There are several villages in this Bay, but that of Golonasy was destroyed by the Dutch on the 25th January, 1808.

Between the south end of Gillolo, and the southern extremity of Bachian Island, is formed the Strait of Patientia.

BACHIAN is a high island, about eighteen leagues in length; and the largest of the little Moluccas. Gold-dust is said to be found here. To the north, the little island of Machian rises like a conical mountain, from the sea. This was regarded as the chief Dutch settlement, before Amboyna became the metropolis of the Moluccas.

Xulla islands are four in number, of which Xulla Bessey is the most considerable. It is in length about eleven leagues; in good cultivation, and well inhabited. The Dutch fort is near a village adjacent to the south-east point, where ships may procure refreshments. The island abounds with wax and honey.

AMBOYNA, wherein is situated the capital and seat of Government of all the Spice Islands, is about sixty miles in extent, north and south, and is the next settlement to Batavia in wealth and consequence. The face of the island is beautiful; exhibiting a fine variety of woody mountains and verdant vales, interspersed with hamlets and enriched by cultivation. The entrance into the bay is between two high and steep points, distant about six miles from each other, and gradually narrowing towards the town, where the distance across the bay is about two miles, without any soundings in mid-channel. This bay, stretching about seven leagues into the island, separates it nearly into two parts. On the south shore of this bay, in latitude 3 deg. 40 min. S., and longitude 128 deg. 15 min. E., is situated Fort Victoria, mounting sixty pieces of cannon ; in which the Dutch maintained a garrison of six hundred men ; while a number of redoubts defended the other parts of the island.

The capture of this settlement by the small squadron under Captain Tucker, merits particular commendation. The troops employed on this service landed, at 2 P.M., on the 16th February, 1810, consisting of,

	Men.	
Detachment Madras Artillery -	46	Lieut. Stewart.
Madras European Regiment - -	130	
Seamen and Royal Marines, from his Majesty's ship Dover - -	85	
Ditto ditto, from his Majesty's ship Cornwallis - - - -	105	
Seamen from his Majesty's sloop Samarang - - - - -	38	

Total   404 Men.

Captain Court, attended by Captains Philips and Forbes, had previously reconnoitered the enemy's positions and defences on the side of Fort Victoria ; and the landing having been effected without opposition, the troops moved to the attack in two columns. The one in advance under Captain Philips, proceeded against the strong position of Wannetto, a battery situated on the top of a small hill, defended by three hundred soldiers, with five twelve-pounders, two eight-pounders, two six-pounders, and two $5\frac{1}{2}$ inch howitzers ; and the approach to which was rendered more difficult by innumerable trous-de-loup which surrounded it. Surmounting every obstacle, however, this gallant party rushed on in the most determined manner; and Lieutenant Stewart, who led the storming party, was the first that entered the battery. Here this gallant officer was wounded; but, after a severe struggle, and the commandant of the battery being killed, the post was carried.

The possession of Wannetto soon gave our troops the command of the Wayoo battery, which the enemy were not long able to retain, after the guns of the former had been turned upon it; deserting it, therefore, they fled into the town, carrying consternation with them. In front of Wannetto, on an eminence of a great height, lay Fort Batto Gautong, rendered by the nature of the ground on whish it stands assailable only from the heights in the rear. It commenced a heavy fire on the former immediately after it was carried by our troops, and which they returned with equal vigour. Against Fort Batto Gautong, Captain Court had, in the mean time, directed an attack with the second column, having Captain Forbes at their head.

After a most fatiguing march through a thick underwood, without any road, they succeeded, a little after sun-set, in gaining the heights that commanded the Fort, and were forming for the attack, when the enemy, perceiving the advantage his assailants had now obtained, ceased firing on Wannetto, and fled with precipitation from his guns, leaving Captain Court to take possession of this important post; and thereby the Water-castle, becoming also untenable, was in like manner abandoned.

The squadron, immediately after landing the troops and seamen, had proceeded in line-of-battle up the harbour, and opened a tremen dous fire on the fort, town, and batteries. This was as rapidly returned by the whole of the enemy's posts, extending from Batto-Meirah to Wannetto, and in several places with red-hot shot.

The breeze dying away, was succeeded by light baffling airs and calms, which, with a strong current and no anchoring-ground, rendered this a most difficult and trying service ; as the number of officers and seamen landed had left the ships very short of complement, and with hardly steerage-way, they were now exposed to all the fury of a severe and galling cross-fire, which hulled them repeatedly, particularly the Cornwallis.

But the successes of our troops on shore having secured to them the possession of the whole of the enemy's line of defence to the left of Fort Victoria, a secure anchorage was obtained in Portuguese Bay, and the squadron was moored there in safety.

During the night, the necessary arrangements were made for prosecuting hostilities next day; and the guns in Fort Batto Gaudong, having been relieved of the spikes, were brought to bear on the town and Fort Victoria with very considerable effect, which the latter returned with shells. While the ships were preparing for another attack, a flag-of-truce was hoisted, and a summons sent to the Governor, Lavinius Haukurlugt, to which a reply was returned by Colonel Fitz, military Commander-in-Chief in the Moluccas ; and the terms of the capitulation being settled, Fort Victoria was surrendered on the morning of the 19th February, when a most interesting scene took place.

The remains of the British force, originally landed, were drawn up on the glacis of the fort, to receive the garrison they had conquered.

The Dutch force, consisting of Europeans and Malay soldiers, with the crews of several vessels, although four deep, outflanked the English by more than double the length of their line; and the discontent and mortification of the former, on observing the handful of men by whom they had been beaten, could not be restrained. Execrations were vented, while several of the officers were seen to break their swords with vexation; and a determination was strongly manifested by the privates, to take up again the arms they had lain down. This, spirit was, however, soon subdued by the promptitude of our officers, and full possession was at length obtained. Two hundred and eighteen pieces of ordnance were found mounted in the fort and batteries, and the garrison consisted of upwards 2000 men, independent of the burghers, and other Dutch inhabitants.

The settlements depending on Amboyna followed the fate of the principal, and were taken possession of immediately after, by his Majesty's ship Cornwallis. This ship, on the evening of the 1st of March, discovered a strange sail under the island of Amblaw, and, it being calm, Lieutenant the Honourable, now Captain Peachey, Mr. Garland, Master, and Mr. Sanderson, Master's Mate, volunteered, and in the yawl, cutter and jollyboat, proceeded to examine her. After an arduous and anxious chace all night, they found themselves, at day-light on the 2d, close to a Dutch national brig corvette, fully prepared for their reception, and who opened a heavy fire of round and grape. Lieutenant Peachey immediately dashed along-side, closely followed by the other boats, and succeeded in boarding and gallantly carrying her, notwithstanding she was most bravely and obstinately defended from the chains, gangways, and afterwards on

2 z

deck, with musketry, pikes, and other weapons. She proved to be the Margaretta Louisa, commanded by Captain G. Ruiter, pierced for 14 guns, having 8 mounted, with a complement of 40 men; of whom one officer was killed and twenty men wounded. The British loss was only five men wounded. This was considered by the respective services, as one of the most brilliant achievements of the expedition.

While the Dover remained at Amboyna for its protection, the Cornwallis and Samarang, with several of the largest prize-ships, set sail on the 16th April, for Java, to convey thither the late garrison of this place.

The unfortunate Commander, Colonel Filz, was, soon after his arrival at Batavia, tried and shot, by order of General Daendels.

The population, Dutch, Portuguese, Chinese, and Malays, is very considerable; being estimated at about 50,000, of whom one-third are Christians. The climate is deemed very salubrious, and the town and country are very pleasant. The annual produce of cloves at Amboyna, is averaged at a million of pounds, there being 500,000 trees, each of which easily furnishes two pounds of cloves. This spice is in great repute all over India; the profits, therefore, of the trade in that quarter alone, are very considerable, independently of the European market. Coffee and Indigo also grow here; besides which, the Island produces a peculiar wood, that is much used for beautiful cabinet-work, and which is universally admired.

Soon after the capture of Amboyna from the Portuguese, in 1605, and when the Dutch, by their subsequent conquest of all the smaller isles, in 1627, had secured possession of the whole of these valuable spice plantations, they commenced that destructive work already noticed, of laying them waste in most of the Moluccas, properly so called; and confined the cultivation of the clove-tree principally to the Island of Amboyna; and that of the nutmeg to Banda and the neighbouring Isles, their respective dependencies. The latter, which immediately appertain to Amboyna, and are properly called CLOVE ISLANDS, are Orna, or Haraucka, Honimoa, or Saparoa, Malana, on which is Fort Durnstede and Noesa-Laut. The Government of Amboyna also exercises controul over the south and western part of the Island of CERAM.

This island is about 190 miles in length, by forty in breadth. It abounds in curious woods and large forests of the sago-tree. There are also plantations of the clove-tree. The village Selama is at the bottom of Sawa bay, on the north coast, with Sawa village, in 2 deg. 56 min. South latitude.

Very little is known of the interior, being inhabited by a cruel and savage race, whose extreme poverty and wretchedness lead them to every act of barbarity where the temptation of gain is before their eyes; and piracies, therefore, are very frequent *.

The whole of Bouro, which, next to Ceram, is the largest and most westerly of all, constitutes another valuable appendage of the Amboyna Government. On the south-east part of Chajili, or Bouro Bay, is situated Fort Defence, in lat. 3 deg. 24 min. south, long. 127 deg. 4 min. east. Ships are sheltered here during both monsoons, and the land-winds, which prevail in the night, render departure easy, on which account it is much frequented by the South Sea whalers. These

---

* Captain Blakenhagen, of the Bengal service, lately lost his life here, in an unsuccessful attack made against one of the refractory Chieftains of Ceram.

extensive fisheries, stretching from Timor to Gillolo, Ombay, and the other isles tributary to Java, are frequented by more than sixty English whalers, whose joint annual importation of spermaceti, into Great Britain, exceeds in value a million of pounds sterling. All sorts of refreshments abound here ; the water is very good, and the wood is plentiful. The celebrated Caii Pooty tree grows plentifully on this island, and from it the natives extract that valuable oil in great quantities.

Manipa, Amblaw, Kelang, and Bonoe Isles, are all subject to Amboyna.

Banda Isles, form a group, ten in number. The Dutch first possessed themselves of Lontor, by the natives called Bandan, the largest of these isles, which is in length nine miles, and two and a quarter across in the widest part; and erected Fort Hollandia, and many batteries, which are now mostly in ruins. A narrow strait divides this from Neira, an island two miles and a quarter in length, and about three-quarters in the widest part. It is defended by two forts, one called Nassau, which commands the passage between Neira and Great Banda, and the other Belgica, directly above it. Nassau is a square fort, and is entirely commanded by Belgica ; which last is a pentagon, and built of stone. The only entrance into it is by a door in one of the curtains, which being on a level with the terrace of the lower work, a ladder is required for access to it from the outside. This fort is, in its turn, commanded on the north-east by several small hills. Pappenburgh, or Signal Mountain, having had guns mounted on its summit, which commands the whole island, is called Fort Drury, since the period of the late capture of this settlement, in August 1810, by

Captain Christopher Cole, of the Royal Navy, an achievement that may vie with that which added Amboyna to the British possessions in these parts. The hill is steep, and the road on the summit runs through a thick wood, but it has no water. Adjoining to the esplanade round Fort Nassau, and the hill of Belgica, at the south extremity of Neira, is the town, the houses in which are very neat, and consist of one story, on account of the earthquakes, which are here frequent, though of late years they have not done much damage. The quarter on the south-west extremity is inhabited by Chinese and native fishermen. The anchorage is abreast of Goonong Api, a volcanic islet, of a pyramidical form, and in height about one thousand five hundred feet. It is separated from Neira by a narrow strait, and has the appearance of a heap of cinders. The wharf, at the south-west angle of Neira, is in lat. 4 deg. 31 min. south, long 130 deg. east.

Rosingain, Pulo-Ay, and Pulo-Rhun, are small and thinly peopled, but are deemed very healthy, in comparison of the other islands. The former lies about four miles to the eastward of Great Banda, and the two latter to the westward.

The islands of Lontor, or Great Banda, Neira, and Pulo-Ay, which last is nearly circular, and about a mile and a half in diameter, are the richest in the production of spices; the soil being particularly favourable for the culture of the nutmeg-tree, which flourishes not only in the rich black mould of all these isles, but even among the Lava of Goonong. Pulo-Ay, however, is the most fertile of all, and the nutmegs grown there are reckoned by far the best. The present annual export produce of spices is averaged at 300,000 lbs. of nutmegs, and 80,000 lbs of mace.

The plantations on these isles are parcelled out amongst the free burghers, who superintend the cultivation, and live in considerable affluence. These park-keepers, as they are called, are bound by very strict regulations, to deliver the entire produce of their parks into the government storehouses. After the separation of the mace from the nutmegs, and the smoking of them has been gone through, the nuts undergo the further operation of being covered with lime, to preserve them from insects, and insure their keeping a long time. The lime is made of coral rock, mixed with sea-water, to the consistency of pap, into which the nutmegs are immersed, the lime covering them with a thick coat. They are then fit for exportation. The rates fixed for nutmegs delivered into the Government stores are as follow:—

First and middle-sized nutmegs, four stivers per pound.

For mace, ten stivers per pound.

And one additional stiver is granted for deliveries made from Pulo-Ay, and Great Banda. For the broken nutmegs of bad kinds, from one to one and a half stiver per pound is allowed.

The nutmeg-tree grows to the size of a pear-tree, the leaves resembling those of the laurel. Their number in the several parts on the Bandas from under the age of five to that of above twenty years, is estimated at 500,000. Nearly the entire surfaces of these isles are divided into nutmeg plantations, and vegetation is exceedingly luxuriant.

The labour is performed by slaves and convicts, the former amounting to above three thousand. These are distributed among the several parks, under charge of their respective overseers, to attend to the nut-meg plantations. They are fed and clothed from the public stores; but at the expense of the park-keepers; who, reaping the first fruits of their labour, can well afford to pay for their maintenance. They are generally well treated, but the sickly climate very sensibly and rapidly diminishes their number.

None of the Aborigines of these isles are now remaining, the Dutch having long ago exterminated them all. The present inhabitants, besides the slaves and convicts, are a few natives of Holland, and Half-casts, with their descendants. The whole population amounts to above four thousand, of whom about one-fourth are free. Trade is so far from being encouraged, that it is not even permitted, and the reason of this rigorous restraint is to prevent smuggling.

Much distress has at times been felt from the want of provisions; and as the numerous works erected by the Dutch, for the defence of these isles, required a considerable number of troops to be always stationary here, they were often reduced to feed on wild cats and dogs. Fish is not only scarce, but in general far from being good. Bread is baked of a kind of sago meal; but almost every article of sustenance must be brought hither from other islands, principally Java and Baly.

The last of the Dutch factories remaining to be noticed, as apper-taining to Java, is that in Japan; which has been always considered as one of primary importance, in a commercial point of view. The two British ships, which, after the conquest of Java, sailed from Batavia to Japan, with rich cargoes, had for their object, a renewal of those rela-tions which formerly existed between the two islands; and to ascertain

the fate of the Dutch factors, of whom no tidings had been heard for
a long time. These were, however, safely brought back to Batavia in
the above ships, which had lately returned with very rich cargoes.
This highly-civilized, but very suspicious people, had very narrowly
circumscribed the Dutch establishment in this part of the world; nor
was the attempt in the present instance to gain admittance into their
port, under the Dutch flag, that being the only European nation with
whom the Japanese Government would allow of any intercourse, without danger. The suspicions awakened in former times, and the remembrance of the bloody persecutions which ended in the massacre of
the missionaries, and their numerous converts, particularly in 1633, are
still alive; and the Dutch have themselves felt in their turn the
effects of that distrust and jealousy, which they had been at first very
assiduous in exciting against the Portuguese, by whose ruin they
hoped to secure here, as they had done in other parts, an exclusive
commerce. But they who had acted so basely towards others, from
the worst of all motives, soon fell into similar disgrace, and were confined to the little island of Desima, near Nangasacki.

In the Dutch accounts of these transactions, it appears that, at first,
the harbour of Firanda was appropriated to the ships and cargoes of
the two rival nations; and that, on the expulsion of the Portuguese,
those who remained in possession, established there a factory, or ware-
house. The folly, however, of their agent, Peter Nuyts, who was
sent out on the part of the Company, in 1628, nearly ruined their
concerns; for his vanity, in attempting to pass himself off as ambassador from a King of Holland, instead of what he was, the repre-
sentative of a body of merchants, drew upon him the chastisement due

to an impostor, at the Kubo, or Emperor's Court. The same imprudent man next incurred, by various acts of aggression in the government of the Dutch establishment, at Formosa, the indignation of the Japanese; who took him and his son, and one of the members of Council, prisoners; and, after forcing Nuyts to subscribe to the most humiliating terms, he obtained permission to be at large. But the Governor soon after making his escape from the Island, to return to Batavia, the Emperor seized on the shipping and the Dutch property, and closely confined the garrison within the walls of their own factory. Being equally mean and submissive when they could not exercise their wonted treachery and insolence, the Dutch were, on this occasion, ready enough to make the most humiliating sacrifices, for the purpose of securing a lucrative trade. Accordingly, on the arrival of Nuyts at Batavia, he was arrested and sent as a prisoner, with a new cargo, exceedingly rich, to the Emperor of Japan. By this submissive act of the Batavian Government, in delivering up one of their own body, to receive whatever punishment the Emperor might be pleased to inflict on him, they prevented the total ruin of their establishment. The ships were permitted entrance; their cargoes exchanged for one of Japan produce, and returned richer laden than ever had been the case before. Nuyts, who expected nothing less than to be burnt alive, was shortly after liberated, to the surprise of every person. But the friendly intercourse which had been thus established. was of short duration, owing to the imprudence of Mr. Charron; who arrived at the Island of Firanda in the year 1640. He solicited and obtained permission to build himself a stone house, which gradually assumed the solidity and properties of a fort. But the Japanese, unacquainted with the European method of fortification, betrayed no suspicion, till a ship arrived from Batavia with the great guns, which Mr. Charron had secretly sent for, packed up in large chests, strongly secured with iron hoops and bars, and stowed among the spice-chests, and other articles of the ship's cargo. They were landed all safe; but as ill luck would have it, the first chest placed among those which contained spices, being opened by the Japanese overseer of Customs, discovered one of these guns; on which, the fort and the house of the factory were instantly surrounded, and Charron hurried off to Jeddo; where the Emperor, after upbraiding him with his treachery, ordered his beard to be plucked out hair by hair; after which he was paraded with every mark of ignominy through the streets of this immense capital, and then expelled for ever from the Japanese dominions. This event not only prevented the restoration of confidence, but served to increase the jealousy that had long existed; and it ended, in 1741, in the banishment of the Dutch to the little Island of Desima, the only harbour now in which foreign ships are permitted to anchor; which privilege is confined exclusively to the Dutch and Chinese. This isle is, in its greatest length, not more than two hundred and forty, and in breadth eighty paces, with a street through the centre, containing the dwellings of the inhabitants; the lower apartments being used as store-rooms, and the upper for the accommodation of the families. Still even this small spot can by no means be considered as the property of the Company; and, on the contrary, the Japanese regard it as a street appropriated to the Dutch, but belonging to Nangasacki, where alone they are tolerated, without being permitted to go to any other part of that town, with which it is connected by a stone bridge, strongly guarded ; thereby preventing all communication or intercourse that is not especially authorized ; while, on that part next to the island, stands a high stone pillar, on which the Emperor's regulations and restrictions, with regard to the Dutch, are inscribed. The Ottona, or Japanese Magistrate, for the islet, lives here, in a fine house, surrounded by his guards.

Seldom more than forty-five Dutch were living on the island at one time, under a Commissioner ; and these were obliged to be changed every two years, a longer stay here not being permitted to the same persons ; though they may return after three or four years absence. Accordingly, three commissioners, or parties, have been always maintained ; and, while one carries on the duty at Desima, the second is returning to Batavia, and the third sets off again from that place to Japan.

As soon as the Dutch ships arrive, the chief in the town of Nangasaki, dispatches a number of sloops and boats to bring away the guns, arms, sails, anchors, &c. to be placed in security. The merchants, passengers, and crews are then landed, and shut up in Desima. Nor are more than four at a time, after especial permission has been obtained, allowed to walk together about the town. The exchange of the import and export trade is entirely regulated by the Japanese commercial overseers, who repair on board, and take an account of the goods brought by the ships ; and for which they substitute whatever articles in the way of barter they judge to be a fit equivalent in return. Nor is there the least cause to apprehend that any embezzlement or fraud will be committed on the property by the Japanese, whose exemplary conduct in this business, amply justifies the praise universally bestowed on these people for their honesty.

Whilst this is going on at the depot, the commissioner, with two or three merchants, more not being allowed, set out for the Emperor's Court, to deliver the customary presents; during which journey, a guard constantly attends them, and they are not permitted to take a single step out of the high-road. On their arrival at Jeddo, a still stricter watch is kept over them, and they are closely immured till the day of audience, when the presents are delivered to the Emperor, who is behind a gauze curtain, screened from their view, though he can see them well enough, and the presents which are displayed before him. And according to the humour which his Majesty happens to be in, so is the treatment which the Dutch experience, who are obliged to comply with his injunctions, let them be ever so ridiculous and inconsistent with the gravity of their character. When the exhibition is terminated, the Europeans are immediately hurried back with great celerity, to their residence in Desima.

The principal, and most lucrative article of exportation from Japan, is copper, which is very plentiful, and richly impregnated with gold. Besides this very fine and most excellent metal, Japan abounds in gold, silver, and other valuable ores; but no mine can be opened without the Emperor's permission. The scymetars manufactured here are said to be the finest-edged tools in the world. A great variety of other articles and Japan-ware are exported, which sell very high, in exchange for sugar, chiefly of the coarsest kind, imported from Java; and a variety of European and Indian goods. The fur trade with

Japan, which is exceedingly profitable, has been carried on exclusively by the Chinese merchants, who being obliged to transport them from Kamschatka over-land, by the way of Okotsk and Kiackta, to Pekin, a distance of more than two thousand miles, and thence to Japan, shews how advantageous this trade would prove in the hands of an English merchant, if a direct importation of the furs could be made from Kamschatka, which is not above three weeks sail from hence; and from the islands between that part and America, where the sea-otters are caught in abundance, and the most valuable skins can be easily procured.

The population of Japan, like that of China, is immense. Jeddo, the capital, is said to be sixty miles in circumference, and well built; but the houses never exceed two stories, with numerous steps towards the streets. The military force is reckoned at more than half a million of regulars, of which number 50,000 are cavalry; and, unlike their neighbours the Chinese, the Japanese bear a character of great bravery and resolution.

The Government resembles the ancient old feudal system of Europe. The head is the Kubo, or Emperor, who is the sole Monarch of the country, and his residence or court is at Jeddo, while at Miaco, the second city of the empire, is held the court of the Dairi, or principal ecclesiastical dignitary of the empire. Their temples are free from any idols; and they make strict search on the arrival of the Dutch vessels after all sorts of images, paintings, and books, which are on no account suffered to be landed, but are instantly burned. Nor are any foreign women suffered to approach the Japanese shore; and though they do not prohibit their females from having intercourse with strangers; they will neither permit them nor their offspring to leave the country. The salutary law of making parents and relations answerable for the conduct of their children and dependents, whose morals they ought to have superintended, has a powerful effect in the prevention of crimes.

In a similar spirit of justice, neighbours are made responsible for one another's property ; which tends, by one of the strongest of all obligations, to the security of individuals, and the preservation of public tranquillity ; since the temptation to robbery is repressed by the general resentment which is excited against offenders of that description, from the injury which their depredations bring upon the community. But the manners, the laws, and the religious institutions of this extraordinary and insulated people, would require a voluminous detail, even were that empire more open to observation, and the means of exploring the country as free and ample as they have hitherto been few and contracted. The possession of Java by the British might possibly, in time, have contributed somewhat to extend our intercourse with these people, as well as with others in their vicinity ; for a liberal and an enlightened policy, with the superiority of arts and arms, could hardly fail to produce favourable sentiments on the minds of an intelligent race, especially when they should have been enabled to discern the contrast between the new government settled in their neighbourhood, and that which it superseded.

A MORE sublime and instructive spectacle could hardly be exhibited to the moral contemplation, than that which presented itself to the observer of the British Empire in the oriental world at the close of the operations which have been detailed in thepreceding sheets. From the gulph of Persia the dominion of our flag extended over the vast and populous plains of the Indian continent, while stretching from the Indus to the mountains of Napaul, and from Cape Comorin to the banks of the Sutledge, the ancient Hydraotes, but the modern boundary of the territory of the Seiks; then again our authority was acknowledged among the numerous Asiatic isles, comprizing the most valuable and ancient settlements in the east, the whole comprizing a population, certainly not less than one hundred millions of active and intelligent beings. Rome, in her proudest state, could not boast of such an accession of power, or equal means for promoting the general interests of mankind. Proportionate, therefore, to the immensity of our influence in those interesting and productive regions, must be the duties which that commanding position imposes upon us for the benefit of the nations and tribes who have been thus providentially placed within the sphere of our exertions. No man, indeed, that feels any concern for the improvement of the degraded part of the human species, or who wishes for the removal of those obstacles which have hitherto impeded the progress of civilization, can be indifferent to the character and condition of the numerous classes of our fellow-creatures, scattered over those vast regions where our arms have established a dominion, and our commerce has opened new sources of industry. Much beyond all question is required in a moral and political view, to render the authority which we have obtained beneficial to those over whom it is exercised. Many are the evils which call for vigorous but judicious remedies, and enormous are the superstitions which, while they depress those who are blinded by them, cannot but operate to the disadvantage of an enlightened government, and the prevention of a liberal legislation. Still, with the impression of these truths on his mind, every well-informed and rational philanthropist will perceive the extreme danger of adopting crude plans of reform, and visionary projects for the improvement of British India. Whatever system may be judged best calculated to maintain the sway which we at present enjoy, and at the same time to ameliorate the situation of the natives, in our eastern possessions ; it seems most reasonable that the whole of it should be digested, and deliberately arranged in that part of the world to which it is intended to be applied ; for extensive and minute as the information is which the people of this country have on the subject of their foreign settlements, still it cannot be denied that for the internal management and security of our dependencies, local observation and personal enquiry must be indispensably necessary.

Reform, therefore, to be effectual among a people who are naturally attached to the very corruptions which oppress them, must be progressive, and the light of religious truth, from the salutary influence of which so many permanent blessings are justly to be expected, should be diffused with all the wisdom and prudence becoming its divine origin and immense importance. But if, on the contrary, intemperate zeal should presume to subvert institutions, and to attack prejudices, which have for ages been regarded with the profoundest veneration ; and if, instead of illuminating men's minds by a friendly intercourse, the encouragement of science, and the benefit of education, fanaticism is entrusted with a power of assailing the faith of millions, the benevolence of our Legislature will be frustrated, humanity will be outraged, and torrents of human blood will be mingled with the waters of the Ganges.

An energetic and comprehensive administration, centrically situated, and furnished with ample powers to aid the intentions of the Government at home, and to restrain any dangerous innovations that might be occasionally attempted by honest but ill-directed minds, would be of inestimable advantage to the natives of India, and the European residents.

But there are now strong grounds to believe, that the policy of Gr ea Britain towards her colonial settlements and remote connexions, will be productive of mutual confidence, and the most salutary consequences, in enriching the stock of knowledge, improving the morals of various tribes who have now no law but their appetite, and, above all, in spreading over the dark and ignorant divisions of the globe, the benefit of legislative protection, and the blessing of Christian revelation.

FINIS.

PRINTED BY R. WILKS, 89, CHANCERY-LANE.

3 R

List of Plates

Plate I	Sketch of the Island of Java from the latest and best Documents Extant
Plate II	The Army Brigades. The Advance, Commanded by Colonel R. R. Gillespie Major of Brigade Capt. Thorn 25th Dragoons
Plate III	Tract of the British Fleets of the Expedition against Java. 1811
Plate IV	Departure from High Islands or 3., Rendezvous of the Fleet
Plate V	The landing of the British Army at Chillinching on the Island of Java. 4th Aug 1811
Plate VI	Route of the British Army and Correct Plan of the Environs of Batavia
Plate VII	Town House at Batavia
Plate VIII	Castle and Wharf at Batavia
Plate IX	Plan of the Action Near Weltervreeden. 10th Aug 1811
Plate X	Sketch of the Enemy's Position on the Retrenched Heights at Jatty near Samarang, 16th Sep. 1811
Plate XI	Plan of Attack on the Fortified Lines of Cornelis. 26th Aug 1814
Plate XII	Plan of the Environs of Samarang
Plate XIII	The Harbour of Gressie and Plan of the Environs of Sourabaya
Plate XIV	Sketch of the Tract pursued by the British Forces from Batavia. 21st March 1812
Plate XV	Sketch of the River of Palimbang.
Plate XVI	Sketch of the Batteries at Borang, in the Palimbang River. 24th April 1812
Plate XVII	Sketch of the Palaces, Forts and Batteries of Palimbang
Plate XVIII	Fort, Palace and Line of Defence at Palimbang
Plate XIX	Sketch of the Fortified Cratten, of the Sultan of Djoejo Carta, taken by Assault 20th June 1812
Plate XX	Funeral of a Oey Hingho, or Captain of the Chinese, at Batavia, as drawn on the spot
Plate XXI	Fort Cheribon
Plate XXII	Fort Taggal
Plate XXIII	Samarang from the Land Side
Plate XXIV	Fort Salatiga
Plate XXV	Water Palace at Djoejo Carta
Plate XXVI	Fort Damack
Plate XXVII	Fort Japara
Plate XXVIII	Fort Joana
Plate XXIX	Fort Rambang
Plate XXX	Gressie
Plate XXXI	Sourabaya River
Plate XXXII	Passarouang
Plate XXXIII	Eastern Archipelago chart of the British possessions, dependencies on Java
Plate XXXIV	Amboyna
Plate XXXV	Banda Isles

Plate II

The Army Brigaded.

THE ADVANCE,

COMMANDED BY COLONEL R. R. GILLESPIE,

Major of Brigade Cap.t Thorn 25.th Drag.ns

Attached to the Advance Cap.t Taylor 24.th Dra.ns

Right Flank Batt.n		Major Miller
Left Flank Batt.n		Major Fraser
Detach.mt 89.th Reg.nt		Major Butler
Royal Marines		Captain Liardet
Bengal Light Inf.y Vol.r Batt.n		Major Dalton
Dismounted 22.nd Dragoons		Lieutenant Dudley
Governor Gen.ls Bodyguard		Captain Gall
Pioneers		Captain Smithwayte
Horse Artillery		Captain Noble
Detach.mt 22.nd Drag.s		Major Traverse

THE LINE COMMANDED BY MAJOR GENERAL WETHERALL.

Left Brigade.	Right Brigade.
Commanded by L.t Colonel Adams,	Commanded by Colonel Gibbs,
Major of Brigade Cap.t Bethune.	Major of Brigade Cap.t Douglas.

H.M. 78.th Regiment.	6.th Batt.n Bengal V.rs	H.M. 69.th Regiment.	H.M. 59.th Regiment.	5.th Batt.n Beng.l V.rs	H.M. 14.th Regiment.
Major Lindsey	Major Raban	Lieu.t Colonel M.c Leod.	Lieu.t Colonel M.c Leod.	Cap.t Griffiths	Lieu.t Colonel Watson

The Reserve Commanded by Colonel Wood,

Major of Brigade L.t Williamson.

4.th B. B. Vol.r	1.st B. 20.th or Marine Reg.t	3.rd B.B. Vol.r	Flank Batt.n
Major Grant	Lieu.t Colonel Loveday		Major Yule

Tent Lascar	Dooly Bearer	Pioneers	Bengal Artill.y	Royal Artill.y	Engineers
			Major Caldwell	Col.l Makenzie	

LIEU.t GENERAL SIR SAMUEL AUCHMUTY COMMANDER IN CHIEF,

Adjutant General Colonel Agnew.	Quartermaster General Colonel Eden.
Deputy Adjutant Gen.l Major Agnew.	Deputy Quartermaster General Major Burslem.
Assis.t Adjutant Gen.l Captain Carroll.	Assis.t Quartermaster General Lieu.t Hanson.
Milit.y Sec.y and A.D.C. Captain Tylden.	D.o .... D.o ...... Lieu.t Wetherall.
Aid de Camp Captain Dickson.	Attached to Qu.rmr Gen.l Departm.t Lieu.t Bayley.
D.o .... Captain Knatchbull.	D.o ...... D.o .... D.o ...... L.t Dalcairns.
D.o .... Lieutenant Blakiston.	Major Farquhar in charge of the Guides &
Major Campbell Commissary General.	Intelligence Department.
Cap.t Limond Commissary of Stores.	Aids de Camp L.ts Wetherall to the Major Gen.l
Dep.t Paymaster General Major Johnson.	Superintending Surgeon Doctor Hunter.

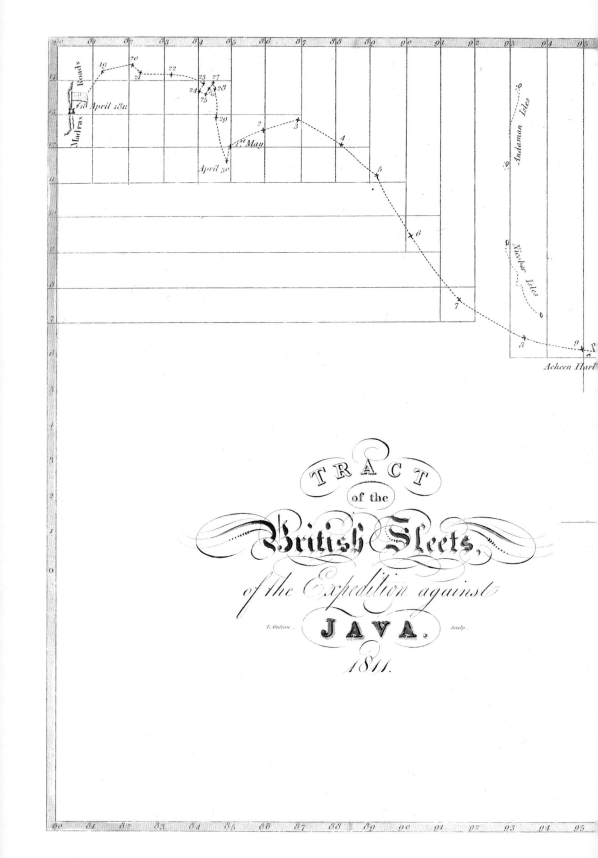

TRACT
of the
British Fleets,
of the Expedition against
JAVA.
1811.

E. Gillan.   Sculp.

Plate III

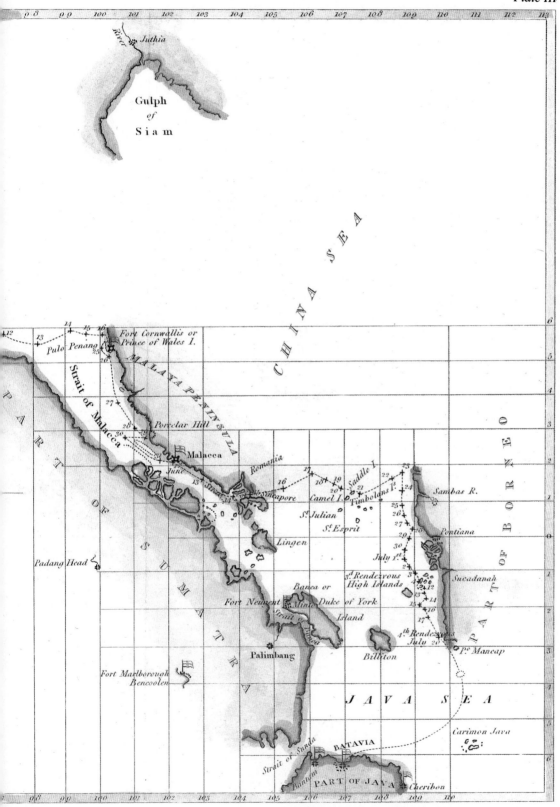

Gulph
of
S i a m

C H I N A   S E A

River Juthia

12 · 13 · 14 · 15 · 16 · Fort Cornwallis or
Pulo Penang · Prince of Wales I.
25
26

MALAYA PENINSULA

Strait

of

Malacca

27

28 · Porclar Hill
30 · 29
31 · Malacca
June · Romania
13 · 16 · 17 · Saddle I.
28 · 19 · 22 · 23
Singapore · 20 · Timbolans I.s · 18 · 24
Camel I. · St Julian · 21 · 25 · Sambas R.
St Esprit · 26 · 27
Lingen · 29 · 28 · Pontiana
30
July 1st

P
A
R
T

O
F

S
U
M
A
T
R
A

Padang Head

Banca or · 3d Rendezvous · 3 · Sucadanah
Fort Neument · Duke of York · High Islands · 4
Strait · Minto · Island · 11 · 12
Banca · 13 · 14
15 · 16
Palimbang · 17
4th Rendezvous · 10
July 20
Billiton · Po Mancap

Fort Marlborough
Bencoolen

J A V A   S E A

Carimon Java

Strait of Sunda · BATAVIA
Bantam · Cheribon
PART OF JAVA

P A R T   O F   B O R N E O

Departure from High Islands or 3 "Rendervous of the Fleets

Plate IV

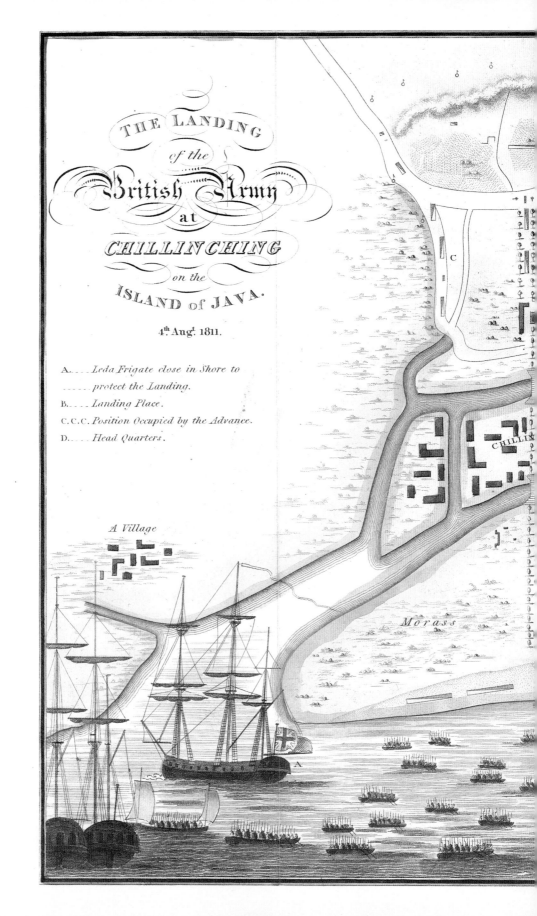

THE LANDING
of the
Britiſh Army
at
CHILLINCHING
on the
ISLAND of JAVA.

4ᵗʰ Augᵗ 1811.

A..... *Leda Frigate close in Shore to*
..... *protect the Landing.*
B..... *Landing Place.*
C.C.C. *Position Occupied by the Advance.*
D..... *Head Quarters.*

A Village

Morass

CHILLI

Plate V

Road to Cornelis

C

Road to Batavia

Route of the Brigades of the Line

Garden House

Praden Stein

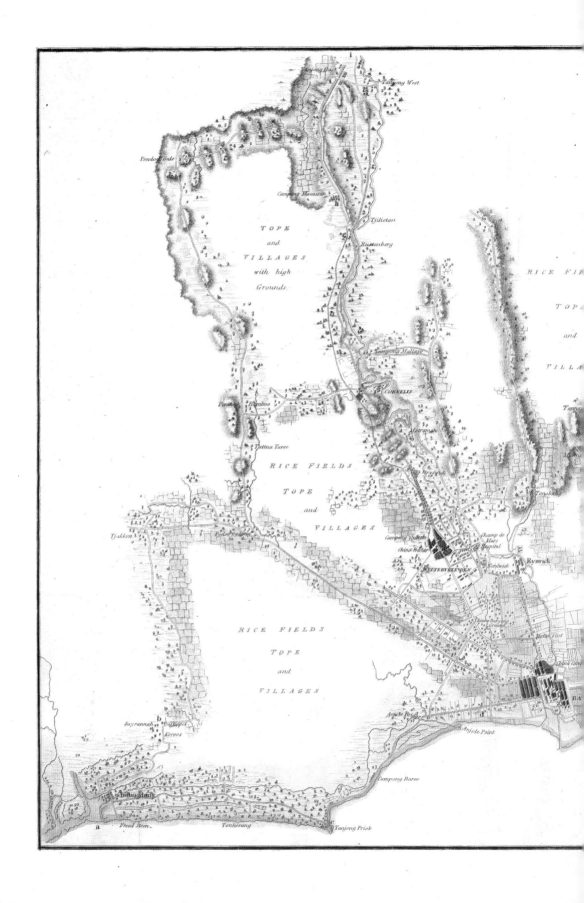

Plate VI

Route
of the
BRITISH ARMY,
AND
Correct Plan of the Environs
of
Batavia.

a   Landing Place and 1st Position at Chillingching, 4th August 1811.

b   March of part of the Advance to Susrannah Chapel, 5th August.

c   Advance Position of the British Army, 6th August.

d   Passage of the Anjole River and Position occupied in the Suburbs 7th August.

e   City of Batavia taken possession of 8th August.

f   Action of the 10th August near Weltevreeden.

g   Battle of Cornelis 26th August.

h   Charge of the British Cavalry in the Pursuit.

i   Extent of the Pursuit, terminating in the total Defeat and destruction of the whole French Army, 26th August 1811.

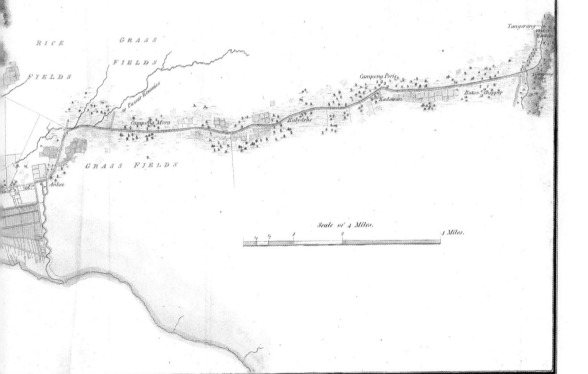

to Buytenzorg

to M. Canterfiejer

to Alljamie

RICE FIELDS

GRASS FIELDS

FIELDS

GRASS FIELDS

Ankee

Campong Morn

Passar Economis

Halydrus

Kadaeian

Campong Poria

Batoe Thipper

Tangerang

Scale of 4 Miles.

4 Miles.

Town House at Batavia

Plate VII

Engraved by J. Jeakes

Castle and Wharf at Batavia

Plate VIII

Engraved by J. Jeakes

Plate IX

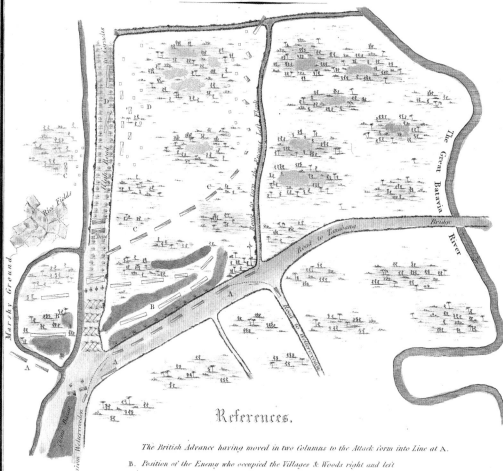

Plan

OF THE ACTION NEAR WELTERVREEDEN.

Between the British Advance Commanded by **COLONEL R. R. GILLESPIE,** *and the French*

Advanced Division, Strongly posted under **GENERAL JUMEL.** 10th Augt 1811.

References.

The British Advance having moved in two Columns to the Attack form into Line at A.

B. *Position of the Enemy who occupied the Villages & Woods right and left*

of the high road to Cornelis, their Guns covered by an Abatis.

C. *Second Formation of the British in pursuit of the Enemy.*

D. *The French entirely routed with the Loss of their Guns.*

and driven back within the fortified Lines of Cornelis.

E. Gullan sculpt.

Plate X

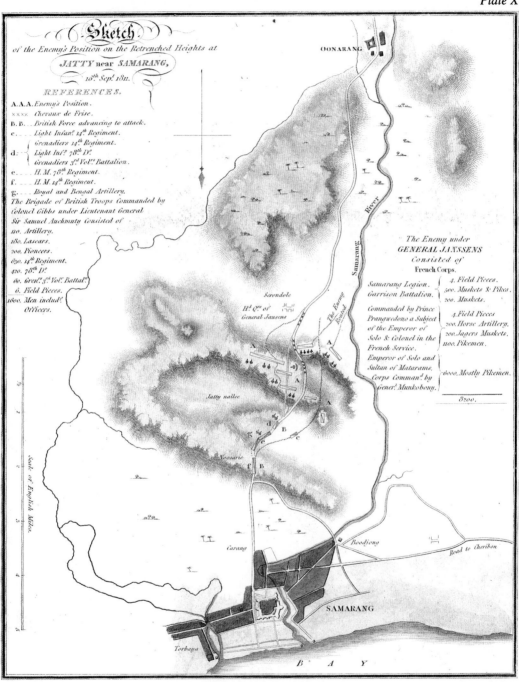

Sketch

of the Enemy's Position on the Retrenched Heights at

JATTY near SAMARANG,

10th Sept. 1811.

REFERENCES.

A.A.A. *Enemy's Position.*
×××× *Chevaux de Frise.*
B.B. *British Force advancing to attack.*
c. *Light Infant. 14th Regiment.*
    Grenadiers 14th Regiment.
d. *Light Inf.ª 78th Do.*
    Grenadiers 3d Vol.rs Battalion.
e. *H. M. 78th Regiment.*
f. *H. M. 14th Regiment.*
g. *Royal and Bengal Artillery.*

The Brigade of British Troops Commanded by
Colonel Gibbs under Lieutenant General
Sir Samuel Auchmuty Consisted of
110. *Artillery.*
180. *Lascars.*
200. *Pioneers.*
630. *14th Regiment.*
420. *78th Do.*
60. *Gren.ª 3d Vol.rs Battal.n*
6. *Field Pieces.*
1600. *Men includ.ª*
      Officers.

OONARANG

Samarang River

Serendole

H.ª Q.rs of General Jausens

The Enemy Routed

Jatty nallee

Yonarie

The Enemy under
GENERAL JANSSENS
Consisted of
French Corps.

	4. *Field Pieces.*
Samarang Legion.	500. *Muskets & Pikes.*
Garrison Battalion.	200. *Muskets.*

	4. *Field Pieces.*
Commanded by Prince	200. *Horse Artillery.*
Prangwedono a Subject	200. *Jagers Muskets.*
of the Emperor of	1100. *Pikemen.*
Solo & Colonel in the	
French Service.	

Emperor of Solo and	
Sultan of Matarams,	6000. *Mostly Pikemen.*
Corps Comman.ª by	
Gener.ª Munkobony.	

8200.

Scale of English Miles.

Carang

Boodjong

Road to Cheribon

SAMARANG

Torbaya

B A Y

E. Gullan sculp.ᵗ

PLAN OF ATTACK

on the FORTIFIED LINES of

Cornelis,

Taken by Assault by the **BRITISH ARMY** *under the Orders of*

LIEU.ᵗ GENERAL SIR SAMUEL AUCHMUTY

Commander in Chief &c.

26. August 1811.

References

A. *Principal Attack Commanded by Col! Robert Rollo Gillespie.*

CONSISTING,

Leading Column,

1. *Rifle Company H.M. 14.ᵗʰ Regiment Lieu! Coglan.*
2. *Detachm! Madras Pioneers Cap! Smythwayte.*
3. *Grenadier Company H.M. 78.ᵗʰ Reg! Cap! M.ᶜ Leod.*
4. *Right Flank Battalion, Major Miller 14.ᵗʰ Regiment.*
5. *Left Flank Battalion, Cap! Forbes 78.ᵗʰ Regiment.*
6. *Detachm! H.M. 89.ᵗʰ Reg! (5 Companies) Major Butler.*
7. *Royal Marines Captain Bunce.*
8. *Detachm! Dismounted Dragoons 22.ⁿᵈ Reg! L! Dudley.*
9. *D.ᵒ _____ Gov.ʳ Gen.ˡˢ Body Guard Cap! Gall.*
10. *One Wing Light Infan.ʳʸ Vol.ʳ Battal.ⁿˢ Cap! Fraser.*
11. *D.ᵒ _____ 4.ᵗʰ Bengal. D.ᵒ _____ Major P. Grant.*
12. *Detachment Royal Artillery. _____ Cap! Byers.*

Colonel Gibbs's Brigade,

13. *Grenadier Company H.M. 14.ᵗʰ Reg! Cap! Kennedy.*
14. *D.ᵒ _____ 59.ᵗʰ D.ᵒ Captain Olphert.*
15. *D.ᵒ _____ 69.ᵗʰ D.ᵒ Captain Ross.*
16. *H.M. 59.ᵗʰ Reg! Lieu! Colonel Alexander M.ᶜ Leod.*
17. *One Wing Light Infan.ʳʸ Vol.ʳ Battal.ⁿˢ Major Dalton.*
18. *D.ᵒ _____ 4.ᵗʰ Bengal. D.ᵒ _____ Captain Knight.*
19. *Detachment Royal Artillery.*

B. *Attack on the Enemy's Left Commanded by Lieutenant Colonel W.ᵐ M.ᶜ Leod at the Head of H.M. 69.ᵗʰ Reg!*

C. *Attack on the Enemy's Rear at Campong Malayo by the Column under Major Yule.*

CONSISTING,

1. *Detachment Pioneers.*
2. *Grenadiers 20.ᵗʰ Regiment Bengal N.I.*
3. *Two Guns Madras Horse Artillery.*
4. *A Troop H.M. 22.ⁿᵈ Dragoons.*
5. *Two Companies H.M. 69.ᵗʰ Regiment.*
6. *Flank Battalion of the Reserve.*

D. *_____ British Batteries & Entrench.ᵗˢ the Remainder ... tioned here under Major Gen! Wetherall joined ... Seamen under Cap! Sayer R.N. threat.ᵈ the Front*

E. *_____ Corps in Reserve occupying the Lines at Str... The Fortified Lines of Cornelis Comprize abo... Circumference Defended by 280 Pieces of Can... The French Army Concentrated within the W... to above 13000 regular Troopes, Command... Jansens Governor General.*

a. *_____ The Front Face of the Enemy's Position was ... Brigadier Gen! Jauffret, under the General o... Gen! Jumel Commander in Chief, Brigadier o... Commanded the Face of the Slokkan, Colon... side of the Great River his Chief Post was N... The Post of Cantpong Maiayo was under ... Major Schultz of the Engineers with orde... the Bridge in Fire the instant the British... appeared which prevented Major Yule fro... by that Route, A Cavalry Picquet was P... the Junction of the Roads behind Campu... with two Pieces of Light Artillery and a ... Detachment of an Officer and Forty Cha... the direction of Major Schultz.*

b. *_____ The Reserve under Brigadier General Lut... in Rear of the Park Guns covered by*

c. *_____ The small Fort of Cornelis and*

d. *_____ The Barracks on the right hand side of ...*

e. *_____ Four Horse Artillery Guns directly Facing ... Bridge over the Slokkan.*

f. *_____ Enemy's Cavalry threatening to Charge.*

g. *_____ Powder Magazine.*

h.h.h. *Barracks.*

i.i.i. *Numerous Batteries.*

l.l. *Deep Cuts across the Roads.*

m.m. *Trous de Loup and chausse Trapes*

E. Gulton & Bloxh's 63d. Fetter Lane, London.

Plate XI

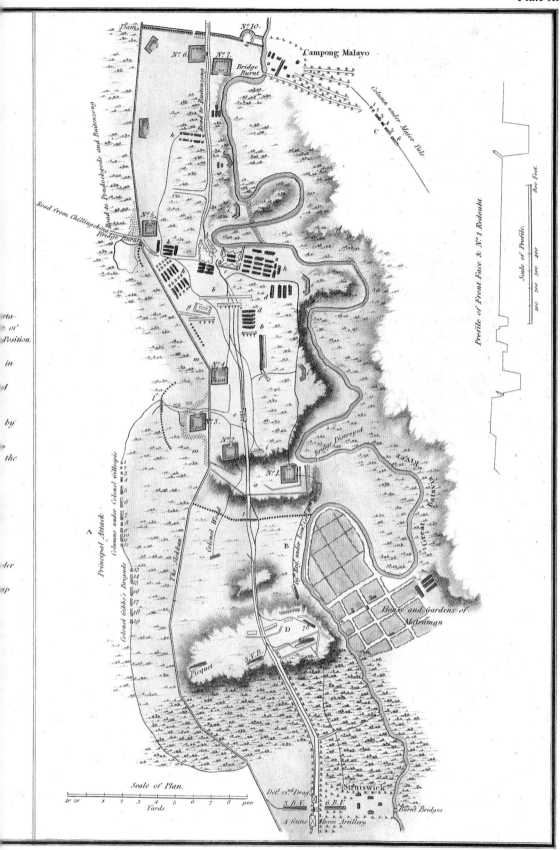

Campong Malayo

Column under Major Yule

Profile of Front Face & Nº 1 Redoubt

Scale of Profile.

100 200 300 400 500 Feet.

Road from Chillingching

Road to Pondokgede and Buitenzorg

Road to Buitenzorg

Nº 10.
Dam
Nº 6.
Nº 7.
Bridge Burnt
Nº 5.
Bridge Burnt
Nº 4.
Nº 3.
Nº 2.
Nº 1.
Colonel Wald

Bridge Destroyed

RIVER (Great) Batavia

House and Gardens of Mtraman

Principal Attack

Columns under Colonel Gillespie

Colonel Gibbs's Brigade

The Mokhan

Picquet

D

5. B. V.

B

10ᵗʰ Reg. under Lieut Colonel Maclean

Det. 22ᵈ Drag.
3. B. V.
4 Guns
6. B. V.
Struiswick
Burnt Bridges
Horse Artillery

Scale of Plan.

40 50   1   2   3   4   5   6   7   8   900
Yards.

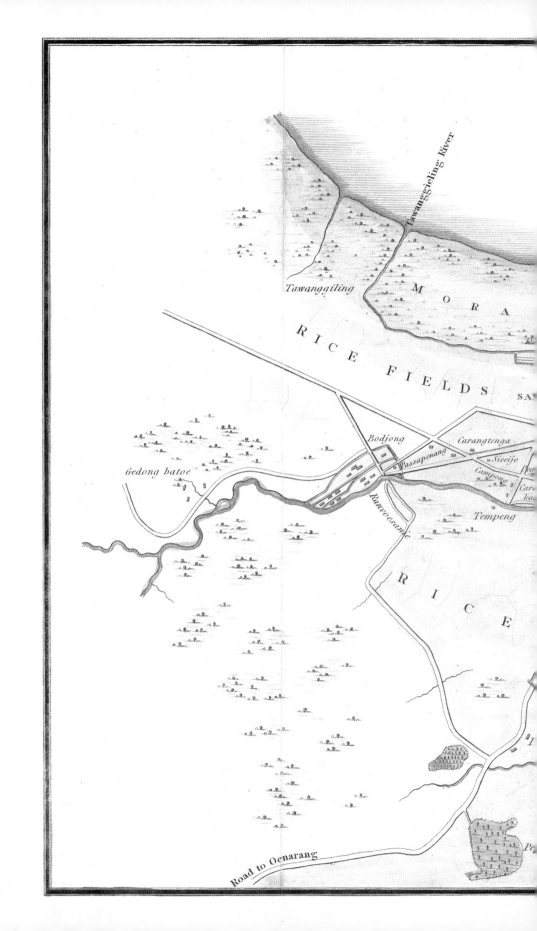

Plate XII

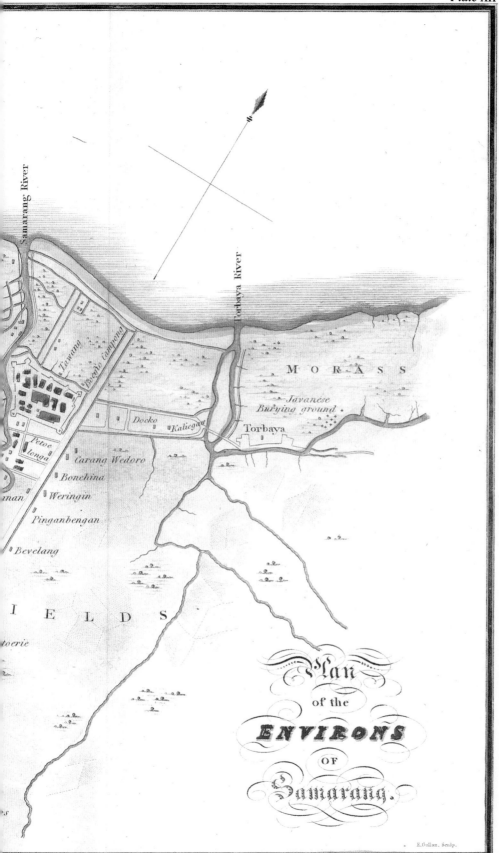

Samarang River

Torbaya River

Tawang

Bugho Campong

M O R A S S

Javanese
Burying ground

Docko

Kaliegan

Torbaya

Petoe
longa

Carang Wedoro

Bonchina

Weringin

Pinganbengan

Bevelang

F I E L D S

Plan
of the
ENVIRONS
OF
Samarang.

E. Gullan. Sculp.

E. Gullan sculp.[t]

Plate XIII

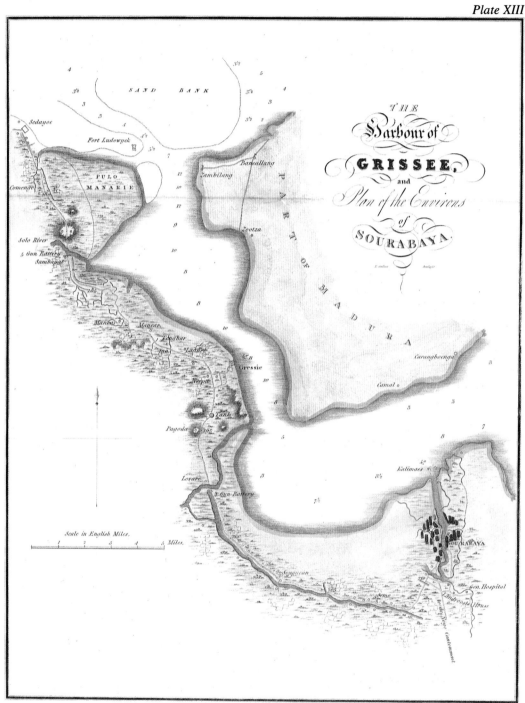

THE
Harbour of
GRISSEE,
and
Plan of the Environs
of
SOURABAYA.

Plate XIV

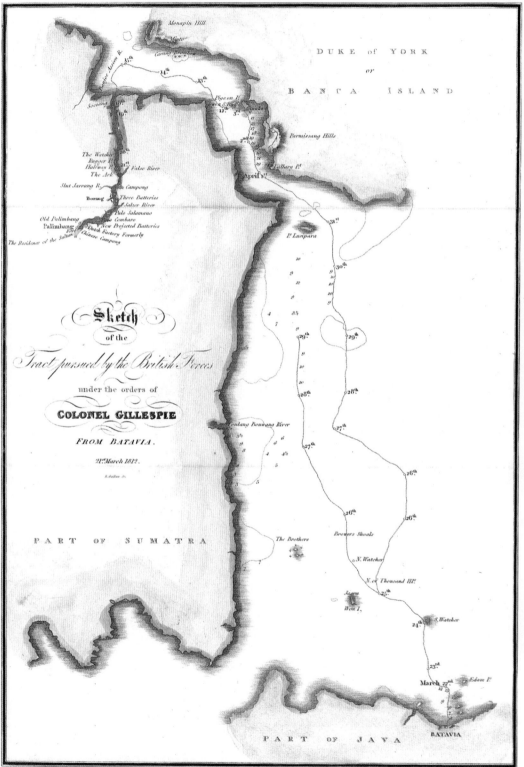

Menapin Hill

DUKE of YORK

or

BANCA ISLAND

Carang Trusang

Socrang

Pigeon I.

Nanka

Parmissang Hills

Lallary Pt

April 1st

The Watcher

Ranger I.

Halfway R. False River

The Ark

Slut Jarrang R. Campong

Borang Three Batteries

Salzer River

Pulo Salamano

Old Palimbang Pulo Combaro

Palimbang New Projected Batteries

Dutch Factory Formerly

The Residence of the Sultan Chinese Campong

P. Lusipara

10

9

9

85

9

29th 29th

10

9

10

28th 28th

Tulang Bouwang River 27th

9 6 6

8 4 4½

27th 27th

5

26th

5

26th 26th

The Brothers Broures Shoals

N. Watcher

PART OF SUMATRA N. of Thousand Id.

Java 25th

West I.

24th S. Watcher

23rd

March 22nd Edam I.

BATAVIA

PART OF JAVA

Sketch
of the

Tract pursued by the British Forces

under the orders of

COLONEL GILLESPIE

FROM BATAVIA.

21st March 1812.

Plate XV

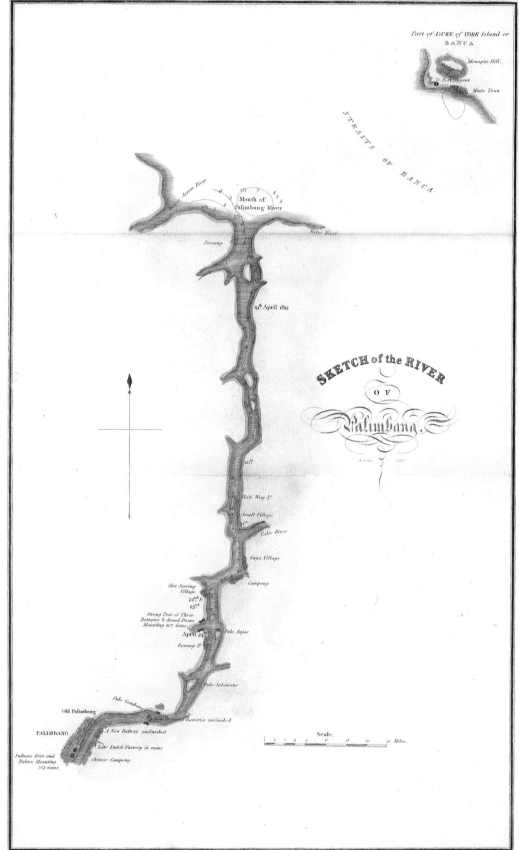

Part of DUKE of YORK Island or
BANCA

Monapin Hill

Fort Nugent

Minto Town

STRAITS OF BANCA

Araen River

Mouth of
Palimbang River

False River

Soosang

19th April 1812

SKETCH of the RIVER
OF
Palimbang.

20th

Half Way I.

Small Village

21st

False River

Gaqu Village

Campong

Shot Jarring
Village

22nd &
23rd

Strong Post of Three
Batteries & Armed Prows
Mounting 102 Guns

April 24

Pulo Anjar

Borang I.

Pulo Salamane

Pulo Combang

Old Palimbang

PALIMBANG

A New Battery unfinished

Two Pointed Batteries unfinished

Late Dutch Factory in ruins

Sultans Fort and
Palace Mounting
242 Guns.

Chinese Campong

Scale.
1 2 3 4 6 8 10 12 Miles.

Plate XVI

Plate XVI

SKETCH of the Batteries at BORANG,
in the
PALIMBANG RIVER.
Taken Possession of by the British Troops,
under
COLONEL GILLESPIE.
24th April, 1812.

JUNGLE

Small Island

Fire Rails

Route of a part of the British advance to take Possession of the principal Battery

Fire Rails

THICK JUNGLE

Piles

Fire Rails

Powder Magazine

Town or Village

Floating Batteries

Armed Prows

Part of BORANG ISLAND

Piles

Fire Rails

Scale
100   200   300 Paces

An Arab Ship, armed by order of the Sultan.

REMARKS.

The three Batteries are advantageously situated to oppose the passage up the River, and the numerous Fire Rafts were filled with Combustibles to fire the Shipping attempting to pass; the Wooden Piles driven in the River are for the purpose of obstructing the approach to the Works: floating Batteries, armed Prows, and a large Arab Ship, armed, were all stationed there by order of the Sultan to add to the defence, in all 102 Guns, mounted, and Plenty of Amunition.——— N.B. On both banks of the River there is a thick impenetrable Jungle, and at high water is entirely overflowed.

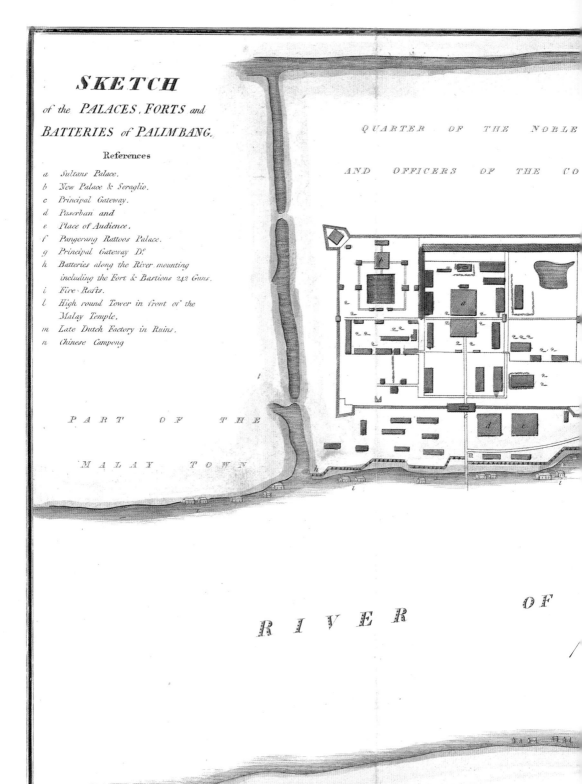

SKETCH
of the PALACES, FORTS and
BATTERIES of PALIMBANG.

References

a   Sultans Palace.
b   New Palace & Seraglio.
c   Principal Gateway.
d   Paserban and
e   Place of Audience.
f   Pangerang Rattoos Palace.
g   Principal Gateway Do.
h   Batteries along the River mounting
    including the Fort & Bastions 242 Guns.
i   Fire Rafts.
l   High round Tower in front of the
    Malay Temple.
m   Late Dutch Factory in Ruins.
n   Chinese Campong

QUARTER OF THE NOBLE

AND OFFICERS OF THE CO

PART OF THE

MALAY TOWN

RIVER OF

Plate XVII

PART OF THE

MALAY

TOWN

f

h

i

PALIMBANG.

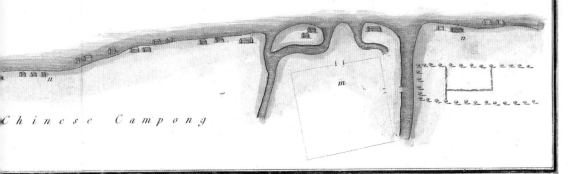

n

n

m

Chinese Campong

Fort, Palace and Line of Defence at Palimbang

Plate XVIII

References.

A. *The Cratten.*

B. *Small Fort possessed by the British.*

C. *British Residency House.*

D. *Principal Attack under Lieu.! Colonel Watson, Grenadier 14.!ʰ Regiment & Leading Column here Crossed the Ditch and escaladed the Ramparts Covered by the Sharp Shooters 14.!ʰ Regiment distributed to the Right and Left of the Assault.*

E. *Enemys Powder Magazine Blown up in the N.E. Bastion, a Part of Bengal Light In--fantry Battalion Crossed the Ditch and running along the Berm Let down the Draw Bridge at the Princes Gate for the admission of Lieu.! Colonel M.ᶜ Leods Column.*

F. *Princes Gate Lieu.! Colonel M.ᶜ Leod's Column passing over the Draw Bridge ascended the Ramparts upon one another's shoulders, whilst a Gun was endeavouring to blow open the Gate which was Strongly barricaded inside, but it was Soon removed by the Assailants.*

G. *Lieutenant Colonel Duwar's Column proceeding by a detour to the Rear or South Side of the Cratten.*

H. *Camp of the Tomoogong Semoot Deningrat, who was Killed and his Troops defeated by the Column under Lieu.! Colonel Duwar who afterwards entered at the South Gate which was opened for their admission by Colonel Watson's Column.*

I. *Attack under Major Grant at the Principal Entrance, to Serve as a Diversion.*

L. *Horse Artillery and Cavalry Cutting off the Enemy's Retreat on the High Roads. Surrounding the Cratten.*

M. *Extensive Campongs enclosed with Walls & occupied by an immence Armed Population.*

N. *A Mosque the Last Stand of the Enemy's Troops.*

O. *The Sultans Palace.*

P. *Insulated Palace with Subaqueous Entrances.*

Q. *New Insulated Tower.*

R. *Prince's Palace.*

S. *Foundery.*

T. *Dutch Town.*

Ninety two Guns Mounted on the Enemys Works.

Plate XIX

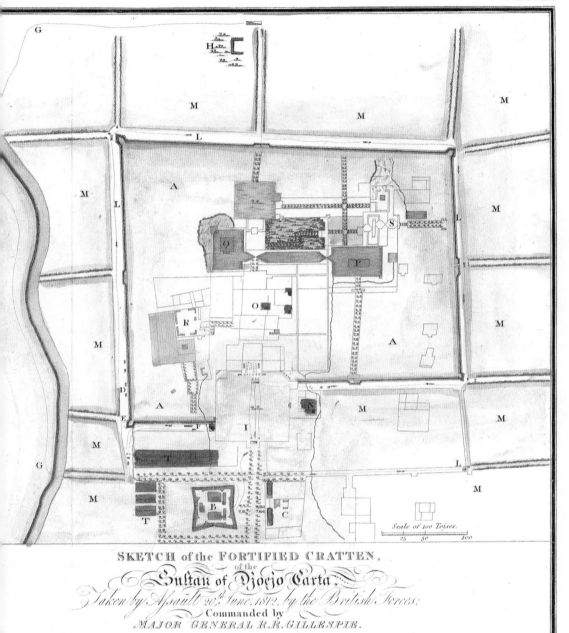

SKETCH of the FORTIFIED CRATTEN,
of the
Sultan of Djoejo Carta.

Taken by Assault 20th June, 1812, by the British Forces:
Commanded by
MAJOR GENERAL R.R. GILLESPIE.

Scale of 100 Toises.
25   50   100

Funeral of a Oey Hingho, or Captain of the Chinese, at Batavia, as drawn on the

Plate XX

Fort Cheribon

Plate XXI

Fort Tapara

Plate XXII

Samarang from the Land Side

Plate XXIII

Engraved by J. Jeakes

Fort Salatiga

Plate XXIV

Water Palace at Djoejo Carta

Plate XXV

Fort Damack

Plate XXVI

Engraved by J. Jeakes

Fort Japara

Plate XXVII

Fort Joana

Plate XXVIII

Engraved by J. Jeakes

Fort Rambang

Plate XXIX

Engraved by J. Jeakes

Gressie

Plate XXX

Sourabaya River

Plate XXXI

Engraved by J. Jeakes

Passarouang

Plate XXXII

Engraved by J. Jeakes

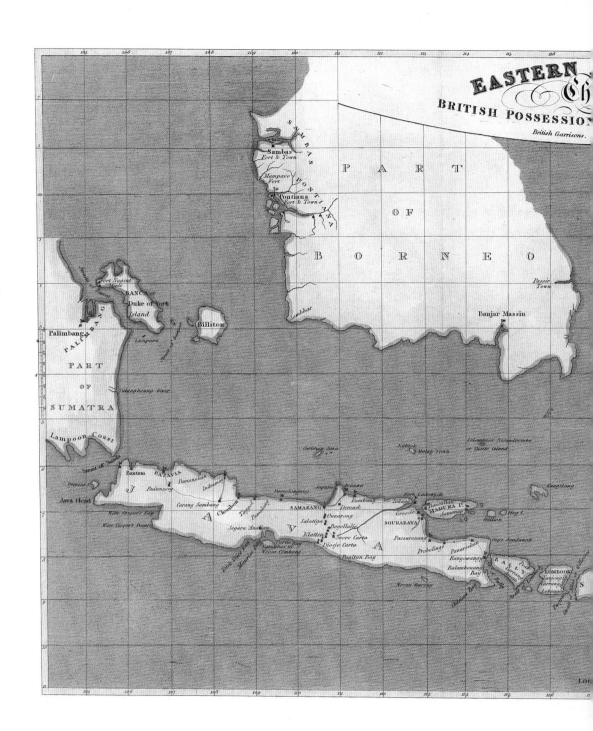

EASTERN &c.

BRITISH POSSESSION

British Garrisons.

PART OF BORNEO

Passir Town

Banjar Massin

Samihbar

SAMBAS
Sambas
Fort & Town
Mampavo
Fort
Pontiana
Fort & Town

BONTIANA

Fort Nugent
Minto
BANCA or
Duke of York
Island

Billiton

Palimbang

PALIMBANG

PART
OF
SUMATRA

Lampoon Coast

Strait of Sunda

Prince's I.
Java Head
White Peeper's Bay
Wine Peeper's Point

Bantam   BATAVIA
Buitenzorg   *Pamanoukan*
Indramaw

Carang Sambang
Checbon
Tagal   Pamanong

Carang Java

Lubeck   Malay Town
*Salombeer Nossentombo
or Cistle island*

Pacoulongan

Sumana   Sumana
Zedang   Fort Ludewyck

Gressie
Pancallak   MADURA P.   Samanap
Jottien   Hog I.

SAMARANG
Salatiga   Ounsarang   Demack
Klatten   Boyollalir
Sooro Carta
Diodjo Carta

Paritan Bay

SOURABAYA
Passaronang
Probelingo   Panarockan
Banyowangy
Balambonang
Bay

Bangerlang

Cape Sandanah

BALLY

LOMBOOK
*Lampon
Carrang
Cobeanc*

Noesa Baron

LOI

Plate XXXIII

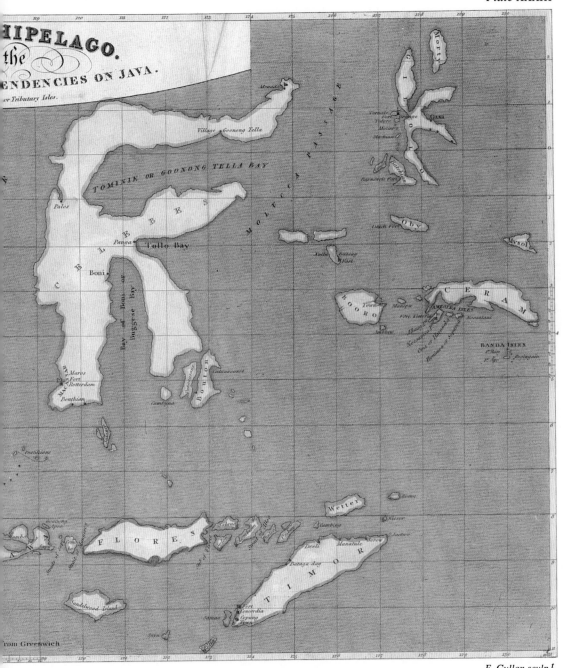

HIPELAGO.

the

ENDENCIES ON JAVA.

or Tributary Isles.

Menada

Village Goonong Tella

TOMINIK OR GOONONG TELLA BAY

MOLUCCA PASSAGE

Verselte
Fort
Totere

Gilongloe

Tidore

Motiere

Machiani

Cassa

MORTY

SIAO

Batchian

Eisenwelt Fort

Pulos

C E L E B E S

Panga

Tollo Bay

Boni

Bay of Boni or Duggrace Bay

Maros
Fort
Rotterdam

Benthian

Gumbina

Bouton

Saleyasoe

Saleyasoe

Selatasoesoe

Pastilious

Xulla

Xulla
Bessiar
Port

Linch Fort

O B Y

MYSOL

B O O R O

Town

Imbow

Manpa

Fort Victoria

Albanij

AMBOINA ISLES

C E R A M

Nossalaut

Nosseneive

Oma or Haroeko

Harooa or Saparoa

BANDA ISLES

Ir Baar

1er Agy

Rosingain

FLORES

Kambonij

Appa

Sombo

Sabrao

Lanham

Vidong

Solor

Ombay

Wetter

Somau

Kisser

Sambien

Deeli

Manatule

Serow

Jacobra

T I M O R

Pataga-day

Sandelwood Island

Samae

Fort
Concordia
Copang
Copao

Sam

from Greenwich

E. Gullan sculp.[t]

Plate XXXIV

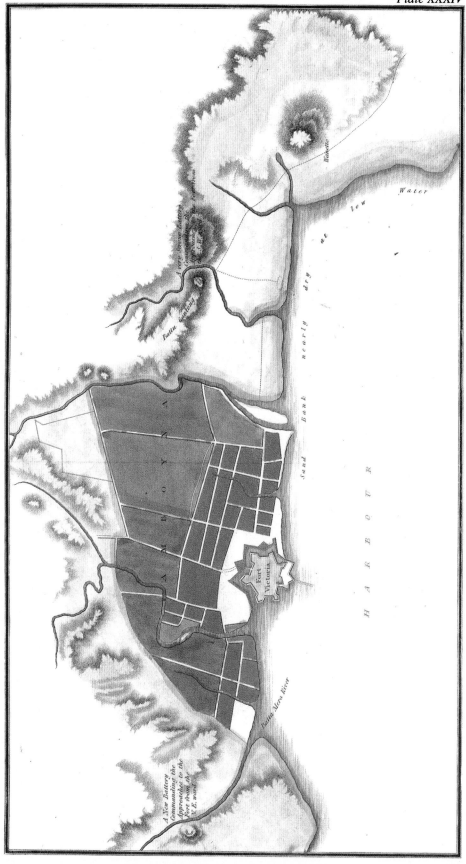

Water

Weinette

low

ae

dry

nearly

Bank

Sand

A very Strong Battery the Fort Town

A Commanding Battery

Battu behind

A M B O Y N A

HARBOUR

Fort Victoria

Battu Mera River

A New Battery
Commanding the
Approaches to the
Fort from the
N.E. West

Plate XXXV

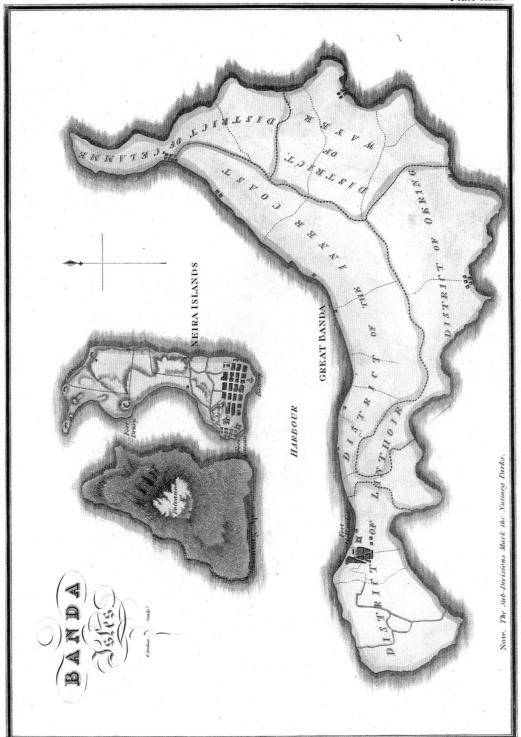

NEIRA ISLANDS

GREAT BANDA

HARBOUR

DISTRICT OF GELAMME

DISTRICT OF WAYER

DISTRICT OF OERING

THE INNER COAST

DISTRICT OF LANTHOIR

DISTRICT OF

DISTRICT OF

Volcano

Fort Belgica

Fort Nassau

Fort Orange

BANDA Isles

E. Wallace Sculp.t

Note. The Sub-Divisions Mark the Nutmeg Parks.

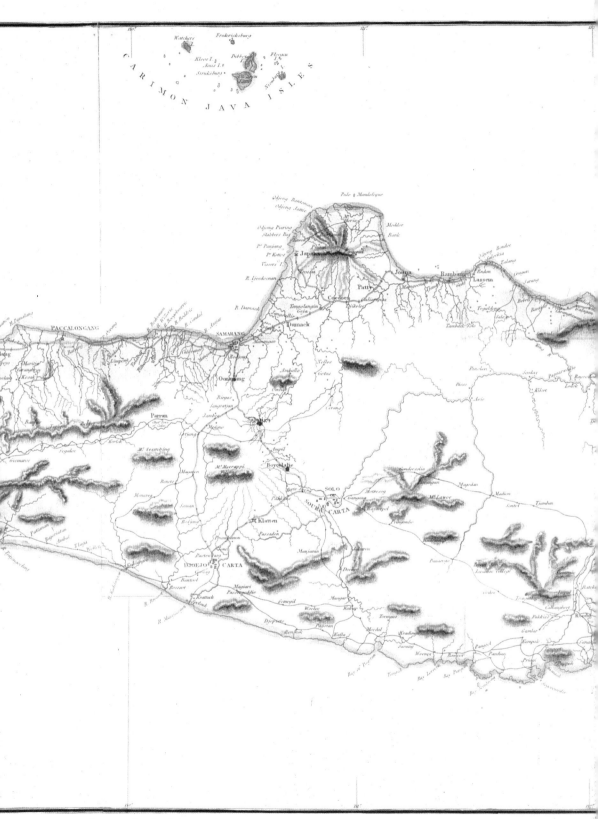

map continues on front endpapers